WELLESLEY STUDIES IN CRITICAL THEORY,
LITERARY HISTORY, AND CULTURE
(VOL. 2)

TEACHING THE
CONFLICTS

GARLAND REFERENCE LIBRARY
OF THE HUMANITIES
(VOL. 1782)

WELLESLEY STUDIES IN CRITICAL THEORY, LITERARY HISTORY, AND CULTURE

GENERAL EDITOR, WILLIAM E. CAIN

TEACHING THE CONFLICTS

Gerald Graff, Curricular Reform, and the Culture Wars

Edited by
William E. Cain

GARLAND PUBLISHING, Inc.
New York & London / 1994

Library of Congress Cataloging-in-Publication Data

Teaching the conflicts : Gerald Graff, curricular reform, and the
culture wars / edited by William E. Cain.
p. cm. — (Garland reference library of the humanities; vol. 1782.
Wellesley studies in critical theory, literary history,
and culture; vol. 2)
Includes essays by Gerald Graff.
Includes bibliographical references and index.
ISBN 0-8153-1466-3
1. Education, Higher—Social aspects—United States. 2. Education,
Higher—Political aspects—United States. 3. Education, Higher—
United States—Curricula. 4. Critical pedagogy—United States.
5. English literature—Study and teaching (Higher)—United States.
6. Critical theory. 7. Graff, Gerald. I. Cain, William E.
II. Graff, Gerald. III. Series: Garland reference library
of the humanities; vol. 1782.
IV. Series: Garland reference library of the humanities. Wellesley
studies in critical theory, literary history, and culture; vol. 2.
LC191.4.T43 1994
378.1'99'0973—dc20   93-29157

Printed on acid-free, 250-year-life paper
Manufactured in the United States of America

Contents

General Editor's Introduction

The volumes in this series, Wellesley Studies in Critical Theory, Literary History, and Culture, are designed to reflect, develop, and extend important trends and tendencies in contemporary criticism. The careful scrutiny of literary texts in their own right remains today a crucial part of the work that critics and teachers perform: this traditional task has not been devalued or neglected. But other types of interdisciplinary and contextual work are now being done, in large measure as a result of the emphasis on "theory" that began in the late 1960s and early 1970s and that has accelerated since that time. Critics and teachers now examine texts of all sorts—literary and non-literary alike—and, more generally, have taken the entire complex, multi-faceted field of culture as the object for their analytical attention. The discipline of literary studies has radically changed, and the scale and scope of this series is intended to illustrate this challenging fact.

Theory has signified many things, but one of the most crucial has been the insistent questioning of familiar categories and distinctions. As theory has grown in its scope and intensified in importance, it has reoriented the idea of the literary canon: there is no longer a single canon, but many canons. It has also opened up and complicated the meanings of history, and the materials and forms that constitute it. Literary history continues to be vigorously written, but now as a kind of history that intersects with other histories that involve politics, economics, race relations, the role of women in society, and many more. And the breadth of this historical inquiry has impelled many in literary studies to view themselves more as cultural critics and general intellectuals than as literary scholars.

Theory, history, culture: these are the formidable terms around which the volumes in this series have been organized. A number of these volumes will be the product of a single author or editor. But perhaps even more of them will be collaborative ventures, emerging from the joint enterprise of editors, essayists, and respondents or commentators. In each volume, and as a whole, the series will aim to highlight both distinctive contributions to knowledge and a process of exchange, discussion, and debate. It will make available new kinds of work, as well as fresh approaches to criticism's traditional tasks, and indicate new ways through which such work can be done.

William E. Cain
Wellesley College

Introduction

William E. Cain

This collection of essays is intended to examine and assess Gerald Graff's proposals for educational reform, in particular his "conflict model," which emphasizes the need to make the conflicts that have racked and riven higher education the *basis* for a coherent curriculum. Graff has been describing and arguing for his proposals for a number of years. He gestured toward them in *Literature against Itself* (1979) and, even more, in *Professing Literature* (1987), and developed them further in a series of provocative articles in scholarly journals and magazines. His recent book, *Beyond the Culture Wars: How Teaching the Conflicts Can Revitalize American Education* (1992), summarizes and amplifies upon his case in compelling detail.

Graff has won many supporters. Paul Berman, for example, in his introduction to an anthology on the "political correctness" disputes, states that Graff's proposal is "the soul of sense." "The debate over political correctness," he explains, "has managed to raise nearly every important question connected to culture and education—the proper relation of culture to a democratic society, the relation of literature to life, the purpose of higher education"(26). And, says Berman, Graff has recognized that education can make fertile use of this debate, situating it in the curriculum itself. The crisis of higher education thus can be a means to make education better, as crucial questions are raised, researched, analyzed, and discussed, though not necessarily settled as neatly as the warring parties in the crisis might wish.

In *Community of Learning*, a study of the American college and the liberal arts tradition, Francis Oakley also praises Graff's work. Like Berman, he believes that the virtue of Graff's ideas is that they prompt teachers and students to address "stubbornly intractable disagreements directly" (159). Oakley concedes some fear that this will confuse students, yet he adds, seconding one of Graff's notions, that students are already confused, moving as they do from one disconnected course to another, and one discipline to another, often maneuvering "among radically divergent theories of knowledge without being fully conscious of so doing, and without getting adequate help in the process" (161). Drawing upon Graff's recent essays, Oakley argues that teachers in all fields need to confront, for and with students, the conflicts embedded in their disciplinary and departmental work. Not only would foregrounding the conflicts "deepen and further the education of our students"(161), but it would also underscore for faculty the importance of civil, generous discourse, a mode of intellectual exchange in which all perspectives on serious issues are voiced, attended to, and examined.

Graff also has his share of foes, however. The central objection to his ideas is that "it is not enough to 'teach the conflicts,' we must solve them" (MacDonald 20). But this misses the point that Graff, and those who have read him carefully, have made. It is in fact a crucial tenet of Graff's position that we will not be able to "solve" the conflicts—not unless one side, conservative or radical, right or left, vanquishes the other and forces it to abide by the victor's rules. That is why we have little choice *but* to teach the conflicts. They cannot be overcome or magically made to disappear, whatever the preferences of this or that imperial "we" determined to "solve" them once and for all.

Graff acknowledges that the curriculum is indeed confused and shapeless, a source of strife and contention. But he stresses that reform will not be achieved by demanding that it serve one faction in the culture wars at the expense of others. The differences among (and within) factions in the academy, and among their followers on the outside, are simply too intense for one side ever to prevail. As James Davison Hunter has noted, "the battles in the ivory tower" are connected to battles about traditions and beliefs in the culture as a whole. The representatives of each side fervently insist that they alone uphold the true principles that others have betrayed or surrendered in favor of political agendas. The debate, Hunter observes, thus "has an interminable character" (220).

It is this situation to which Graff directs his attention, and he has devised a powerful means to transform the heated yet stalemated debate into a remodelled curriculum, a curriculum built upon the values of strong democracy and open, informed exchange. He has seen the paradoxical truth that the conflicts in American higher education that so many people have lamented and sought somehow to "solve" can function as an opportunity for learning. If we are willing to take risks and if we abandon tired remedies that have never succeeded, we might well find, says Graff, that what divides us can bring us together and give education the hardy integrity that, at present, it conspicuously lacks.

As an emblem of the polarized debates to which both Hunter and Graff refer, and which Graff can help us to work *with*, one can cite the attacks on, and defenses of, the two-volume *Heath Anthology of American Literature* (1990), a major publishing project designed to open up the canon of American writers and texts.

The nineteenth-century part of the Heath anthology includes familiar figures—Irving, Cooper, Poe, Emerson, Thoreau, Hawthorne, Melville, and Whitman. But it also includes female, African-American, and Native-American writers who have rarely appeared, or not appeared at all, in earlier anthologies.

The Heath editors, furthermore, devote a sizable section to "the literature of abolition," which provides samples of poetry and prose by David Walker, William Lloyd Garrison, Lydia Maria Child, John Greenleaf Whittier, Angelina Grimké Weld, Sarah Moore Grimké, Henry Highland Garnet, Wendell Phillips, Thomas Wentworth Higginson, Mary Boykin Chesnut, and Abraham Lincoln. The work of these writers, the editors claim, is historically important *and* interesting in literary terms. It has not usually been studied for the plain reason that the critics and scholars who defined American literature and legitimated it in the academy perceived slavery and abolition as social and political issues. These were not deemed the sorts of things that writers of truly "literary" texts would engage.

The editors, in my view, make good arguments, and there is much additional evidence with which they could have bolstered their decisions. After all, very few, if any, black professors taught at the elite institutions where the case for American literature was prosecuted in the 1920s, 1930s, and 1940s. The white majority did not see the contribution to literature that black writers had made, nor were they able to bring into focus the literary achievement of white essayists and lecturers, like Garrison, aligned with blacks in the antislavery cause.

This same white majority also misread and underread the writings of canonical authors. Emerson's and Thoreau's abolitionist speeches were marginalized; Melville's account of a slave mutiny and its aftermath in *Benito Cereno* was explicated as a universal tale about the conundrums of appearance and reality, not as a story about slave rebellion and murderous revenge against white oppressors. Hawthorne was admired for his novels and stories, yet no one asked how the writer who crafted these texts could be the same writer who in 1852 composed a laudatory campaign biography of Franklin Pierce (a friend of Hawthorne's and a Democrat whom the abolitionists detested) and, later, a querulous essay on the Civil War, "Chiefly about War Matters," published in *The Atlantic Monthly* in 1862.

The editors of the Heath anthology have added an array of writers and texts to the field of nineteenth-century American literature, and thereby have furnished a fertile context for the essays, stories, and poems of the so-called traditional canon. Emerson, in "The Poet" (1844), and Whitman, in his preface to the 1855 edition of *Leaves of Grass*, both called for a truly "American" literature that would shake off the burden of English literature and be faithful in style and theme to the spirit of American democracy and freedom. These frequently taught polemical and prophetic pieces can now be located in the Heath anthology alongside the abolitionist writings that were regarded by many in the nineteenth century as the foremost "literature" of America.

When Wendell Phillips, for example, summarized the "philosophy of the abolition movement" in 1853, he stated that the antislavery speeches and texts answered the summons for a distinctive American literature: "This discussion has been one of the noblest contributions to a literature really American" (51). Two years later, in his own review of the antislavery movement, Frederick Douglass declared that the 1850s would "be looked to by after-coming generations, as the age of antislavery literature" (2: 356). To Phillips and Douglass, as well as to many who did not share their abolitionism, it was inconceivable that an appraisal of the "literature" of the 1840s and 1850s would fail to accent the literature of slavery.

The publication of the Heath anthology is, I think, highly positive: it includes the masterpieces *and* weaves among them many other new and little-known texts. The result—to make a point that Graff has made often about the "canon" question—is that teachers and students have before them the prospect for lively conversation about the standards for objective value, the ranking of authors, the nature of literary experience, the impact of history on literary production, and the content (and intent) of a strictly "literary" evaluation of texts. These are all important topics that merit serious inquiry, and that the quarrels about the canon have reinvigorated.

But conservative reviewers of, and commentators on, the Heath anthology have replied that there is nothing to discuss, nothing worth inquiring into. They have spurned the claims about literature that the Heath anthology embodies and have indicted it as a literary travesty and cultural nightmare, an illustration of everything that is wrong in the humanities.

In the October 1990 issue of *The New Criterion*, for instance, an editorial spotlights the Heath anthology as "the latest example of what the politics of ethnic and sexual redress has done to the academy" (3). The editorial goes on to refer to it as "a monument to the intellectual bankruptcy of the multicultural imperatives it champions" (3). It is "a shabby production, intellectually shallow, politically tendentious; it deserves the scorn of everyone who cares about the preservation and transmission of American literature" (5).

For me, the striking feature of *The New Criterion*'s editorial is the absence of any analysis to sustain the vituperation and complaint. As the alternative to what the Heath editors have done, the writer conjures up "literary value" and "literary excellence." He does not indicate what these terms mean. Their meaning, it is assumed, is crystal clear, and dissent or difference of judgment is unthinkable.

This absence of explanation is an index to the depth of the dispute, to the ingrained feeling on the part of conservatives that a book like the Heath anthology is obviously and incontrovertibly wrongheaded, and hence is beneath the dignity of logical argument. To the conservatives, the momentum of multiculturalism and canon revision must be halted and reversed, and the bitter charges they have hurled against the Heath anthology reaffirm those they have cast at similar books.

In the December 1990 issue of *The New Criterion*, Paul Lauter, one of the Heath's editors, replied to the October editorial. He noted that the canon which *The New Criterion* maintains must be protected at all costs has in fact been altered over the years: "Let's remember that in 1920 Longfellow's 'Hiawatha' would have been acclaimed, whereas the work of Melville was all but forgotten" (87). Lauter also tendered the key institutional point that the Heath anthology is the first such book to include a nonwhite scholar on its editorial board; and, he added, until the Heath project, only two white women had served as editors of American literary anthologies.

Should literary choices be made only by white male scholars? Should the historical component of canon formation and definitions of "the literary" be ignored? If Melville's work is absolutely and unequivocally great, then why, asked Lauter, were critics, scholars, and intellectuals, decade after decade, unable to cherish and comprehend it (87)? Why was Melville (who died in 1891) barely known as a writer until the revival of interest in his books that surged in the 1920s and 1930s?

The editors of *The New Criterion* had no sympathy for this argument, however, and answered Lauter by repeating that the Heath anthology is, on its face, perverse and indefensible, a sin against "artistic and intellectual quality" (88).

This truancy of argument in the conservatives' broadsides can prove frustrating—unless one is already converted to their cause and enjoys hearing the old song sung yet again. It's assumed that only a flaming ideologue would sanction changes like those that the Heath anthology incorporates and that Lauter justifies—which means that the conservatives are exempted from having to offer reasoned explanations for their views.

Roger Kimball, the managing editor of *The New Criterion*, returned to the subject of the canon, so much at the center of the exchange about the Heath anthology, in an essay in the January 1991 issue. "There is a body of works from the Western tradition," he emphasized, "that should form the core of a liberal-arts education" (10). That's a given for Kimball, something that sane persons agree upon. But nowhere does he catalog the texts, not even a few of them, that are members of this "body of works." "The criterion for membership" is whether a text "has proved to be of permanent interest. It happens that some works have demonstrated their insight, beauty, or truth to so many educated people for so long that failing to read them is tantamount to consigning oneself to the ranks of the ill-educated" (10–11).

Why Kimball's failure to name names? The reason is that there is, and always has been, much disagreement about the texts that count the most. In literary studies, once you get past Shakespeare, you find lots of disagreement. (And which of Shakespeare's plays should be taught?) This, too, is a point that Graff has made, but made in order to urge that we capitalize upon it, taking advantage of disagreement, as we strive to make our curriculum and teaching *better*, richer, and more rewarding for faculty and students. But it is a point that Kimball can concede only at the expense of his entire argument: if he were to concede it, he would be admitting that there is, and has been, dispute about what he says is indisputable.

A similarly revealing moment occurs in former Secretary of Education William J. Bennett's *To Reclaim a Legacy* (1984), an influential pamphlet that most conservatives endorsed when it was published and still stoutly support today. To his credit, Bennett does name the authors whom he judges to belong in the Western traditional canon.

The works and authors I have in mind include, but are not limited to, the following: from classical antiquity—Homer, Sophocles, Thucydides, Plato, Aristotle, and Vergil; from medieval, Renaissance, and seventeenth-century Europe—Dante, Chaucer, Machiavelli, Montaigne, Shakespeare, Hobbes, Milton, and Locke; from eighteenth- through twentieth-century Europe—Swift, Rousseau, Austen, Wordsworth, Tocqueville, Dickens, Marx, George Eliot, Dostoyevsky, Tolstoy, Nietzsche, Mann, and T. S. Eliot; from American literature and historical documents—the Declaration of Independence, the Federalist Papers, the Constitution, the Lincoln-Douglas debates, Lincoln's Gettysburg Address and second inaugural address, Martin Luther King, Jr.'s "Letter from the Birmingham Jail" and "I have a dream . . ." speech, and such authors as Hawthorne, Melville, Twain, and Faulkner. Finally, I must mention the Bible, which is the basis for so much subsequent history, literature, and philosophy. At a college or university, what weight is given to which authors must of course depend on faculty competence and interest. But, should not every humanities faculty possess some members qualified to teach at least something of these authors? (10–11)

There is plenty to recommend on Bennett's list, but much is missing from it as well. What about Cervantes, Marlowe, Donne, Pope, Goethe, Charlotte and Emily Brontë, Coleridge, Dickinson, Whitman, Tennyson, Ibsen, Chekhov, Henry and William James, Proust, Yeats, Joyce, and Kafka? Bennett remarks that the canonical authors "are not limited to" this named group alone. But where does the list end? Are there choices to be made, and what are the grounds for them?

It is easy enough to wave the banner of the great authors and insist that "every humanities faculty" should have people who are equipped to "teach at least something" about them. But one wants to know what this "something" is. Bennett's term begs the question as to which books by these authors students should read. Does it make any difference whether students are assigned *Oliver Twist, Bleak House,* or *Great Expectations*? Or *Adam Bede, Felix Holt, Middlemarch,* or *Daniel Deronda*? It is intellectually impoverished to say that it makes *no* difference—that one novel is as worthwhile as any other—and to imply that it does not matter what the student knows about these authors, just so long as he or she knows "something." This would seem to invite the very relativism of opinion-making and unmoored judgment that the conservatives have deplored.

Kimball and Bennett are convinced that the Left dominates the academy, and they are hardly alone in believing that colleges and universities have been captured by Marxist partisans. But to those on the Left, it's the Right that is clearly in charge. And the stinging sharpness of the Left's rebuttals demonstrates, from the other side, the polarized form of the debate that Graff has identified and queried, and that his "conflict model" is designed to restructure.

Henry A. Giroux, for example, has called in a series of books for a radical approach to teaching to combat the status quo. In his estimation, it is imperative that we advocate "emancipatory rationality" and "citizenship education." "Emancipatory rationality," he states, criticizes "that which is restrictive and oppressive while at the same time supporting action in the service of individual freedom and well-being" (*Theory* 190). "Citizenship education" in turn measures the promise of American democracy against the rotten reality, and envisions education as necessarily involved in the struggle for social and political change (*Theory* 193–94). Giroux understands teaching as a means of leftist reconstruction, and maintains that it should not be confined to schools. It should transpire, too, in "oppositional public spheres" that an enlightened, committed citizenry occupies:

> If a radical pedagogy is to become conscious of its own limitations and strengths within the existing society, it must be viewed as having an important but limited role in the struggle for oppressed groups to reclaim the ideological and material conditions for organizing their own experiences. . . . Struggles within the schools have to be understood and linked to alliances and social formations which can affect policy decisions relating to the control and content of schooling. . . . Radical teachers will have to be deeply involved in struggles outside of the apparatuses of the state to develop alternative public spheres and counter-educational institutions that provide the conditions and issues around which people could

organize in ways that reflect their own needs and actual experiences. (*Theory* 237–38)

As Giroux elsewhere contends, "the notion of the liberal arts has to be reconstituted around a knowledge-power relationship in which the question of curriculum is seen as a form of cultural and political production grounded in a radical conception of citizenship and public wisdom" ("Liberal Arts" 121).

Another scholar on the Left, Evan Watkins, also champions radicalizing the humanities. Borrowing extensively from the Italian Marxist Antonio Gramsci, Watkins explains in his book *Work Time* that his own position springs from "the recognition that what circulates systematically from English is not necessarily what circulates in English, but rather the result of the abstract form of value determined by the social organization of work. Political praxis then involves learning to use the peculiar features of work as a means to disrupt wherever and whenever possible the circulation of abstract value *from* English. That is, it disrupts the formation of 'human capital.' . . . It is necessary to learn *to use* work where we are, to disrupt what the social organization of labor is designed to circulate" (22–23).

Watkins seems to be suggesting that members of English departments should create interferences that will obstruct, or at least limit, the metamorphosis of students into durable subjects for capitalism. The job of faculty is to mount resistances within their institutions to the capitalist ideology embedded in them.

This, I wager, will strike a fair number of like-minded leftist readers as a worthy aspiration. They probably would concur with Watkins that the Left must act against the Right's dominance inside and outside the academy. But it is a sign of the polarized nature of the rhetoric and position-taking in the culture wars that Watkins never asks whether his proposals could, or should, gain universal acceptance. The more one ponders his words, the more one is uncertain about the audience he imagines he is addressing. To whom is he delivering his injunctions about what is and is not "necessary"? How many people share his goals, and what about the others who do not?

Watkins affirms that "the political values of our work are contingent on our *location* of work, and that location I think dictates that we function in the education of a support structure. It will mean giving up the dream of transubstantiation, of a cultural avant-garde suddenly and miraculously emerging as also a political vanguard. But for a change it might also mean that the work we do has consequences for revolutionary change" (28–29). Watkins counsels that we should cease hoping that literary and cultural work will one day enable us to *become* political: we are politically engaged already, and by acknowledging this truth we can fight openly for the radical renovation of society.

But, again, Watkins's program takes for granted that his audience shares his yearning for revolution. He relies upon first-person plural pronouns that imply "we" agree about "our" political aims, and in this respect his assumptions are as unexamined as Bennett's and Kimball's on the Right. For him, as for them, everybody—at least every sensible person!—should already be enlisted in the one good cause or else needs just a bit of prodding before signing on the dotted line. Watkins assumes that faculty in general relish the idea of "revolutionary change," as though there were now a consensus in favor of it. One wants to ask him how many persons in literary studies really look forward to the day of revolution? And how many of *them* have thought about what this would mean for their lives?

The presence in the academy of scholars with views like Watkins's and Giroux's enrages the conservatives, and the level of conservative protest gives Watkins and Giroux their proof that the Right does rule. Each side denounces the other and harps on the correctness of, and necessity for, its position as the sole basis for reform and renewal in colleges and universities.[1] And so the culture wars continue, with both the Right and the Left in an angry stalemate.

Graff has a sturdy response to this unproductive state of affairs. With admirable directness, he says that we either can persist in conflicts that no one can end, with the curriculum the unwinnable prize, or we can locate the conflicts at the center of the curriculum, knowing that winning is not the issue, nor a likelihood. Stage the debate itself, involve students in it, and represent the polarized positions along with any that fall between. Expose students to what their elders are squabbling about, and empower them to grasp and articulate why these issues matter so they can gauge where they stand themselves. Make education truly *democratic*, based on free exchange of ideas, and recognize that the alternative is an impasse. And a strange impasse, too, in that each side is avowedly fighting on behalf of democratic values that, if it were somehow to gain victory, it would deny to others. The result would be an *undemocratic* situation in which this single side is represented and other sides silenced, their ideas muffled.

Consider how Graff's proposal might play itself out in practice. What would happen if the controversies about the Heath anthology were made the basis for a course, or a section of the curriculum, or a conference that would put into circulation the arguments *for* and *against* it? What if Kimball and Lauter were invited to campus to spell out their positions, with faculty and students taking part in the debate and conducting panels? In this way, the arguments and the principles underlying them could be discussed openly. Students would learn about them and thereby become agents and participants in debates that are now swirling around them, debates which affect them but from which they are excluded.

From this perspective, teaching books would mean getting animated dialogue underway about what's at stake in the choice of which books to read and how to interpret them. Such a dialogue might well prompt students to read more, and read more intensively, than they are doing now. What does the reception of the Heath anthology display about the contested meaning of studying literature, writing criticism, and valuing some texts more than others? This is a short but by no means simple question that implies a great deal and that could stimulate a wide range of reading and frank, adventurous discussion. Everybody would *want* to be delving into the materials gathered in the Heath anthology, and doubtless would be drawn to look up, consult, and peruse lots of other texts—canonical and noncanonical—that the Heath omits. This additional reading and research would be required for comparison, criticism, and contrast in the currents of cross-campus conversation.

In his commentaries on the culture wars, and in his own set of practical examples, Graff has always highlighted improving communication between faculty and students and enriching the sense of intellectual community. As he has cogently said, nearly all of the teaching in the humanities occurs in isolated classrooms. In them a single teacher tends to a bevy of students who drift from course to course, room to room, from this teacher to that one, with little sense of what organizes and connects these discrete experiences. For most of the struggling students, there is not much clarity of aim in the education that they receive. They regard themselves as mystified outsiders, unsure of the nature of the discourse that the teacher offers and that they somehow must obtain in order to prosper.

The teacher's position is often as confined and balked as the students'. Graff has frequently remarked that individual teachers in their public, professional lives engage in debates and controversies about *what* should be taught and *how* it should be taught. But rarely is any of this told to students, and this omission makes each teacher's job harder. It's as though revealing to students the differences in viewpoint that exist among professors, inside and outside their home institution, would mean a loss of authority from which education would never recover. Yet it might be just these differences, and the conversation they imply and make possible, that could motivate the students as they are not being motivated now.

Each teacher comes to class, Graff explains, armed with assumptions that he or she might be defending at meetings and conferences, but that he or she automatically assumes, or deliberately keeps hidden, when in front of the students. The subject for the day in a literature course might be a novel by Henry James or Ernest Hemingway that has generated rousing controversy. Yet so often the controversies themselves (How should this novel be interpreted? Which method is best?), and battles about the author (Why should we be reading him and not someone else?), do not figure as an essential *part* of the subject. These are at the heart of much scholarly work, of professional "research," and they have loomed large in disagreements about the literary canon and critical approaches to it. But most professors defensively judge that it is their duty to keep a decorous hush about "specialized" research and to suppress disagreements about authors, texts, interpretations, and judgments. Again, they do not see the constructive role their own research can help them to perform in their pedagogical labors. They reject a rich resource, keeping private on their home campus what they circulate in public at other campuses and at meetings, conferences, and symposia.

One of the merits of Graff's proposals is that they invite faculty members to link their public, professional, and research lives to their teaching. Graff doesn't demand—as some in the culture wars do—that faculty cut back on their scholarly pursuits in order to devote themselves full-scale to teaching. Faculty make good scapegoats, Graff concedes; it is convenient to blame them for what's gone wrong in higher education, and to pitch research against teaching in yet another polarity. But Graff replies that it is impossible to change by mere fiat the procedures of modern professional scholarship: faculty undertake research because they find it rewarding, as well as necessary to their careers. They would not become transformed into contented, effective teachers if they were refused the chance to do the research that they find fruitful and that, furthermore, contributes in valuable ways to the growth of knowledge.

In addition, says Graff, the real issue is not that faculty are narrowly specialized, but that the important social, political, and ethical implications of their scholarship have not been conveyed to students or, for that matter, to the general public. There is a gap between research and teaching, between how each is explained and represented, that needs to be bridged, so that the exciting dividends of scholarly work, as well as its conflicts and controversies, can be made known to students, in forms accessible to them.

Graff's recent publications, especially *Beyond the Culture Wars*, constitute a strong argument on behalf of the humanities, enabling those in these disciplines to portray themselves more successfully, because more accurately, to students and to outsiders. In this respect, Graff's plan for "teaching the conflicts" carries forward a concern he expressed in his first book, *Poetic Statement and Critical Dogma*, published more than two decades ago, in 1970. In it Graff closely analyzed the "antipropositional" poetic theories of I. A. Richards, Northrop Frye, Cleanth Brooks, and other influential modern critics. By "antipropositional," Graff meant theories that "deny that poetry asserts anything or makes propositional truth claims" (xiii). Though he did not elaborate the point, Graff noted that such theories had worsened the plight of humanists, who had defined themselves in a manner that separated them from "the everyday demands of objectivity and public reality" (xiv). If humanists shunned making claims for the truth of the knowledge that the arts offer, or else if they did so only hesitantly, then they could hardly complain, Graff stated, when their activities were regarded as ornamental and, at bottom, trivial.

But it was not until *Literature against Itself*, which appeared in 1979, that Graff developed a sweeping critique of and reorientation for the humanities, and probed the ideas that had distorted literary studies. His aim, like Matthew Arnold's in the mid-nineteenth century, was to consider the function of "literary thinking" at the present time (1). And he rendered his judgment in barbed terms:

> Almost as if a formal partition-treaty had been negotiated, the creative faction (or the creative side of the individual) has renounced its claim to be a seeker of rational understanding and identified itself with an outlook that makes rational understanding sound contemptible. There is no deterministic theory of degeneration at work in my diagnosis. Our literary thinking has gone wrong because we have, by our own free will and conscious reasoning, sold ourselves a certain conceptual bill of goods. (28–29)

Graff outlined several failings in the study of literature— the decline of standards, the rarefied and recondite character of vanguard literary theories, the jettisoning of purpose in criticism and teaching. But the fundamental charge that Graff made was that literary theorists had divorced literature from society and culture and had thereby prevented it from having robust relevance to the world.

To restore precision and order to literary studies, and to slant it again toward the real world, Graff argued in *Literature against Itself* that critics and teachers should promote "a historical view." He urged that the student be "returned to his history" and shown the critical perspective "from which to assess the richness and poverty of the contemporary, to see what has been gained from this break with the past and what has been lost—and might be regained" (124). English teachers should work in "collaboration" with teachers in other departments and indicate to students the complex, pluralistic, interdisciplinary nature of what may at first seem purely "literary" questions.

> The fact that scholars do not agree on the nature of history does not defeat such a program, for its purpose would not be to indoctrinate the student with a single theory but to bring him into the debate, to introduce him to the issues, and to equip him with the means to form his judgment of them and see his personal connection with them. The point is not to destroy pluralism but to transform it into a pluralism defined by a community of debate rather than a pluralism of incommensurable positions. (125)

Here one can glimpse Graff's early preoccupation with, and emphasis on, *debate* and intellectual exchange. The point of education should not be to convert students to one position or another, but to aid them in speaking forcefully and persuasively about the issues. It is this commitment to a powerful pluralism, as realized by and enacted within a college or university community, that Graff increasingly pursued in his writing after *Literature against Itself*, and that he fleshed out in *Beyond the Culture Wars*.

Because *Literature against Itself* stressed discussion of issues rather than their solution, it was attacked by both the Right and the Left. The Right approved of Graff's stringent commentary on the adverse impact of new methodologies on the teaching of literature, yet, at the same time, quarreled with his linkage of the sorry condition of criticism to the dynamics of capitalism. "One of my central arguments," Graff said in his opening chapter, "is that the real 'avant-garde' is advanced capitalism, with its built-in need to destroy all vestiges of tradition, all orthodox ideologies, all continuous and stable forms of reality in order to stimulate higher levels of consumption" (8). But despite anticapitalist sentences like this one, Graff became, along with E.D. Hirsch, author of *Validity in Interpretation* (1967) and *The Aims of Interpretation* (1976), one of the literary Left's villains. He stood as a target of opportunity for the Left, and was assailed as a political reactionary, an authoritarian, and an ambassador of neoconservatism from the court of Ronald Reagan.

What accounts for these contradictory judgments? In part, the problem lay in Graff's unsteady rhetoric, as he shifted his angle of criticism from one set of foes to another, and from the academy to the culture, without clarifying his own political stand. But even more, Graff faced attacks from the Right and the Left because he was not stating a position that either side could comfortably recognize. This led each side to make him over in the counterimage they were determined to perceive. If he indicted capitalism, he must be on the Left, so the Right concluded. If he maintained that much contemporary literary theory was defective, and that criticism should be committed to the quest for "referential value" and the knowability of "the real," then, according to the Left's verdict, he must be on the Right, a positivist opponent of change. Graff was in neither camp, yet fell victim to both of them.

In *Literature against Itself*, Graff made his first sustained attempt to depict the multiple complexities of higher education that the Left and the Right seemed driven to simplify. When he appealed for collective discussion, historical analysis, and interdisciplinary collaboration (124–27), he was, in effect, saying: "Look, it's not possible for all of us to agree that the college or university is a right-wing or a left-wing stronghold; and it's neither possible nor desirable for us to transform it into something that serves only the goals of the Right or the Left. The situation we're in is not that elementary. So let's instead seize upon the conflicts that separate us and define them as issues that we can explore with one another and with students. Let's make the institution a place for serious learning and for political self-consciousness without insisting that it become single-mindedly politicized, captive to a single ideology."

Graff's somewhat wavering and not fully developed efforts in *Literature against Itself* to express how we might work with conflicts did not satisfy many readers. Yet it seemed to me then, and does so even more in its honed formulations, to be the only type of proposal for educational reform that makes room for the Right and the Left, and for the shades between. The telling feature of Graff's argument, in this preliminary version and in later ones, too, is that he does not mandate that everybody agree about what the college or university is before change occurs. He understands a point that is neglected by reformers of all political stripes—that it will never be possible to get the faculty members within a department and discipline to embrace the same theory of literature and criticism, value the same body of texts, and teach in an identical fashion. Graff takes difference and disagreement and asks how we might forge a consensus *through* and *with* them—a consensus based on the agreement to voice and debate differences.

Graff's next book, *Professing Literature: An Institutional History*, published in 1987, situated a version of this proposal within a detailed account of the rise of literary studies in America. It did not win the plaudits accorded to Allan Bloom's *The Closing of the American Mind* or Hirsch's *Cultural Literacy*, both of which were also published in 1987 and reached the best-seller list. But *Professing Literature* was more interesting and important, and more historically grounded in its arguments, than either of them.

Hirsch and, especially, Bloom said superficial but vivid things that prompted people to believe that the failures of American education boiled down to a loss of nerve. Unlike Bloom, Graff did not censure faculty, mock students, and stamp the 1960s as the period when ethical disintegration and educational collapse commenced. Nor did he announce—as Bloom did—that a saving remnant might find its humanistic haven through rapt absorption in a five-foot shelf of Great Books. Graff also rejected Hirsch's claim that the fault lies in an absence of information among students—a fault that Hirsch says can be remedied by stocking minds with bits of decontextualized facts.

Professing Literature enabled readers to see the marked weakness, and also the familiarity, of Bloom's and Hirsch's ideas. Indeed, it was the sheer commonness of what Bloom and Hirsch were proposing (i.e., that coddled students are reading the wrong books, that students don't know enough brute facts) that gave them their aura as persuasive messengers and prophets. People are attracted to the old remedies, even when these have never worked as advertised.

In making his different, more original case, Graff focused in *Professing Literature* on the growth of the institution of literary studies, starting with the classical college of the early nineteenth century and closing with a survey of the burgeoning field of literary criticism and theory in the 1980s. Scholars learned much from Graff's careful labor of historical recovery, as he went back to dusty volumes in the archives to map how literary study came to its present form. But *Professing Literature* considered a host of cultural, social, and political issues, and its lucidly conducted, broad narrative signalled Graff's effort to reach non-specialist readers—the general public to whom he makes an even more forthright appeal in *Beyond the Culture Wars*.

In *Professing Literature*, Graff contended that it is misleading to exhort teachers and students to embrace "tradition" and reinstate educational methods that supposedly prevailed, and made everybody happy, in the past. Graff was exactly right on this score and properly insisted that we achieve a greater accuracy and honesty in our collective cultural memory. When conservatives bemoan the loss of meticulous, close, rigorous interpretation of the literary classics, they are forgetting that this practice of "close reading" was itself judged to be terribly radical when it hit the academic scene in the 1920s, 1930s, and 1940s. "Close reading" then seemed either to invite impressionism, with each reader discovering his or her own meanings in texts, or to scant the luminous beauties and moral gems in the texts that critics and students were setting out so industriously to explicate.

What is now naturalized as a traditional truth that we have lost was, in fact, an educational trend that met fierce opposition. We cannot reform education, Graff explained, by looking backward to a past that never was, idealizing approaches that were very much in dispute and regarded as breaks with tradition, as the historical record, when it is actually studied, time and again attests.

Changes in methods, approaches, and, perhaps above all, in reading lists are hard to accept, as I think Graff would agree. The books we admire get lodged in our scale of values, and we do not like to feel them jostled. Yet it is often forgotten that traditions, canons, and curricula have been dramatically amended, and that texts that strike us as "great" were once treated unsympathetically.

In 1895, for example, a young professor at Yale named William Lyon Phelps, later an eminent man of letters and newspaper columnist, offered a course on "the modern novel" that centered on Twain, Conrad, and Hardy. This was considered so shocking that it was reported on the front page of the *New York Times*, and it so agitated Phelps's senior colleagues that he nearly lost his job. Twain, Conrad, and Hardy are writers we instinctively list as part of the American and English literary traditions, yet when Phelps first taught them, he was said to be violating tradition and—caught in the grip of "modern" ideas— replacing fundamental literary values with the merely fashionable.

One might recall, too, the tale told by the literary scholar F.O. Matthiessen, the author of *American Renaissance: Art and Expression in the Age of Emerson and Whitman* (1941) and monographs on Eliot, James, and Dreiser, who went hunting in the Yale University library in 1930 for a copy of Melville's *Moby-Dick*. He found it shelved in the "cetology" section. To the staff at Yale's library, *Moby-Dick* was not a literary masterpiece but a seaman's chest of information and hearty lore about whales. The place of Melville's book on reading lists is now secure, yet it was not always deemed a salient work in the American literary tradition—or even recognized as a literary work.

My own experiences in school in the 1970s are, I suspect, fairly representative of what most people experienced during this decade, and I mention them here because they support the arguments about the changing nature of tradition and institutional policy and practice that Graff has mobilized—and the shortcomings of the manner of education that nostalgic recollection has honored. I received an excellent education in both college and graduate school, studying with good professors and reading the classic texts that Bennett, Kimball, and Bloom prize. But it is now clear that I did not read widely enough. During my years as an undergraduate (1970–74) and as a graduate student (1974–78), I took twenty-five courses in English and American literature without ever reading a poem, play, story, novel, or critical essay by an African-American writer.

This meant that I never read Frederick Douglass, W.E.B. Du Bois, Langston Hughes, Zora Neale Hurston, Richard Wright, Ralph Ellison, Gwendolyn Brooks, or James Baldwin. In all my years of schooling, the only book by an African American that I encountered was Ellison's *Invisible Man* (1952), which I read in my sophomore year of high school. Clearly this was an injustice—not only to white students like myself, but to black students whose culture was slighted and devalued.

It was a *literary* injustice, for the absence of African-American writers from reading lists forestalled students from knowing the full dimensions of the subject of "English and American literature." It also ensured that faculty members who taught courses in, for example, the American novel or modern poetry lacked command of the field in which they claimed expertise. They knew less than they needed to know to teach their courses well.

Consider my undergraduate course in American literary realism and naturalism. At no time did the teacher mention Richard Wright, even though Wright, as *Black Boy* (1945) bears witness, located himself within this literary tradition and perceived Theodore Dreiser, Frank Norris, Sinclair Lewis, and other novelists whom we did read as his major influences. When Wright's *Native Son* appeared in 1940, it was an immediate best-seller and was identified as a masterpiece of "naturalism." Yet it was not even cited in the course that I took in the 1970s.

I managed to major in English and American literature and acquire a doctorate in the field without hearing about slave narratives, African-American autobiographies, the Harlem Renaissance, or the Black Arts movement. African-American writers were not treated in separate courses, nor were they introduced in courses that purported to examine the entire scope of the American literary experience. Langston Hughes loved Walt Whitman's poetry, and he saw himself as advancing Whitman's aesthetic project. But when we explored how Whitman reverberates in modern poetry, we highlighted Hart Crane. Hughes never came up. He was as invisible in my poetry course as was Du Bois in my course on American cultural criticism, and as were Ellison and Baldwin in my course on postwar fiction.

It is crucial that we realize, as Graff has said, that we cannot time-travel to the traditions of a bygone era. The shortcomings of that era demonstrate that we should not *want to*. This kind of dreamy thinking does, Graff admits, have a certain seductive appeal, but it is an appeal that we should be suspicious of. It can mislead us into clutching at false solutions that will only perpetuate the cycle of educational despair.

When, in *Professing Literature*, Graff reviewed the Great Books programs at the University of Chicago in the 1930s and at Harvard in the 1940s, he noted that the idea seemed then (and now) wonderfully attractive: base the curriculum on the masterworks of the West and guide the students toward a steady appreciation of them. But this apparently good idea failed at both universities, and it would surely fail again, for it fatally assumed that the Great Books would "teach themselves" and thus did not connect students to the books, to what makes them interesting.

No matter how great the Great Books are, Graff observed, they do not declare how we should read them. To read them profitably, we must think about, and choose among, interpretive methods and contexts. We need, in a word, to involve ourselves in discussion of and debate about all of the difficult, contested issues that the zealots of the Great Books and core curriculum models assert we can (and should) dispense with.

Here, as often, Graff dismantled a popular axiom. Teachers, he stated, fondly trust that all they need to do is to hand the books to the student with a sage smile, allowing him or her to read without preconceptions. But if a student has no guidance about what to look for, he or she probably will be unable to enter with enthusiasm into the text and the concerns it addresses. The student may feel little impulse to read the text at all, if not granted some encouraging signs as to why it is significant and how it has been (and could be) approached.

In *Professing Literature* and in subsequent articles, Graff asked, What is to be done? Picking up on the hints he gave in *Literature against Itself*, he advised that a good first step would be to acknowledge the peculiar way in which faculty screen "conflicts" from students. The academy and the media are filled with arguments about how education in the humanities should proceed: Should the Great Books be at the center or not? How much emphasis should be placed on race, class, gender, and ethnicity? What is multiculturalism, and does it strengthen or damage education in America? Why all of the fuss and furor about literary "theory"? But while these questions are constantly being debated, they hardly ever get into the classroom and curricula. They are questions *about* education that are not *in* education.

In *Professing Literature*, and as again in *Beyond the Culture Wars*, Graff recalled his own experiences as a student in the mid-1950s. He said that he assembled a solid-looking English major, yet nevertheless felt his work was fragmented and unclear in its purpose. It was only years later that he learned of the debates about education, literary studies, and critical methods that had been going on when he was a student. Even in the 1950s—the period that Allan Bloom idealizes—there was heady talk about educational change and reform. Graff speculated that it was precisely this position-taking about the central issues of humanities education that might have given his study the context that it needed—and that also might have bonded it to the political and cultural life of the society as a whole.

Graff noticed something important about the structure of literary studies and, by implication, other departments in the college and university. When faculty confront the challenge of a new theory or methodology, they do not reconceive their discipline and curriculum, but, instead, "add on" the challenge itself. By adding a feminist critic to their ranks and a few courses on women's literature, for example, the members of a department can keep their curriculum up-to-date even as they then feel free to ignore whatever the feminist critic might be doing.

This practice is connected, Graff averred, to the principle of "field coverage," through which faculty convince themselves they have organized the curriculum and unified the major. The job of the department, all assume, is to cover the various periods, making space for new topics and methods, and for new definitions of the conventional periods when it seems incumbent to do so. There is an admirable tolerance built into this very familiar scheme: there is room for just about everything, as long as it does not jar against something that someone else is doing. But such a strategy has intellectual costs: adding courses means continuing the curriculum's incoherence. And it also has financial costs, which are all the more weighty in a time of cutbacks in, and declining budgets for, higher education. It is unlikely that departments can keep adding new courses to cover the field without subtracting others, and they may be impelled to subtract courses even when they do not have others to add.

Graff stated that we must imagine how we can profitably make education coherent through foregrounding conflict and employing it as a principle. If there is conflict between feminists and others in a department who take different approaches to literature, then utilize it in the organization of courses, in the curriculum, and in conferences that will involve students and faculty alike. Disagreement, Graff concluded, is not dangerous; or, rather, it is so only when it is masked, with each teacher ensconced in his or her classroom, instructing students in patterned isolation from everybody else. Don't seek simply to tack on more to what is now being done, but, instead, Graff advised, reorder and rearrange it. Theorize the curriculum, rather than just putting theory in a course.

Graff is seeking to move teachers and students past the predicament in which they are now trapped—past, one might say, the culture of blame and exasperation that badly limits education today. Unaware, or only vaguely so, of the lively debates that might energize and integrate their work in various courses, students have struck their elders as aimless and uninterested. An Allan Bloom or E. D. Hirsch then arrives on the scene with a resolute answer to the present crisis, an answer that receives a wide hearing—especially if it includes an attack on the faculty!—but that effects no change, relying as it does on a set of values that satisfies one faction and not others, and on a method that has been implemented and has failed before. We thus end where we started, with bemused and discontented students, and with faculty upset about the incoherence of their enterprise. And we wait for the next militant spokesperson for bracing discipline to make his or her presence felt, for someone who will assign lots of blame and advise us to march back to the basics—the Great Books, the core facts—that we have neglected.

Through his proposals, Graff suggests how we might build our different views about educational theory and practice *into* the curriculum rather than concealing them and cordoning them off, outside and away from students. Graff shows us why we should be skeptical of the stock solutions, and he points us in positive new directions, inviting us to weigh the opportunities for change that lie in the divisions and differences that have always seemed to make change impossible. He describes how we can capitalize upon the conflicts that we are warring over, and, in the process, demonstrates how they can draw us together.

The selections that follow begin with three pieces by Graff himself that provide an overview of his criticisms of higher education and proposals for reform. Taken as a group, these essays make for a cogent single narrative. But it is also instructive to witness Graff's engagement with a somewhat different audience in each of them. He writes primarily for chairpersons of and teachers in literature departments in "Taking Cover in Coverage," which originally appeared in *Profession 86* (1986); for teachers of and specialists in literary theory and criticism in "Other Voices, Other Rooms: Organizing and Teaching the Humanities Conflict," which appeared in *New Literary History* in 1990; and for a general audience of faculty, students, and administrators campus-wide in "How Curricular Disconnection Disempowers Students," an article first published under a slightly different title in *The Chronicle of Higher Education* in February 1991.

The second part of this volume consists of analyses and critiques of Graff's ideas, especially his "conflict model." Each contributor received copies of the three pieces by Graff, though he or she was not obliged to confine commentary to them alone.

In his essay, Carl Freedman assesses Graff's role in the development of contemporary literary theory and scrutiny of the mission of literary studies. Freedman commends Graff's concern for the flexible use of theory, and, furthermore, sees the advantages of Graff's approach. Yet he concludes that it is missing the crucial category of *power*, a category that the dialogical mode defined by Mikhail Bakhtin supplies. Freedman stresses that the classroom, as Graff pictures it, is too pleasant, is without relationship to the hard struggles of particular times and places. There are, according to Freedman, more ties between the profession of literary studies—its terms, values, and structures—and the larger society than Graff seems able or willing to acknowledge. The conflict model is, in sum, too good to be true.

Harold Fromm also discusses Graff's work in the context of literary theory and departmental/disciplinary policy and practice. But his vision is at odds with Freedman's, and hence he criticizes Graff from a quite different direction. He appreciates some of Graff's suggestions as a means to overcome the isolation of faculty and students. But in Fromm's opinion, the basic need is getting undergraduates to read lots of important books—which he regards as the traditional task that nearly all proposals for educational change, including Graff's, have overlooked. Fromm adds that interpretive "conflicts" like those Graff espouses have been deployed in the past, in, for example, the "casebooks" that lined up a battery of interpretations of a major literary work. The real heart of the matter, he concludes, has less to do with "conflict" than with the leftist orthodoxy that Graff endorses, and the political itinerary that, at the expense of the books that the faculty should be teaching and that the students should be reading, Graff prescribes for the profession.

Whereas Fromm attacks Graff, and other theorists like him, for having done something *to* literary studies, Steven Mailloux accents Graff's contribution for the *betterment* of literary studies. Mailloux takes special note of the rhetoric that Graff has used, a rhetoric that features such terms as "debate," "conversation," and "dialogue." He suggests that Graff could strengthen his plan for educational change if he tapped into rhetoric—and the topics it raises—as part of "teaching the conflicts." One of the useful aspects of Mailloux's essay is that it gives an account of a major curricular initiative under way at Syracuse University that Mailloux himself helped to launch, and that Graff has cited favorably. Both Graff and Mailloux seek to reorient work in the humanities and in the emerging field of cultural studies, and, in Mailloux's case, in the human sciences as well.

Mailloux closes, as does Freedman, by recommending greater analytical and curricular contact between composition, literary, and cultural studies. And this is the issue that John Schilb explores in detail in his essay. Though Schilb admires the thrust of Graff's proposals, he worries that these could deepen the rift between literature and composition, and further marginalize the students enrolled in composition courses.

Like Mailloux to an extent, Schilb hopes to capitalize on the discipline of rhetoric. He believes that it can connect the theory of composition, which depicts writing as persuasion, and advanced literary theory, which delves into the tropes and figures of speech that organize written texts. Schilb also contends that there are more separations and conflicts within departments, and within their hierarchy of rewards, than Graff recognizes. Perhaps the central one exists between faculty and students, whose perception of what counts as an issue or a conflict the faculty usually disregard or dismiss. Schilb judges, indeed, that Graff underestimates students, and the resources they possess.

Andrea A. Lunsford and Suellynn Duffey make a version of this same point when they warn against the risk of the teacher merely enacting the conflicts before a group of passive students. They note that Graff's language is itself somewhat conflicted and contradictory; it includes imagery of battle and war as well as of conversation and mutually instructive dialogue. As Lunsford and Duffey suggest, for the conflict model to achieve its full potential, it must lead to a truly profound rearrangement of the relationship of teachers and students, with the students playing an active role in the conversations, rather than simply giving a slightly different cast to the familiar arrangement of dominant teacher and subordinate students.

Through their account of first-year writing courses at Ohio State University, Lunsford and Duffey provide concrete guidance and practical tips for classroom work that defines teachers and students as "co-constructors of knowledge." Engaging conflict, they conclude, involves challenging hierarchy of all kinds; if this is not done, then the conflicts will be only partially treated, and teachers and students, like teachers of writing and teachers of literature courses, will remain separate from one another. They will not be joined in a common endeavor—the goal to which Graff aspires.

In her own way, Deborah H. Holdstein also perceives conflicts in higher education that Graff fails to consider fully. She notes that many institutions face severe financial and administrative crises; and at such times, major changes are exceedingly hard to propose, develop, and implement. It's hard enough, she indicates, just to retain the main elements of the structure already in place. Nevertheless, Holdstein does believe that Graff's ideas can figure in specific courses, if not in the curriculum as a whole, and that the adjustments made in these courses can aid students in making better sense of their academic work in general. For her, as for others, one of the main rewards of Graff's ideas is that they help to kindle important kinds of discussion in the classroom—about, for example, the meanings of "high culture"—and impel students to connect writers, texts, and issues that are too often compartmentalized.

Patrick J. Hill, like Holdstein, argues that Graff has not gotten to the bottom of the conflicts to which he refers. But Hill's point has less to do with the conflicts in departments and disciplines than with the conflicts between faculty and an increasingly diverse, multicultural, and multiethnic student body. Have we, Hill asks, really given sustained, serious thought to the challenges of teaching the "new" students, from America and abroad, who are now attending colleges and universities? He raises another important commonsense question: how can Graff convince faculty to make significant change, given that most believe that programs for change and reform, and for dealing with conflict, are meant for someone else, are someone else's business? Hill maintains that Graff has failed to tackle these basic questions, and has glided past the burdens and responsibilities that afflict American and global societies. When Graff invokes "conflict," he is touching on something important, but, says Hill, Graff is dealing more with the pale reflection of racial, ecological, and economic conflicts than with their full, painful reality.

Like others in this volume, Timothy D. Johnston pays special attention to the "field coverage" model of education that Graff has criticized. Johnston not only agrees with Graff about its shortcomings, but observes that faculty have done little to aid students in acquiring the cognitive skills needed to sort through and integrate knowledge. Johnston is a psychologist, and hence brings to bear on the discussion a keen feeling for the problems that teachers outside the humanities confront.

Johnston's account, like Mailloux's, considers a new curricular initiative, a freshman seminar program at the University of North Carolina at Greensboro that draws upon Graff's ideas. Johnston professes that Graff has correctly noted the merits of *engaging* students in the discourse of the academic disciplines, and he appreciates the ways in which Graff's proposals can increase the prospects for truly "participatory learning."

Lynette Felber, however, is more guarded and skeptical. She welcomes the opportunities for dialogue that Graff's reforms afford, but, somewhat like Hill, she judges that the conflicts are more profound than Graff realizes. She surveys the limits on the expression of ideas on campus, especially for junior faculty who may hesitate to disagree with senior colleagues: they may pay a stiff price for the conflicts they perceive and dare to kindle.

In Felber's estimation, the problems that Graff has diagnosed, such as those caused by the "field coverage" model, can only be resolved if other problems are solved first—the split between research and teaching, the exploitation of part-time faculty, the lack of parity between male and female faculty, the decision-making power vested in senior faculty, and the lowly status of junior faculty. She sees great potential for worthwhile "destabilization" in Graff's recommendations, but maintains that more must be done. Implicit in her argument is the notion that it matters greatly who holds power and hence *who names* the conflicts—who decides just what are the conflicts that teachers and students should delve into and organize the curriculum around. In closing, Felber offers ideas of her own for a "core course" for undergraduate and graduate students; and like Johnston in psychology, she, in the field of literary studies, calls for a better means to "integrate" the work that students undertake.

D. G. Myers's essay in one sense hearkens back to Mailloux's, in that Myers, too, inspects the rhetoric, the verbal form, through which Graff states his views. But Myers's piece is also linked to Hill's and Felber's, because it fastens on the inadequacies of Graff's conception of conflict. Graff suggests that education should "represent" conflicts in which the various sides have their say, but, according to Myers, he does not consider how each side might (or should) appraise the truth or falsity of its own claims. If Graff's proposals are not coupled to a crisp understanding of the canons of rational argument, says Myers, they will not achieve the goals established for them. It's fine to recommend that students take part in debates about educational conflicts, but, in Myers's judgment, they cannot profitably participate if they are not trained in logic. They will not be introduced to, or make discriminations within, the disciplines and will not advance in their knowledge.

James J. Sosnoski propels the discussion into the future, as he forecasts the conditions in which education will occur at the turn of the century. Like Johnston and Felber, he too spotlights the integration of knowledge, yet points out that it will be achieved in the years ahead through an array of new and developing technologies—computers, VCRs, CD-ROM disks, and audio systems. As we ponder Graff's recommendations, we must be mindful, Sosnoski states, of the "university of the future" and its modified tools and instruments. Sosnoski explores how the notions of a learning community, of intellectual collaboration, of teacher/student interaction—all of which Graff underscores—can be implemented via the new "conceptual environments" that computers make available. Such changes will not be easy by any means, in part because of lingering uneasiness about technology among humanities scholars, but in part, too, because the technology itself can deepen the very isolation that Graff wants to overcome. Sosnoski concludes that the benefits outweigh the hazards, and he describes the dazzling communication, collaboration, and community that highly computerized "time and space" create.

The volume ends with Graff's reply to his critics, in which he corrects common misconceptions about his ideas, and takes up a number of the issues that the essayists here have articulated. His thinking about educational reform has been in process for decades—always gaining, I think, in force and clarity—and the commentaries assembled here provide him with another important occasion to test and reframe his views.

While working closely with Graff's ideas, and gauging how they might effectively be put into practice, I have been led, like others here, to ask just what the future in American education will hold. One of the aims of this volume is to stimulate readers to scout the territory ahead, and to think about what education in the 1990s and in the new century should look like and should accomplish. It may be that the culture wars will rage on, each side locked into defense of its own agenda and demanding changes in educational theory and practice that would mean the elimination of the other side. That is the prospect that Graff has warned against, and that his proposed reforms are geared to curtail and transform into something better. The grave danger of the current state of war about values, goals, policies, and curricula is narrowness, rigidity, and reductionism—which result from the statement and restatement of positions that are closed to exploratory analytical contact with the positions of the other side.

On the Right and on the Left, there is far too much preaching to the already converted, and it is disturbing to imagine that this might continue unabated, with no end in sight, and with the true exercise of critical consciousness blocked. Just as disturbing is the possibility that students will remain outside the debates that affect them, missing the opportunities for acquiring skills and knowledge, and for learning to express themselves cogently in speech and writing, that working *with* the conflicts can offer to them. We wonder why students are not better than they are, even as we deny them a fair chance to surprise us.

NOTES

1. One could readily list other examples of extreme rhetoric, such as Bruce Bawer's essay-review of *The Columbia History of the American*

Novel, a volume that Bawer terms "the single most frightening document yet to emerge from the Marxist assault on American higher education. . . . To read it is to step into an Orwellian nightmare where freedom is slavery, wealth is poverty, and knowledge is ignorance; it is to feel as if one is motoring through some Iron Curtain metropolis of the mind, down a boulevard lined with interchangeably gray and desolate edifices" (20; see also Toynton).

WORKS CITED

Bawer, Bruce. "Columbia's Assault on the American Novel." *The New Criterion* 10 (December 1991): 20–31.

Bennett, William J. *To Reclaim a Legacy: A Report on the Humanities in Higher Education.* Washington, D.C.: National Endowment for the Humanities. November 1984.

Berman, Paul, ed. Introduction to *Debating P.C.: The Controversy over Political Correctness on College Campuses.* New York: Dell, 1992. 1–26.

Douglass, Frederick. *Writings.* Ed. Philip S. Foner. Vols. 1–5. New York: International, 1975.

Giroux, Henry A. "Liberal Arts Education and the Struggle for Public Life: Dreaming about Democracy." *South Atlantic Quarterly* 89 (Winter 1990): 133–38.

———. *Theory and Resistance in Education: A Pedagogy for the Opposition.* South Hadley, MA: Bergin, 1983.

Graff, Gerald. *Beyond the Culture Wars: How Teaching the Conflicts Can Revitalize American Education.* New York: Norton, 1992.

———. *Literature against Itself: Literary Ideas in Modern Society.* Chicago: University of Chicago Press, 1979.

———. *Poetic Statement and Critical Dogma.* Evanston, IL: Northwestern University Press, 1970.

———. *Professing Literature: An Institutional History.* Chicago: University of Chicago Press, 1987.

"*The Heath Anthology.*" Reply to Paul Lauter. *The New Criterion* 9 (December 1990): 87–88.

"The Heath Travesty of American Literature." *The New Criterion* 9 (October 1990): 3–5.

Hirsch, E. D. *The Aims of Interpretation*. Chicago: University of Chicago Press, 1976.

———. *Validity in Interpretation*. 1967. New Haven, CT: Yale University Press, 1974.

Hunter, James Davison. *Culture Wars: The Struggle to Define America*. New York: Basic, 1991.

Kimball, Roger. "*Tenured Radicals*: A Postscript." *The New Criterion* 9 (January 1991): 4–13.

Lauter, Paul. Letter on *The Heath Anthology*. *The New Criterion* 9 (December 1990): 87.

Lauter, Paul, et al., eds. *The Heath Anthology of American Literature*. 2 vols. Lexington, MA: Heath, 1990.

MacDonald, Heather. "D'Souza's Critics: PC Fights Back." *Academic Questions* 5 (Summer 1992): 9–22.

Oakley, Francis. *Community of Learning: The American College and the Liberal Arts Tradition*. New York: Oxford University Press, 1992.

Phillips, Wendell. *Wendell Phillips on Civil Rights and Freedom*. Ed. Louis Filler. New York: Hill and Wang, 1965.

Toynton, Evelyn. "Policing Literature." *Commentary* (July 1992): 60–62.

Watkins, Evan. *Work Time: English Departments and the Circulation of Cultural Value*. Palo Alto, CA: Stanford University Press, 1989.

I. Gerald Graff: Selections

Taking Cover in Coverage*

Gerald Graff

In addressing the topic "The Value of Theory in English Studies," I want to say at the outset that the antagonism usually presumed to exist between literary theory and humanistic tradition has been exaggerated. It is perfectly possible to defend the infusion of theory into the curriculum on traditional grounds, namely, that students need theoretical frameworks in order to conceptualize, and talk about, literature. Until recently, in fact, it was traditionalists like Irving Babbitt and Norman Foerster who called for more "theory," in opposition to the disconnected empiricism of positivist literary history and formalistic explication, where the faith seemed to be that "the facts, once in, would of themselves mean something" (Foerster 11–12). Most scholars "have left virtually uninspected the theory upon which their practice rests" or have proceeded "as if that theory were an absolute good for all time" (Foerster et al. v). While a great deal of current theory does radically attack the premises and values of traditional literary humanism, that attack revives the kinds of questions about literature and its cultural functions that used to concern traditional humanistic critics.

The real enemy of tradition has been the established forms of literary study, which has neglected traditional theoretical questions about the ends and social functions of literature and criticism. There is something strange about the belief that we are

*Originally presented as a panel discussion on "The Value of Theory in English Studies" and published in *Profession 86* (1986): 41–45. Reprinted by permission of the Modern Language Association of America.

being traditional when we isolate literary works from their contexts and explicate them in a vacuum or with a modicum of background information. Matthew Arnold would have recognized little traditional or humanistic in these established forms of pedagogy. Obviously I am not saying that recent literary theory is nothing more than the application of Arnoldian culture by other means. What I am saying is that recent theory has reawakened some of the large questions that Arnold raised, while rejecting the Arnoldian answers as no longer sufficient.

In fact, it was the breakdown of agreement on the Arnoldian answers that inspired the current popularity of theory and ensures, I think, that this interest will not be a passing fad. By one definition that seems to me to be valid, "literary theory" is simply the kind of discourse that is generated when presuppositions that were once tacitly shared about literature, criticism, and culture become open to question. Theory is what breaks out when agreement about such terms as *text, reading, history, interpretation, tradition* and *literature* can no longer be taken for granted, so that their meanings have to be formulated and debated. Admittedly, the term *theory* is used here in a very broad sense, denoting an examination of legitimating presuppositions, beliefs, and ideologies. By this definition, even antitheorists like Arnold and F.R. Leavis qualify as theorists, having theorized about the premises of literature and culture and the place of literature and culture in modern societies. And in this sense all teachers of literature operate on theories, whether they choose to examine these theories or not.

Clearly, we need to reserve another sense of theory to denote the technical, abstruse, and systematic speculation typical of recent Continental thought. But here is another misconception—that theory is necessarily obscure, technical and abstruse, and therefore too advanced or esoteric for the average college or high school student of literature. This belief fails to recognize that all teaching involves popularization and that even the most difficult current theories are not intrinsically more resistant to popularization than the New Criticism, which had its own abstruse conceptual origins in Kant, Coleridge, and Croce.

It is the average-to-poor student who suffers most from the established curriculum's poverty of theory, for such a student lacks command of the conceptual contexts that make it possible to integrate perceptions and generalize from them. All the close concentration in the world on the particularities of literary texts will not help a student make sense of these particularities without the categories that give them meaning.

Current antitheorists have things exactly backward when they oppose theory to tradition and to close literary analysis and demand that we minister to the ills of literary studies by desisting from theoretical chatter and getting back to teaching literature itself. It was the isolation of "literature itself" in a conceptual vacuum that stranded students without a context for talking about literature and that still forces many of them to *Cliffs Notes* and other such cribs. It is easy to disdain these cribs, but marketing pressures have actually forced their producers to think through the problems facing the average literature student more realistically than have many department curricular planners. *Cliffs Notes* supply students with the generalized things to say about literary works that the literature program takes for granted they will somehow get on their own.

The irony of the current cry of "back to literature itself" is that it was the exclusive concentration on literature itself that helped create a situation in which the *Cliffs Notes* on given works of literature are more readily available in campus bookstores than are the works themselves. Perhaps I am naive to suggest that a more theoretically contextualized curriculum would cause such cribs to wither away. I can certainly imagine a *Cliffs Notes* on deconstruction, supplementing the ones on Keats and Dickens. But for the moment I think we should view this eventuality as a possibility to be recognized and avoided rather than as an inevitability.

These opening reflections will probably persuade only those who already agree with them. My purpose here, however, is not to make a case for theory in the literature program but to point up some difficulties that arise once we have decided that such a goal is desirable. In addressing the pedagogical uses of recent literary theory, we tend to treat the issue as if it were primarily a matter of figuring out how to integrate this theory into individual classrooms. We form conference "workshops," which concentrate on technical questions like how to use reader-response criticism to teach *Hamlet*, or poststructuralist theory to teach the romantic lyric, or feminist critiques of the established canon to restructure the nineteenth-century-novel course. Such reforms can be useful and necessary, but if we do not go beyond them we will limit theory to its instrumental uses, making it into a means of sprucing up ritualized procedures of explication. We will apply theory within the existing structure but will fail to make a theoretical examination of the structure itself.

I want to suggest that one of the first things we need to do with literary theory is to train it on the literature department itself, particularly on the way that the department and other departments and the university are organized. Insofar as a literature department represents a certain organization of literature, it is itself a kind of theory, though it has been largely an incoherent theory, and this incoherence in fact has reinforced the impression that the department has no theory.

In deciding to call ourselves departments of English, French, and German—rather than of literature, cultural studies, or something else—and in subdividing these national units into periods and genres, we have already made significant theoretical choices. But we do not see these choices as choices, much less as theoretical ones, because the categories that mark them— English, eighteenth century, poetry, novel—operate as administrative conveniences and eventually as facts of nature that we can take for granted. We need to recognize that the way we organize and departmentalize literature is not only a crucial theoretical choice but one that largely determines our professional activity and the way students and the laity see it or fail to see it.

To make this statement is not to agree with those who think that the departmentalization of literature itself was a kind of original sin and who look back nostalgically to the days before the creative imagination was bureaucratized. Anyone seriously committed to the idea of democratic mass education has to acknowledge the obvious necessity for some form of bureaucratic departmental organization and the specialized division of labor that that entails. But the form that organization takes is neither self-evident nor inevitable, and it will have a lot to do with considerations of theory.

I use the term field coverage as a convenient description of the model of organization that has governed literature departments since the dawn of the modern university, in the last two decades of the nineteenth century. According to the field-coverage model, a department considers itself adequately staffed when it has acquired the personnel to "cover" an adequate number of designated fields of literature, and it assumes that the core of the curriculum will consist of the student's coverage of some portion of those fields. The field-coverage model arose as an adaptation to the modern university's ideal of research specialization, for dividing the territory of literature into fields supervised by specialists imitated the organizational form that had made the sciences efficient in producing advanced research. But the field-coverage principle had a humanistic justification as well, the argument that a student who covered the fields represented by the average department would get a reasonably balanced exposure to the literary-humanistic tradition.

It was the operational advantages, however, that made the field-coverage model irresistible, especially in a newly expanding university where short-term expediency rarely afforded leisure for discussion of first principles and where first principles in any case were becoming increasingly open to dispute. One of the most conspicuous operational advantages was the way field coverage made the department virtually self-regulating. By assigning instructors the roles predetermined by their literary fields, the model created a system in which the job of instruction could proceed as if on automatic pilot, with no need for instructors to confer with their peers or superiors. Assuming that individual instructors had been competently trained—and by about 1900 or so the American system of graduate study had matured sufficiently to see to that—they could be left on their own to carry out their teaching and research jobs without elaborate supervision and management.

A second advantage of the field-coverage model was that it made the department immensely flexible to innovation. By making individuals functionally independent of one another in carrying out their tasks, the model enabled the department to assimilate new subjects, ideas, and methodologies without risking the conflicts that would otherwise have had to be debated and worked through. It thus allowed the modern university to overcome the chronic stagnation that had beset the old nineteenth-century college, where new ideas that challenged the established Christian orthodoxy were usually excluded or suppressed. The coverage model solved the problem of how to make the university open to innovation and diverse viewpoints without incurring paralyzing conflicts.

Unfortunately, these advantages came at a severe cost that we have been paying ever since. The same arrangement that allowed instructors to do their jobs efficiently and independently also relieved them of the need to discuss matters of fundamental direction either with their own members or with members of other departments, and it is a rule of bureaucratic organizations that whatever such organizations are not structurally required to do they will tend not to do. Moral exhortation unaccompanied by structural change will be largely wasted. The department was open to innovation as the college had not been before, but under circumstances that were almost as effective in muffling the confrontations provoked by innovation as the old system of repressive control had been. Previously there had been little open debate over first principles because dissenters had been excluded. Now dissenters were invited in, but the departmental structure kept them too isolated from their colleagues for open debate to take place.

Vigorous controversy did arise, but usually only behind the scenes of education, in specialized journals, department meetings, or private gossip—all places where students derived little benefit from it, usually knew nothing of its existence, and certainly did not participate in it. Instructors were freer than they had been from administrative tyranny, but at the sacrifice of certain possibilities of intellectual community.

To put it another way, the field-coverage model solved the problem of theory. Departmental organization took the place of theory, for the presence of an ordered array of fields, fully staffed, made it unnecessary for anyone to have a theory about what the department should do to permit the work of teaching and research to go on. The theoretical choices had already been taken care of in the grid of periods, genres, and other catalog rubrics, which embodied a clear and seemingly uncontroversial conceptualization of what the department was about. With literature courses ranged in periods and genres, instructors did not need to ask what "period" or "genre" meant or what justified the established demarcations. The connections and contrasts between periods and genres, so important for understanding these categories, fell between the cracks, as did other large issues in the university, such as the relation between the sciences and the humanities, which was the responsibility of neither the sciences nor the humanities.

Latent conflicts of method and ideology that had divided the faculty from the outset and the cultural conflicts that these often exemplified did not have to be confronted and taught. Fundamental disagreements over the study of literature were embodied, for example, in the conflict between the research "scholar," who adhered to a positivistic methodology, and the generalist man or woman of letters, who scorned this methodology, and, later, in the conflict between both these types and the hyperanalytical New Critic. But while the department enacted these conflicts, it did not explicitly foreground and engage them. As long as scholars, generalists, and critics covered their turfs within self-enclosed classrooms, the average student did not need to be aware of the clashes of principle, much less use them as a larger context for literary study.

This explanation accounts for the otherwise inexplicable persistence of the fiction of shared humanistic values and purposes during a period when conflicts in method and ideology were becoming progressively more frequent and antagonistic. Since the official premise that humanistic values governed the department did not have to be theorized or subjected to periodical review and discussion, there was no particular reason to acknowledge that the premise was wearing increasingly thin. Not only did the structure provide no necessary occasion for questioning the content of that humanism which, according to the catalog, theoretically held the diverse and conflicting viewpoints of departments together, but the illusion could be maintained that nobody even had a theory.

And of course it was true that the department did not have *a* theory, for it harbored many theories without any clear way to integrate them. Here we arrive at the central problem: how does a department institutionalize theory when there is no agreement on what the theory is to be? The question becomes answerable, however, only if it is assumed that a department must achieve theoretical *consensus* before it can achieve theoretical coherence.

The perennial assumption seems to have been that professional and cultural conflicts have to be *resolved* before they can be presented to the students; students, apparently, must be exposed only to the results of the conflicts dividing their teachers, not to the process of conflict itself, which presumably would confuse or demoralize them. Surely one reason why we tend, as I noted earlier, to reduce pedagogical questions to questions about workshop techniques for individual courses is that we doubt the possibility of agreement on larger collective goals. Our doubts are well founded in experience, but why need we assume that we have to agree in order to integrate our activities? Must we have consensus to have coherence?

The unfortunate thing is not that our conflicts of method and ideology have often proved unresolvable but that we have been able to exploit so little of the potential educational value of our unresolved conflicts. Part of the reason stems from the literary mind's temperamental resistance to airing differences; the old-fashioned version of this attitude held that open debate is unseemly, while the more up-to-date version holds that there are no privileged metalanguages, or no fact-of-the-matter outside interpretations, or no "decidable" answers to questions, so that there is nothing to argue about anyway. But even if these sources of resistance to debate were to disappear, there would remain a problem of structure. Our structure prevents exemplary differences of method, ideology, and value from emerging into view even when we want them to.

The literature curriculum mirrors and reproduces the evasion of conflict characteristic of the departmental structure. Hypothetically, the curriculum expresses a unified humanistic tradition, yet anyone who looks at it can see that in every era down to the present it has never expressed a unity of humanistic values but always a set of political trade-offs and compromises among competing professional factions. We need not enter into the now disputed question of whether the curriculum can or should be determined by any more lofty principle than political trade-offs, for again this is precisely the type of theoretical and cultural question that does not have to be resolved in order to play an effective part in education. If the curriculum is going to continue to express political trade-offs, as it seems likely to do unless one faction in the current disciplinary conflict can wholly liquidate its opposition, then why not bring students in on whatever may be instructive in the conflict of political principles involved?

Instead of confronting such conflicts and building them into the curriculum, however, the department (and the university at large) has always responded to pressures by adding new subjects and keeping them safely sealed off from one another. This practice can be justified educationally only on the increasingly hollow pretense that exposure to an aggregate of teachers, periods, genres, methods, and points of view figures to come together in the student's mind as a coherent humanistic experience. The tacit faith is that students will make sense of the aggregate even if their instructors cannot. The surprising thing is that some students manage to do just that, but most do not. Recognition of this failure stimulates further curricular innovation, which in turn, however, is assimilated to the cycle of accretion and marginalization. So we beat on, boats against the current, etc., etc.

Over the hundred-year span of our institutional history we have had a succession of methodological models, each with a corresponding pedagogy, from linguistic philology to positivist literary history to New Critical explication, all of which now remain as geological strata overlaid by the new theories and methodologies. Each of these revisions has marked a paradigm shift in which the conception of what counts as "literature," "scholarship," and "criticism" altered radically. Yet, as I attempt to show in a forthcoming institutional history of academic literary studies in the United States [i.e., *Professing Literature*, published in 1987], the one constant through all this change has been the field-coverage model. The contents have been radically reshuffled, but the envelope has remained the same, and with it the method of assimilating innovation. Arguably the changes represent considerable progress in critical sophistication and cultural range, but if I am correct the benefits for the average student have been less than they might have been.

Nor is it just the students who have paid a price under the field-coverage system, it is the faculty as well. The principles of selection for amassing a literature faculty have systematically screened out intellectual commonality and programmed professional loneliness. A self-destructive principle is built into the mighty effort departments make to achieve a balanced spread of interests. If the interests of candidate X overlap those of faculty Y, their shared ground is an argument for not hiring X—"We already have Y who does that." The calculus of needs determining appointment priorities thus tends to preselect exactly those instructors who have the least basis for talking to one another. In compensation the department gets a salutary diversity, but the potential benefits of diversity are not really exploited. Nor is the problem merely abstract; the recent proliferation of humanities conferences and symposia suggests that these gatherings have become substitutes for the kind of general discussion that does not take place at home.

The moral is that if the introduction of theory is to make a real difference at the average student's level, we must find some way to modify the field-coverage model, if not to scrap it entirely. Otherwise, theory will be institutionalized as yet another field, equivalent to literary periods and genres—which is to say, it will become one more option that can safely be ignored. We will lose theory's potential for drawing the disconnected parts of the literature curriculum into relation and providing students with the needed contexts. So, I would argue, the real threat that theory faces today comes not from its outright opponents, some of whom are at least willing to argue with it, but from those who are perfectly willing to grant theory an honored place in the scheme of departmental coverage so that they can then forget about it.

This pattern seems to be establishing itself now, as departments clamor to hire theorists to get the new field covered, after which they sit back and assume that the relation of theory to the interests of the rest of the department will take care of itself. In practice, this policy passes the buck to the students, leaving them to figure out how theory courses correlate with the others. And of course as long as theory is conceived of as a special field, the rest of the department can go on thinking that its work has no connection with theory.

Offering students doses of theory in individual courses without helping them make the requisite connections and relations between courses will tend to produce a confused response, which antitheorists will quickly take as proof that theory is inherently over the head of the average student. For the average student to profit from theory, especially from recent theory, the courses that incorporate it must be not only linked with other courses, both theoretical and untheoretical, but also positioned to operate as a central means of correlation and contextualization.

In other words, literature departments should stop kidding themselves. They should stop pretending that, as long as individual courses are reasonably well conceived and well taught, the aggregate can be counted on to take care of itself. If they are serious about incorporating theory, they should not let it remain an option but should make it central to all their activities, not by putting theory specialists in charge but by recognizing that all their members are theorists.

To put it another way, introducing more theory will only compound our problems unless we rethink the assumption that the essential unit of all teaching has to be the single, self-sufficient course that the students correlate with other courses on their own. We can fail just as badly teaching a new canon in a theoretical way as we have failed in teaching an old canon in a nontheoretical way. Unless literature teachers change their means of connecting institutionally with one another, I am afraid that even the most radical theories and canon revisions will not significantly affect the way most students take in what is put before them.

To close, then, I offer a few schematic suggestions:

1. In relation to other courses in the department, theory courses should be central, not peripheral; their function should be to contextualize and pull together the students' work in other courses (outside as well as inside the literature department). Wherever possible, therefore, they should be required courses rather than electives.

2. In taking stock of its strengths, a department should evaluate not just how well it is covering standard fields and approaches but also what potential conflicts of ideological and methodological perspectives it harbors; it should then ask itself what curricular arrangements might exploit these conflicts. There need be no single way of doing this—but one idea (suggested by Brook Thomas) is to couple courses to bring out conceptual relations and contrasts—between, say, views of literature in earlier and modern literary periods or between competing and complementary methodologies of interpretation.

3. A department harboring a conflict between theorists and antitheorists should look for ways to build this conflict into its courses, so that students can situate themselves in relation to the controversy and eventually participate in it. The department should also look for ways such disputes can be used to complicate and challenge period and genre distinctions without necessarily eliminating them.

4. A department should consider the unit of teaching to be the issue or context, not the isolated text; texts to be taught should be chosen not only for their intrinsic value but for their usefulness in illustrating exemplary problems and issues.

5. As a means of accomplishing goal 4 on a structural scale, the university should subsume literary studies under cultural studies and cultural history, conceived not as a privileged approach but as a framework that encourages ideological dialectic while retaining enough chronological structure to keep focus and continuity from being lost.

The point is that theory is not only a field to be covered, though it is that at one level. It is something that all teachers of literature and all readers practice and that all have a stake in. The worst thing we could do would be to institutionalize theory in a compartmentalized way that would keep theorists and antitheorists from having to hear what they are saying about each other—and would keep students from observing and joining in the battle.

WORKS CITED

Foerster, Norman et al., eds. *Literary Scholarship: Its Aims and Methods.* Chapel Hill: University of North Carolina Press, 1941.

Graff, Gerald. *Professing Literature: An Institutional History.* Chicago: University of Chicago Press, 1987.

Other Voices, Other Rooms: Organizing and Teaching the Humanities Conflict*

Gerald Graff

In the faculty lounge the other day, a dispute arose between a couple of my colleagues that typifies the warfare currently agitating the educational world. It began when an older male professor complained that he had just come from teaching Matthew Arnold's "Dover Beach" and had been appalled to discover that the poem was virtually incomprehensible to his class. Here was yet another sorry illustration of the deplorably ill-prepared state of today's students. Why, can you believe it, said the older male professor (taking a page from the personal ads, let us call him OMP for short), my students were at a loss as to what to make of Arnold's famous concluding lines, which he proceeded to recite with slightly self-mocking grandiloquence:

> Ah, love, let us be true
> To one another! for the world, which seems
> To lie before us like a land of dreams,
> So various, so beautiful, so new,
> Hath really neither joy, nor love, nor light,
> Nor certitude, nor peace, nor help for pain;
> And we are here as on a darkling plain
> Swept with confused alarms of struggle and flight
> Where ignorant armies clash by night.

*Originally published in *New Literary History* 21 (1990): 817–839; and republished in revised form in *Beyond the Culture Wars: How Teaching the Conflicts Can Revitalize American Education* (New York: W.W. Norton, 1992); reprinted with permission.

My other colleague, a young woman who has just recently joined our department (let us call her YFP), replied that she could appreciate the students' reaction. She recalled that she had been forced to study "Dover Beach" in high school and had consequently formed a dislike for poetry that it had taken her years to overcome. Why teach "Dover Beach" anyway, YFP asked. No wonder so many of our students hate poetry when this is the way "poetry" is presented to them!

Furiously stirring his coffee-mate, OMP replied that in *his* humble opinion—reactionary though he supposed it now was— "Dover Beach" was one of the great masterpieces of the Western tradition, a work that, until recently at least, every seriously educated person took for granted as part of the cultural heritage. YFP retorted that while that might be so, it was not altogether to the credit of the cultural heritage. Take those lines addressed to the woman by the speaker, she said: "Ah, love, let us be true to one another . . . ," and so on. In other words, protect and console me, my dear—as we know it's the function of your naturally more spiritual sex to do—from the "struggle and flight" of politics and history that we men have regrettably been assigned the unpleasant duty of dealing with. YFP added that she would have a hard time finding a better example of what feminists mean when they speak of the ideological construction of the feminine as by nature private and domestic and therefore justly disqualified from sharing male power. Here, however, she paused and corrected herself: "Actually," she said, "we *should* teach 'Dover Beach.' We should teach it as the arch example of phallocentric discourse that it is."

OMP responded that YFP seemed to be treating "Dover Beach" as if it were a piece of political propaganda rather than a work of art. To take Arnold's poem as if it were a species of "phallocentric discourse," whatever that is, misses the whole point of poetry, OMP said, which is to rise above local and transitory problems by transmuting them into universal structures of language and image. Arnold's poem is no more about gender politics, declared OMP, than *Macbeth* is about the Stuart monarchical succession.

But *Macbeth is* about the Stuart monarchical succession, retorted YFP—as its original audience surely would have thought. It's about gender politics too—why else does Lady Macbeth need to "unsex" herself before she can participate in murdering Duncan? Not to mention all the business about men born of woman and from their mothers' womb untimely ripped. The fact is, Professor OMP, that what you presume to be the universal human experience in Arnold and Shakespeare is male experience presented as if it were universal. You don't need to notice the politics of sexuality because for you patriarchy is the normal state of affairs. You can afford to ignore the sexual politics of literature, or to "transmute" them, as you put it, onto a universal plane, but that's a luxury I don't enjoy. . . .

Theory Has Broken Out

There are many possible ways to describe what happened here, but one of them would be to say that "theory" had broken out. What we have come to call "theory," I would suggest, is the kind of reflective, second-order discourse about practices that is generated when a consensus that was once taken for granted in a community breaks down. When this happens, assumptions that previously have been taken for granted as the "normal state of affairs"—in this case OMP's assumption that literature is above sexual politics—have to be explicitly formulated and argued about. What had formerly gone without saying now has to be *argued for*.

OMP would probably complain that this trend diverts attention from literature itself. But YFP could reply that literature itself was not being ignored in their debate but discussed in a new way. It was not that she and OMP stopped talking about poetry and starting talking theory. It was rather that because their conflicting theoretical assumptions differed about how to talk about poetry, they had to talk about it in a way that foregrounded those theories.

Not sharing the same assumptions about literature, criticism, and the aims of education, OMP and YFP could not discuss "Dover Beach" without being drawn into matters of theory—the very matters of theory, in fact, which have preoccupied the literary theorizing of the last several decades:

the nature of literary value and meaning and its relation to questions of politics, canonicity, and pedagogy. But then, the very question of whether this kind of discussion should properly be called "talking about literature in a new way" or "abandoning literature for theory" is doubtless another of the questions that OMP and YFP would disagree about.

The recent prominence of theory, then, is the result of a climate of radical disagreement, and the complaint that theory is pervasive finally reduces to the complaint that literature and criticism have become too controversial. Yet the complaint only has the effect of generating more theory and more of the theoretical disagreement being deplored. Forced by the disagreement to articulate his principles, OMP, the traditional humanist, was "doing theory" just as much as YFP, articulating assumptions that previously he could have taken as given. That opposition to theory is itself a theory is increasingly borne out today, as opposition to theory becomes an attitude one has to argue for, or at least explicitly assert, with the effect not of drawing the discussion back to "literature itself" but only to add to the theory-talk.[1] For this reason, the belief that the theory trend is a mere passing fad is likely to be wishful thinking.

The question is who and what are hurt by this situation. Who and what are damaged by conflicts like the one in the faculty lounge? The obvious answer would seem to be "Dover Beach." But this answer raises the question of just how well "Dover Beach" was doing in college (and high school) literature classes before radical teachers like YFP came along. We need only look at the complaint by OMP that triggered the lounge-debate to be reminded that such classics have often inspired deep apathy in students even when taught in the most reverential fashion—perhaps especially when taught in that fashion.

Anyone who has studied the history of modern education will know that professorial complaints about student apathy and incomprehension in the face of the classics have been chronic since American education became a mass enterprise after the turn of the century, when humanists began to feel beleaguered by the philistine culture of vocationalism, fraternity-sorority life, and football.[2] If the problems seem to us to be more grave in

1990 than they were in 1920, this may be only because the number of students available to be bored by works like "Dover Beach" is so much larger in 1990 than it was in 1920. Long before academic feminism and Marxism, pressure to open the canon has stemmed from the recognition of students' problems with classics like "Dover Beach."

Considered in this light, one might argue that "Dover Beach" has little to lose from the debate between OMP and YFP and a good deal to gain. In an odd way, YFP is doing "Dover Beach" a favor: in treating Arnold's poem as a significant instance of ideological mystification, her critique does more to make the poem *a live issue* in the culture again than does the respectful treatment of traditionalist teachers like OMP, which, as he himself complains, fails to arouse his class.

But will "Dover Beach" survive in the course at all if the YFPs of the world have their way? The question is difficult to discuss in the atmosphere of hysterical exaggeration created by wildly misinformed journalistic reports, but its logic is not as clear-cut as it has been made out to be, for the question of what will be read and taught is not easily separable from the question of how and in what context it will be read and taught.[3] If YFP expects to alert students to the phallocentrism of "Dover Beach," she will have to assign the poem. Conversely, it is OMP whose interest is served by dropping the poem from the syllabus. For if teaching it is going to mean demystifying it, then taking it off the reading list would at least have the effect of damage control. Such speculation may be perverse, but it is far from obvious that an attitude of polite deference is more favorable to the survival of a classic like "Dover Beach" than an attitude of ideological interrogation. That survival may well depend on the extent to which "Dover Beach" remains interestingly pertinent to such challenging concerns as those raised by YFP.

What the debate between OMP and YFP really threatens is not "Dover Beach," I think, but OMP's conception of "Dover Beach" as a repository of universal values that transcend the circumstances of its creation and reception. Whereas this decontextualized concept of culture was once axiomatic in humanistic education, it has now become one theory among others, a proposition that has to be argued for rather than taken as given. What is threatened by the canon-controversy, in other words, is not the classics but their unquestioned status. But again, when the classics enjoyed that unquestioned status there is little evidence that it made them seem more compelling to students than they seem now. In short, from an educational point of view, the classics have less to fear from new-fangled ideological hostility than from old-fashioned indifference.

I would argue that what is most unfortunate about the conflict between OMP and YFP is not *that* it is taking place but *where* it is taking place, behind the educational scenes where students cannot learn anything from it. What is really injurious to students' interests is not the conflict over culture but the fact that students are not more active participants in it. For the canon-conflict is not something that is taking place apart from culture, but is necessarily part of what we mean by "culture" in a multicultural society where controversy is increasingly not the exception but the rule. In a society increasingly being forced to come to terms with cultural difference nothing could be more practical than an education that treats cultural and ideological conflict as part of its object of study.

My thought as I watched OMP and YFP go back and forth in the faculty lounge was that if OMP's students could witness this debate they would be more likely to get worked up over "Dover Beach" than they are now. They might even find it easier to gain access to the poem, for the controversy over it might give them a context for reading it that they do not now possess.

Then again, it might not. The controversy would have to be presented in a way that avoids pedantry, obscurity, and technicality, and this is difficult to do. And even when it is done, many students will still have as much trouble seeing why they should take an interest in critical debates over "Dover Beach" as they do seeing why they should take an interest in "Dover Beach" itself. This may be less of a problem as the conflict over the canon becomes ever more urgent and public and its relation becomes clearer to issues whose importance everybody can recognize, like the politics of multiculturalism. But the alienation of students from academic culture often remains deep, and it may deepen further as the terms of that culture become more confusingly in dispute than in the past.

Here lies both the challenge and the difficulty of the newly contested situation of the humanities. As academic culture has become more democratic and plural in content, more engaged in the most challenging problems of the present, and more prone to political conflict, the humanities have become potentially more relevant to the lives of students than the relatively antiquarian and restricted humanities of a generation ago. Yet the very conflicts that betoken the humanities' increase in potential relevance also make them more confusing and hard to penetrate.

The issue here is one of institutional legibility: how do institutional discourses become readable to people not already initiated into them? To what extent does a loss of tacit consensus impair an institution's readability to outsiders? Unless steps are taken to counteract it, an increased degree and intensity of conflict within an intellectual institution figures to make it harder to make the institution's discourses intelligible to its constituencies. It is hard in any period to clarify something so complex as intellectual culture to people not already at home in it, and sometimes not sure they wish to be. It figures to be all the harder to clarify that culture when there is less and less philosophical common ground to fall back on. In the humanities today, that common ground has so diminished that the very question of what counts as a "clarification" is part of what is politically contested. My clarification may be your ideological obfuscation.

In such a situation, helping students gain access to academic discourse communities means clarifying conflicts like the one between OMP and YFP (and numerous others not so neatly polarized), even as what counts as true clarification remains itself open to debate. If the aim is to help students become interested participants in the present cultural conversation instead of puzzled and alienated spectators—or as passive recipients of a one-way transmission in which "our" culture trickles down to "them"—the aim should be to *organize* such conflicts of principle in the curriculum itself.

Just opening reading lists to noncanonical works— necessary as that step is—will not in itself solve the problem. Merely replacing "Dover Beach" with *The Color Purple* does not necessarily help the student who has difficulty with the intellectual vocabularies in which both those texts are discussed in the academic environment. What makes reading and interpretation difficult for many students is not the kind of text being read, whether canonical or non-canonical, highbrow or popular, but the heavily thematic and allegorical ways in which all texts irrespective of status level are discussed in the academic setting—the student phrase for it is looking for "hidden meaning." Academics are so accustomed to attributing certain kinds of abstract meanings to all phenomena, not just texts, that they easily forget that this activity does not seem natural or self-evidently justifiable to everyone. If the practice of looking for hidden meaning seems strange to you, it will seem no less strange to look for it in *The Color Purple* than in *Hamlet*.

This last point needs underscoring, because educational progressives have been too quick to blame student alienation from academic literacy on the elitist or conservative aspects of that literacy. But students can be as alienated from democratized forms of academic literacy as from conservative forms, and from permissive as well as restrictive classrooms. What alienates such students is academic literacy *as such*, with its unavoidably abstract and analytical ways of talking and writing, regardless of whether that literacy comes in traditional or populist forms.

Perhaps too much educational writing is done by people who either never experienced this alienation from academic literacy or who forgot what it was like once they overcame it. My own recollection of school days is that *not* reading the assignments felt to me and my classmates like a heroic gesture of resistance against the sterile intellectualism being forced on us. I suspect this attitude still persists even where the content of what is taught is politically unexceptionable. Overlaid on the disparity between "radical" and "conservative" culture is an older disparity between the discourses of "intellectuals" and "lay" people.

In the heat of today's antagonisms it is easy to get so caught up defending one or another proposed list of books to be taught that one forgets that for many students it is *the life of books* itself that is strange and alien, regardless which side gets to draw up the list. One becomes so embroiled in the battle between traditionalist and revisionist views of culture that one forgets that for many students categories like "traditionalist," "revisionist," and "culture" itself are remote and mysterious, no matter which view is in charge.[4]

There is no question of occupying a neutral position here: in my view, the shift from the traditionalist to the revisionist view of culture is very much a change for the better. But from the vantage point of students who feel estranged from the intellectual life as such, revisionist culture can easily seem like the same old stuff in a new guise. To such students a Roland Barthes and an Allan Bloom will seem far more similar to one another than to people like themselves, their parents, and friends. In their eyes, a Barthes and a Bloom would be just a couple of intellectuals speaking a very different language from their own about problems they have a hard time regarding as problems. Though the intellectual distance separating an OMP from a YFP may look vast to us and to OMP and YFP themselves, to these students it would seem relatively insignificant. The very issues that make it possible for OMP and YFP to attack one another so vigorously constitute a bond that puts them in another world from most of their students.

To those who are not at home in it, intellectual discourse is like a foreign language—some of it literally *is* foreign language. The best way to learn a foreign language is to live in the country in which it is spoken. In theory, the classroom is the "country" that mediates between the foreign languages of intellectual culture (I have elsewhere termed them Intellectualspeak) and the students. But making the classroom into an effective intellectual community is an uphill battle as long as the classroom has no functional connection to the larger "country" of other classrooms and to the general intellectual life of the university, a situation that intensifies the dependency of students on their teachers.

If the curriculum represents itself to students as a set of disjunctive discourses, it will naturally be difficult for them to recognize it as a community at all, much less one that seems attractive to join. The problem is obviously compounded to the extent that joining the academic intellectual community threatens to estrange students from the communities they already belong to—church, family, peer group, job. On the other hand, one senses that many students are not resistant to joining the academic intellectual community, but find it forbidding and hard to penetrate. Granted, some students manage to make their own individual sense of the curriculum. It is the many who do not with whom I am concerned with here.

In other words, we pay a steeper educational price today than in the past for a disjunctive curriculum in which students encounter each course as an isolated unit and therefore have trouble seeing its conversational relation to other courses and discourses. For as the conflicts inside and outside the academy become more antagonistic, the amount of perceptible carryover and translatability from one course to another is less and less likely to take care of itself. Courses that in principle speak to common or related concerns will not always appear to do so unless something is done to make the convergence explicit. In a radically dissensual climate, the ground rules will change confusingly without notice from one course to the next.

The new climate of ideological contention in the university seems to me a sign of democratic vitality rather than the symptom of "disarray," relativism, and declining standards that the critics on the Right take it to be. But the university *has* failed so far to make a focused curriculum out of its contentiousness. For this reason, I doubt that it is tapping its full potential for drawing students into its culture.

Pluralism at the End of Its Tether

Just how "democratic" the university has become can be questioned. Though the curriculum is significantly more pluralistic, multicultural, and culturally representative than it was a generation ago, the faculty and student body remain preponderantly white and middle class. As Henry Louis Gates observes, "it sometimes seems that blacks are doing better in the college curriculum than they are in the streets."[5] Yet as Gates acknowledges, it is not a negligible fact that today's curriculum, by comparison with that of only a generation ago, is strikingly more responsive to the pressures of the surrounding culture and its democratizing impulses. By contrast with the university of the 1950s, in which the content of the humanities was still a predominantly New England WASP culture, today's humanities take cultural difference far more seriously.

For this reason, I would argue that the primary weakness of the humanities curriculum (at least in the institutions that set the standard) is no longer its failure to embrace cultural and ideological difference, but its failure to take maximum educational advantage of the impressive range of difference that it now does embrace. The curriculum encompasses a far wider range of cultural differences than in the past but instead of engaging those differences it still tends to keep their components in non-communicating courses and departments. As a result students are often unable to recognize difference *as* difference, since they experience its components only in separation.

To say this is not to dismiss academic pluralism, an immense progressive improvement over the exclusionary system of the nineteenth century college, but to criticize the failure of pluralism to engage its own pluralities. Pluralism deserves credit for opening academic culture to previously unrepresented groups, methodologies, and viewpoints and greatly expanding its ideological diversity. But it has done so by adding innovative and revisionary subjects and perspectives without asking that the challenges these innovations pose to traditional assumptions and methods be confronted and worked through.[6]

Thus when the New Criticism overcame the resistance of the older historical and philological scholarship and entered literature departments after World War II, it came to coexist peacefully with the traditional courses whose approaches it was challenging. As feminism and post-structuralism have today made their way into the department and the curriculum, they too coexist peacefully with the New Criticism and old historicism which they radically subvert. After a century of it, this system of growth by accretion and assimilation now seems so natural and normal that one in which differences were engaged in the curriculum itself seems virtually unthinkable. It takes an effort of defamiliarization to see something strange in the result—that the humanities have become the site of the most radical cultural transgression without ceasing to be a bastion of traditional values. It is this contradiction that explains how the humanities can be attacked at once from the Left for clinging to hidebound traditions and from the Right for welcoming revolutionary insurrection. Again, academic peaceful coexistence has its benefits (as it does in the global arena), especially when compared to the authoritarian system that preceded it. But the heavy intellectual costs of such a system are passed on to students, who are exposed to the ideological contradictions of the curriculum without enough help in making sense of them, or even recognizing them as contradictions.

The problem has not gone unrecognized—witness the mounting chorus of recent complaints about academic "fragmentation" and "pluralistic disarray" and the "cafeteria-counter" or "garage sale" curriculum that gives students little help in connecting the disparate subjects and values the curriculum offers them. But the terms in which such complaints are framed are themselves inadequate, failing as they do to acknowledge the problem of ideological conflict.

In the liberal-pluralist rhetoric officially adopted by most universities today, the university is characterized as a scene of "diversity" without conflict. The iconography of the college catalog, with its juxtaposition of pastoral and technological imagery, represents the campus as a reconciler of contraries, where ivy and steel, the chapel and the laboratory, the garden and the machine need not clash. This effect is reinforced by the numbered department and course listings, which make it seem unexceptional that conflicting values and methods should coexist side by side. The university is conceived as a site of infinitely multiplying differences that never need to be confronted, since in the end they presumably conduce to commonly shared social goals. As long as the major fields are covered by departments and courses and as long as students cover a reasonable spread of those fields, questions about how these contents converge or conflict can be left to work themselves out on their own, or as each student may work them out by himself.

Conservatives mount an effective attack on the evasive and relativistic implications of this laissez-faire approach to the curriculum (the analogies with cafeterias and garage sales reflecting their patrician disdain for the vulgar marketplace). They point out with justice that it lets educators transfer the responsibility to students for deciding which knowledge is most worth having. But the only alternative proposed by conservatives for this evasion of responsibility is to reinstate a concept of tradition that also ignores or suppresses conflicts. Whereas the liberal appeal to diversity assumes that the clarification of ideological conflicts will work itself out through the free play of individual initiatives, the conservative attempt to reimpose an ideal of "our common culture" denies the very legitimacy of ideological conflicts, and blames their eruption on rabble-rousing Leftists, who are accused of "politicizing" a culture that is naturally above politics. Thus neither liberal-pluralist nor conservative approaches to the curriculum have a strategy for dealing with ideological conflict in education by making it a productive part of the curriculum.

In *Professing Literature,* my narrative of the history of academic literary studies in America traced the way successive attempts to break this pattern of routinized absorption and cooptation had each in turn been absorbed, routinized, and coopted into the structure of conflict-free pluralism. The story traced a kind of institutional compulsion, in which repressed conflicts repeatedly return in the form of neurotic repetition: what initially emerges as a subversive innovation (modern language philology, old historicism, New Criticism) subsequently becomes the traditional humanism of a later period. I speculated at the end of the book that what endangers today's radical literary theories is not that they will be repressed, but that they will be accepted and relegated to the margins where they will no longer need to bother those they challenge. The new theories are ghettoized in the theory course while the other courses go on about their business as before (or they are quietly absorbed into the older forms of work where they spruce up a tired methodology). The picture still seems to me accurate, but it is only part of the story. Like other recent "cooptation" analyses, this one leaves out the extent to which a system can be altered in the very process of coopting innovations.[7]

For as the ideological conflicts within the university have become more open and acrimonious, the university's time-honored strategies of conflict-avoidance are ceasing to work as efficiently as they once did. As these conflicts become too fundamental to be papered over by the device of keeping opposing factions isolated in non-communicating classrooms and departments, students, increasingly, can hardly help knowing there is trouble behind the scenes. Thus the war over the canon has already had a certain educative effect not planned by any curriculum committee, at least in leaking the news that the humanities are not the calm, uncontested terrain that they have pretended to be. The news is not merely leaked, of course, but openly taught in courses like women's studies, post-colonialism, cultural materialism, and other theory-conscious forms of study, and in the standard period and genre courses that increasingly bear their influence.

Even so, I believe it will take more than new courses (and new styles of individual pedagogy) to produce a curriculum that makes more than a small minority of students articulately aware of the controversies surrounding them and able to take an aggressive part in them. For the powerful vocabularies in which the controversies are fought out remain in the control of the faculty rather than the student body. And as long as it continues to be taught in a privatized space, even the best-taught course is limited in its power to help students gain control of those vocabularies.

I doubt the privatized classroom has ever been an effective structure, but at least it made consistent sense in the relatively consensual conditions that existed in the socially restricted academic culture of the past. That is, when academic culture was socially and intellectually homogeneous, it was reasonable to assume that common premises would be randomly repeated and reinforced over a span of courses, so that the latent conversations between different courses did not need to be programmatically actualized. In an institution in which everyone presumably speaks (or wants to learn) a version of the same master discourse, the random effect of their voices speaking it separately figures to produce enough redundancy to convey a coherent picture to students.

All accounts suggest that, at least since the demise of the old college, professors have not shared a master discourse (ruptures appeared immediately between scientists and humanists and professional and anti-professional humanists), and the coherence of the academic humanities has never been apparent to more than a minority of students. Now that the academic humanities can no longer take for granted even the shaky consensus they once had, and now that it is no longer clear that such a consensus would even be desirable, it is all the less likely that an accessible picture of the humanities can emerge for students without an attempt to structure the latent connections between courses and discourses.

Thomas S. Kuhn observes in *The Structure of Scientific Revolutions* that at moments of crisis or paradigm shift in the sciences, "a law that cannot even be demonstrated to one group of scientists may . . . seem intuitively obvious to another."[8] Imagine what happens in the mind of a student caught in the crossfire between several conflicting paradigms, each of which represents itself to him as "intuitively obvious" and uncontroversial. Kuhn's own book is a case in point, having been treated as holy writ by many literary theorists even as it has been ignored or disparaged by some scientists and philosophers of science. A student would be asking for trouble if she assumed that the assumptions about scientific truth and paradigm-change that she learned from her Kuhnian instructor carry over into other courses. In the same way, a student would be asking for trouble if she assumed that what counts as "literature" or "criticism" (or as good literature or genuine criticism) in a course taught by OMP carries over into a course taught by YFP. In OMP's class it may go without saying as uncontroversial that great literature is a repository of universal truths, while in YFP's it may go without saying as equally uncontroversial that this view is pernicious, reactionary, and passé.

The problem is further intensified when a paradigm shift occurs so rapidly that a new set of truths attain the status of commonplaces in one discourse community before other communities have even heard of them. One now hears one's more advanced colleagues saying things like, "I'm getting so tired of hearing about 'hegemonic discourse.' And if I hear one more time that reality is 'socially constructed' I'll pass out." Though the theories that have become so self-evident as to be boring to these professors have never been encountered by most of their students, it would not be surprising if the professors did not explain the theories to their students but presupposed them as going without saying among those in the know. Since no student wants to be exposed as not in the know, he will naturally think twice before asking teachers for clarification.

We might be tempted to write off such behavior as a case of mere bad teaching, correctable by urging the instructors to be more sensitive to their students' difficulties. But as long as she teaches in isolation from her colleagues, even the most sensitive teacher cannot know how much of what she tells her students may be considered controversial by some of those colleagues. In teaching the history of criticism this year, I persistently had the suspicion that many of my colleagues would probably raise their eyebrows at about three-fourths of the picture of literary and cultural history I drew for my class, and probably for very different reasons. I had no way of knowing how much of the picture I drew might or might not jibe with the one my students were getting from other colleagues, but I would be amazed if there were not major discrepancies.

My students probably noticed discrepancies between my account and that of other teachers, but they were too polite to mention them. Rather than ask instructors to confront apparent contradictions among their views when these arise, shrewd students will usually decide that it is safer to put the matter out of mind and give each teacher what he or she "wants." A student in my criticism course last semester told of an earlier teacher who warned her class that she would not tolerate the word "problematize." This student happened to be concurrently taking another course in which it seemed clear that using words like "problematize" would be to his advantage. Not wishing to offend either teacher, he did what any canny student would do: he avoided "problematize" in one course and used it as much as possible in the other.[9]

Note that the instructors in all these cases are protected by the closed nature of their classrooms, which makes it unnecessary (or even impossible) for them to confront the challenges to their assumptions that might be represented by other teachers. The students, on the other hand, having no such protection, become the battleground of the university's increasingly more violent ideological contradictions. They, too, naturally protect themselves by repressing the contradictions, as my student did with his judiciously selective use of "problematize." Taking a series of courses thus becomes a game of psyching out each instructor's paradigm, playing along with it for the duration of the semester, and then forgetting it as soon as possible after the final examination in order to make mental room for the next instructor's paradigm.

But why, it will be objected, could not any teacher represent the views of other teachers to their students? Surely if they are good teachers, OMP and YFP will each represent their dispute over "Dover Beach" to their classes—differently to be sure, but that is all to the better. Does not any good teacher already "teach the conflicts" by presenting students with opposing perspectives on controversial important issues? The flaw in such an objection should be obvious to anyone trained in literary studies over the last generation, where the crucial difference between didactic and dramatic forms of representation has been axiomatic. That is, seeing a conflict described by one person is a very different experience from seeing it acted out in a community and still more different from taking part in that acting out. There is a qualitative difference between having a conflict described to you in a particular register and participating in the actual clash of viewpoints.

The foregoing objection expresses the common habit of reducing educational problems to a matter of good or bad teaching. This reduction of education to teaching, which goes hand in hand with the glorification of the autonomous, self-contained course as the natural locus of education, fails to see that educational problems are systematic ones that involve not just individual teaching but the way that teaching is organized. Individual teaching is arguably the least promising place to start in transforming education, since it is the aspect of the system that is most subject to idiosyncrasies of talent and inclination and thus the least amenable to being programmed.

Even the most radical theorists of socially transformative education make their objective the alteration of teacher and student behavior in closed classrooms rather than the rethinking of the organization of instruction. The system is to be transformed by the sum total of individual teachers employing alternative pedagogies in closed classrooms. This tactic makes sense in a situation in which the closed classroom is the only sphere in which transgression is possible or permissible, but its limits become clear if one reflects that the closed classroom model is rooted in the very bourgeois positivist individualism that these Leftist critics persistently attack. We have no trouble seeing the *department* as an expression of this positivist individualism, but the *course* appears as the alternative to it—the garden over against the machine—instead of an expression of the same forces.

Toward a Dialogical Curriculum

Citing the work of Ira Shor, Paulo Freire, and Henry Giroux, Dale M. Bauer has recently argued for the need "to foreground dialogics in the classroom."[10] Only a dialogical classroom, Bauer argues, can turn education into a place where questions of authority, identification, and resistance are explored rather than repressed or taken for granted. I agree with Bauer's argument, but I maintain that its logic points to something larger than "the classroom" as the locus of dialogue. I doubt whether "the classroom" can become effectively dialogical as long as it is not itself in dialogue with other classrooms.

What is the advantage of a dialogical structure over a monological one? Simply that in a dialogical curriculum, questions that challenge or redefine the premises of the discussion would not arise in one class only to be abruptly dropped in the next, as tends to be the case now. Since such questions would have a chance to become part of other conversations besides the one taking place in the privacy of a single course, the more pertinent ones would figure to be sustained and reinforced. This is the case if only because the inevitable inequalities of authority in the pedagogical situation mean that questions like "So what?" "Who cares?" "Could you clarify that?" "How is that point relevant?" and "Why are we going on about *this* issue to the exclusion of that one?" are more likely to come from other faculty than from students, at least for the moment.

Granted, a dialogical curriculum would also risk inflicting new kinds of boredom and alienation on students. Instead of being turned off by a single instructor, students could now be turned off by a whole phalanx of instructors. And there is no doubt that a dull, pedantic faculty teaching collaboratively will produce no better result than a dull, pedantic faculty teaching separately. But even in this worst-case scenario, the outcome would not be worse than it can already be under the prevailing system. More to the point, for a generation hiring and promotion committees have gone to increased expense and trouble to recruit faculties that are not only intellectually gifted and original, but far more representative of the diversity of culture than in the past. So it does not seem unreasonable to assume a faculty with a reasonable potential for intellectual liveliness. My proposition is that a faculty organized to teach dialogically is more likely to realize this potential than it is working in uncoordinated classrooms.

For the greater the degree of collective interaction, the more likelihood of generating and sustaining self-criticism of whatever is problematic in that interaction, including its lack of relevance to students' interests and needs. To put it another way, a faculty working dialogically figures to be self-correcting in a way that a faculty working in privatized courses is not. That is, given a faculty representative of the present diversity of academic culture, a dialogical curriculum figures to be more theoretically, historically, and politically self-aware than a privatized one. Instead of repressing its own history and politics, such a curriculum would tend to foreground its own history and politics and open it to theoretical debate.

By the same logic, a more collective organization of teaching would figure to foreground questions of political power that a privatized system tends to evoke only intermittently in periodic eruptions. Take the question debated by OMP and YFP about the legitimacy of seeing sexual politics in a poem like "Dover Beach," a central question by anybody's reckoning in the conflict over the humanities. Instead of a situation in which YFP takes it for granted in her course that it is self-evidently a crucial question while OMP takes it for granted in his that it is self-evidently out of order, the crucial debate over the politics of literature would have a chance to become and remain a common context of discussion. This outcome would not in itself redress the power inequalities that concern YFP, but it would at least enable those inequalities to become a theme of general discussion instead of one that erupts now and then only to be buried.

Since some groups and interests are inevitably excluded from any institutional conversation, the metaphor of "conversation" or "dialogue" is often justly criticized as an ideological mystification. But if some groups must be excluded or marginalized, an organization that foregrounds difference and conflict would promise to give the more arbitrary exclusions and marginalizations a better chance than they now have of coming to light and becoming an explicit theme of discussion. Conversation, then, becomes a less politically suspect trope the more the conversation thematizes its own exclusions. The interests of the disempowered tend to be jeopardized most by a privatized system, which offers no public sphere in which their situation can become generally visible.

For this very reason, of course, it will seem to be in OMP's interest to resist entering into dialogue with YFP. Why should the OMPs of the world agree to debate with the YFPs over such an issue as the canon, especially when what bothers the OMPs is that there should *be* a debate over the canon to begin with? Once OMP acknowledges that the canon is a *debate* rather than a self-evident embodiment of value, he has lost the culture war. Why should he lend the debate legitimacy?

For one thing, he may not have a choice. Hiding in his private classroom is not going to make the canon debate go away or cause the issues to become less controversial. OMP can try to deny YFP tenure, but he may not have the power to do so (evidently he could not prevent her from being hired, so he may not be able to prevent her from being promoted), and he may regard such tactics as professionally and morally repugnant. One might argue that it is in OMP's interest to fight for his cause in public where he may be able to persuade students to his view of things, whereas if he withdraws into the privacy of his classroom he figures to lose the war by attrition to his younger opponents. As for YFP, for different reasons it may be in her interest too to fight her battle in public, lest the victory of her faction result in yet another marginalized radical enclave in the university.

Some OMPs and YFPs may not see it this way, of course, and this is their right. Where it is possible, those of us who want to teach more collectively should go on without those who do not. It is not necessary to get unanimous faculty (or student) participation to increase the degree of intellectual community enough to have a significant impact on teaching and learning. Those who want to be left alone should be respected, but it does not follow that the university has to be run for their convenience.

Then, too, their proportions may be smaller now that a generation of teachers has entered the university for whom terms like "dialogical," "rhetoric," "interdisciplinary," "conversation," and "public sphere" pack a positive charge. This development is part of a larger transformation in the conception of knowledge and culture, one that shatters the old partnership which founded the modern university between the positivist idea of knowledge as a series of building blocks added to an ever-accumulating pyramid and the humanistic idea of culture as a fixed set of traditions. Knowledge and culture now look less like a unified package, capable of being formalized in a list of great books or cultural literacy facts, and more like a set of unruly and conflicted social practices. But though the shape of knowledge and culture has been transformed, departmental and curricular structure continues to express an earlier positivist-humanist paradigm, though one that most lay people and conservative academics still hold. This very conflict and the need to work through it demands a model of the curriculum that is neither a cafeteria counter nor a core, but something more like a conversation.

Several promising models are already at hand: in the new English major in "English and Textual Studies" at Syracuse and a comparable one at Carnegie Mellon; in interdisciplinary programs such as the one in Cultural Studies at the University of Pittsburgh that emphasize collective teaching and make use of metacourses in theory and methodology to give coherence to the variety of other courses in the curriculum; in integrated programs that have arisen on campuses off the prestige main line like Evergreen State, Alverno College, Mount St. Mary's of

Maryland, and the University of North Carolina at Greensboro;
in the Ph.D. program in "English Studies" under development at
Illinois State University, which actually takes seriously and
makes part of its object of study what has always been assumed
but honored only in the breach—that graduate students are
being trained to teach literature as well as research it.

The rationale guiding the Syracuse major is worth quoting:
the major attempts to distinguish between a "traditional
pluralism," in which there are many separate viewpoints and
each exists without locating itself in relation to opposing
viewpoints, "and a multiplicity of positions, each of which
acknowledges a contestatory relation to other positions." The
purpose of a curriculum based on the latter model is not to
impose one way of knowing on everyone but to make the
differences between ways of knowing visible and to foreground
what is at stake in one way of knowing against another. The goal
is "to make students aware of how knowledge is produced and
how reading takes place and thus to make them capable of
playing an active role in their society, enabling them to intervene
in the dominant discourses of their culture."[11]

This and other new programs, which need to be discussed
at more length than is possible here, should be studied seriously
by curricular planners. But steps in the direction they point to
can be taken right away without elaborate bureaucratic
complications, and I want to suggest one strategy (I have
observed something like it used successfully in an NEH-funded
freshman seminar program at the University of North Carolina
at Greensboro entitled "Teaching the Canon and the Conflicts").
This idea has the advantage of building on the courses that
happen to be already scheduled in a department or college at a
given moment, and of drawing on a familiar format, the
academic conference.

The idea is to *thematize the semester*. It works this way: a
department or college (or a group of teachers in different
departments or colleges) decides that in the coming semester
some or all of its courses will have a common theme. The theme
should be one that packs contemporary urgency but also has a
history that can be traced and opens out potentially into diverse
lines of inquiry. Sample themes could be Interpretation across

the Disciplines; The Crisis of Traditional Culture; Majority and Minority Cultures; The Canon Controversy; The Politics of Representation; Contemporary Art and Academic Scholarship; Social Constructionism and its Discontents; The Arts in a Business Society. Disagreements will inevitably arise in choosing the theme, but since the theme can change from year to year it should be possible to avoid the kind of deadlock that results when it is assumed the aim must be to formulate definitively the core subjects of a liberal education.

Having determined the theme, instructors (with interested students) choose two or three common texts, which will help give focus to the theme and provide a basis for common meetings of all the courses involved. Two or three of these common meetings are scheduled during the semester at a convenient hour. The common meetings are modelled along the lines of the academic conferences and symposia which so many faculty now find indispensable to our intellectual life, the premise being that if such conferences are so helpful in socializing faculty (and increasingly graduate students) into academic discourses and debates, then if suitably adapted they can perform the same function for undergraduates.

The multicourse symposia would concentrate on common issues across the courses raised by the common texts and on exemplary points of difference and convergence over them. Speakers (possibly an author of one of the texts) could be invited from outside to bring a further perspective to the discussion. It would be of crucial importance that students not remain in a passive relation to this symposium, but their roles can vary depending on degrees of initial aptitude and interest, ranging from writing papers about the conference, to presenting some of the papers and responses in it, to planning and organizing the program itself. The point would be not just to expose students passively to the interplay of diverse discourses, but to help them gain control of these discourses by experiencing them as part of the social practices of a community rather than in closed classrooms. If successful, the experiment might provide the basis for more ambitious changes, such as a required metacourse in "Contested Issues in the Humanities," or a revised major or interdisciplinary program.

Thematizing the semester figures to bring about a number of desirable things that now tend to be missing from day to day academic life. It would create the common sites of discussion that I have been arguing are necessary for the clarification of academic discourse communities, yet it would create those common discussion sites without the need for either a faculty consensus on first principles or a fixed canon or core curriculum.[12] For it would now be the differences of perspective themselves that would give the discussion its coherence and commonality without fixed subjects or texts. Since the common texts and issues would be revisable from semester to semester, conflicting interests would be satisfiable without the sacrifice of intellectual community that results from the "Let's Make a Deal" trade-offs of the laissez-faire curriculum.

To follow the strategy outlined here would be to shift the terms of the recent curriculum debate, which has tended to be fixated on single components of the educational process rather than on the total system as students experience it. Attention would shift from isolated great books, cultural literacy facts, and subjects, and from isolated classrooms, to the special social practices in which books, facts, and subjects are treated by academic communities. For finally what students study is not books, facts, and subjects, but the way an intellectual community at a given moment deals with these components. As long as students remain outsiders to that community, education is likely to remain an alienating process for the majority, regardless of what texts and subjects are studied.

I have operated on the premise that best way to learn a foreign language is to live in the country in which it is spoken. Most students, like most Americans generally, do not speak the language of academic intellectual culture because they do not feel themselves part of the country in which the language is spoken. Those students experience that country through a curriculum that does not appear as a community at all, much less one they can imagine joining. So the curriculum obscures rather than clarifies the country of the academic intellectual community that it potentially represents and helps produce a normal environment whose most energizing features, its political and philosophical conflicts, are hidden from view. The country is not intrinsically impenetrable, but the way it is represented by the curriculum makes it *look* more impenetrable and less interesting than it has to be. If it is to represent the country in its real vitality, the curriculum needs put its own philosophical differences at its center.

NOTES

1.   I have in mind such attacks as Robert Alter's *The Pleasures of Reading in an Ideological Age* (New York, 1989) and the essays and reviews of Denis Donoghue, Roger Shattuck, and others, the effect of which is to provoke more of the metadiscourse about assumptions, values, and principles that these writers regret.

2.   In *Professing Literature: An Institutional History* (Chicago, 1987), I quote a number of statements by professors of this era on the absolute imperviousness of the contemporary college student to literary culture of any kind (pp. 104–118).

3.   Of course one who has been following recent journalistic reports would get the idea that the trendier English departments have virtually stopped assigning anything but rap songs and rock videos. The full story of how the issue has been reported would make an interesting chapter in the annals of disinformation.

For example, in a 1988 editorial in the *Chronicle of Higher Education*, Christopher Clausen, who is Head of the English Department at Pennsylvania State University and thus might have been expected to know better, offered to bet that Alice Walker's novel, *The Color Purple* "is taught in more English courses today than all of Shakespeare's plays combined" ("It is Not Elitist to Place Major Literature at the Center of the English Curriculum," *Chronicle of Higher Education*, 13 Jan. 1988, Sec. A, p. 52). Perhaps Professor Clausen intended his remark as hyperbole—surely even at peak popularity, *The Color Purple* has never been assigned with a third of the frequency of any of Shakespeare's major plays. In any case, before any money could be got down on Clausen's improbable wager, his remark was cited as sober truth by Secretary of Education William J. Bennett, in a widely reported address to the National Association of Independent Colleges and Universities. This was the address in which Bennett charged that a group of "trendy lightweights" was undermining the Western cultural heritage. "The American public is losing faith in colleges and universities," the *Chronicle* reported Bennett as saying, "because faculty members are eliminating classic works from the curriculum and replacing them with 'nonsense' promoted by 'trendy lightweights'" (Robin Wilson, "Bennett: Colleges' 'Trendy Lightweights' Replace Classics with Nonsense," *Chronicle of Higher Education*, 10 Feb. 1988, Sec. A, p. 27).

The same week as Bennett's speech, Clausen's remark was cited once again as truth by David Brooks in another angry denunciation of canon-busting professors in the *Wall Street Journal* (2 Feb. 1988). Brooks's article, entitled "From Western Lit to Westerns as Lit," conveyed the impression that at Duke University and elsewhere the teaching of popular Westerns by such writers as Louis L'Amour had virtually superseded Shakespeare and other major authors.

Only a month earlier, Jonathan Yardley had written in a piece in the *Washington Post* on "The Fall of Literary Standards" that "according to [current] vigilantes of the English departments, literary quality is irrelevant. . . . Makes you want to rush right back to college, doesn't it? To hell with Shakespeare and Milton, Emerson and Faulkner! Let's boogie! Let's take courses in the writers who really matter, the writers whom the WASPish old guard sneers at. Let's get relevant with courses on Gothic novels, bodice-ripper romances, westerns, detective stories—all of which, *The* [New York] *Times* advises us, 'are proliferating' in the English departments" (11 Jan. 1988). Yardley did not identify the *Times* article, but by now the network of self-confirming falsehoods was so thick that it hardly mattered who was quoting whom. It was now common knowledge that the canon-busters were plotting, and perhaps had already achieved, nothing less than the liquidation of the classics. As Terry Teachout put it in the March 1988 issue of *Commentary*, it was the expressed objective of the revisionists "to erase the values of Western culture from the minds of the young by deliberately failing to introduce them to the history and literature in which those values are embodied" (p. 71).

It is of course true that the canonical classics now share time increasingly with the texts of popular culture and minority traditions. Yet the extent and pervasiveness of that displacement has been grossly exaggerated, as a Modern Language Association sampling of undergraduate English offerings has recently documented. See my *Beyond the Culture Wars* for a discussion of this and other surveys (pp. 21–25).

4. Traditional humanists deny responsibility for this problem by blaming the impenetrability of academic culture on the "jargon" of their trendy opponents. They conveniently ignore the fact that to most people

in our society the word "humanist" is no less a form of jargon than the word "deconstruction" or "problematize." This fact was brought home to me recently when, waiting with a group of scholars for a bus to the National Humanities Center in North Carolina, I heard a pager announce, "Will the group going to the National *Humanitarian* Center please come to the baggage claim area."

For a typically smug attack on theory jargon, see Alter, *The Pleasures of Reading* (pp. 16ff). After quoting a specimen from an article on Kafka, Alter says that the perception it contains "has been stated not only more elegantly but also more instructively by critics who do not use this jargon of the new literary technocrats: that Kafka invents a mode of enigmatic fiction which taps an inchoate realm of the unconscious and defies conventional habits of interpretation" (p. 17). I asked my class what they thought of Alter's supposedly more eloquent and instructive version. "It's no better, is it?" they declared. To them, "invents a mode of enigmatic fiction which taps an inchoate realm of the unconscious," etc. was indistinguishable from Alter's most barbaric cases of theory jargon.

5. Henry Louis Gates, Jr., "The Master's Pieces: On Canon Formation and the African-American Tradition," *South Atlantic Quarterly*, 89, no. 1 (Winter 1990), p. 91.

6. Gary Waller has called this strategy the "park bench principle": "When a powerful newcomer shows up, everyone on the bench shuffles over just a little to make room for the latest arrival. Occasionally, if things get a little crowded, the one at the end falls off—Anglo Saxon, perhaps, or philology." Gary Waller, "Powerful Silence: 'Theory' in the English Major," *ADE Bulletin*, 85 (Winter 1986), p. 33.

7. For an analysis of the paradoxes of cooptation theories, see my "Cooptation," in *The New Historicism*, ed. Harold A. Veeser (New York, 1980), pp. 168–81.

8. Thomas S. Kuhn, *The Structure of Scientific Revolutions* (Chicago, 1962).

9. One cannot overlook the possibility that my student got some benefit from trying out conflicting vocabularies without committing himself to any just yet. The question is how well he can try out those vocabularies if he never sees them engaging one another.

10. Dale M. Bauer, "The Other 'F' Word: The Feminist in the Classroom," *College English*, 52, no. 4 (April 1990), p. 387.

11. The Syracuse curriculum is described in the Syracuse *English Newsletter* (from which I have quoted here); the Carnegie-Mellon curriculum is described by Gary Waller in the article cited in n. 6; the

Evergreen State model resembles the "Federated Learning Communities" developed by Patrick J. Hill in the late seventies at the State University of New York at Stony Brook; see Hill, "Medium and Message in General Education," *Liberal Education*, 67, no. 2 (1981), pp. 129–45, and "Communities of Learners: Curriculum as the Infrastructure of Academic Communities," *Opposition to Core Curriculum: Alternative Models of Undergraduate Education*, eds. James W. Hall and Barbara L. Kelves (Westport, Conn., 1982), pp. 108–34.

On course integration at Alverno, see *Teaching Critical Thinking in the Arts and Humanities*, ed. Lucy S. Cromwell (Milwaukee, 1986), especially Chapter 4 by James Roth.

In addition to the essay by Waller just mentioned and conversations with Waller and Steven Mailloux, my thinking has been influenced by the well-known work on "discourse communities" by composition and rhetoric specialists like Patricia Bizzell and David Bartholomae, work that has been in turn influenced by the theorizing on "interpretive communities" of Stanley Fish. The writings of Bakhtin, Rorty, Habermas, and Derrida provide various kinds of stimulus for the idea of a "dialogical curriculum."

12. Adapted to the lower schools, these principles need to be developed as an alternative to E.D. Hirsch's Cultural Literacy project, which in my view wrongly assumes that information can and should be acquired *before* a student enters an intellectual community. My assumption is that decontextualized lists or other inventories of facts are essentially unlearnable in themselves, and can never generate the incentive to learn them. Information is usefully acquired only through an interested engagement in a community's activities and purposes. We should proceed on the assumption that a curriculum structured as a viable intellectual community would itself provide the information necessary to enter the community's discussions, and would generate the incentive to learn that information.

How Curricular Disconnection Disempowers Students*

Gerald Graff

A student recently told me about taking a literature course in which the instructor observed one day: "As we now know, the notion that truth can be objective is a myth that has been exploded by postmodern thought." The student also happened to be taking a political-science course in which the instructor spoke confidently about the objectivity of his discipline as if no such challenge existed. "What did you do?" I asked.

"What could I do?" the student responded. "I trashed objectivity in the one course and assumed it in the other."

Curricular disjunction is not a new problem, but its effects are more damaging as the academic climate becomes more conflict-ridden and teachers share fewer common assumptions about their subjects. A student today can go from a course in which the universality of the Western literary canon is taken for granted (and therefore not stated or argued) into another course in which it is taken for granted (and therefore not stated or argued) that the universality of the canon has been discredited. While this disparity can be exciting, many students become baffled or cynical and decide to give the teacher whatever he or she seems to want, as my student did. It may not even be easy to infer what the teacher wants, since that often "goes without

*Originally published in *The Chronicle of Higher Education* (13 Feb. 1991): A48; under the title "Colleges are Depriving Students of a Connected View of Scholarship"; reprinted by permission of the author.

saying" among those in the know. Think how intimidating it must be to write a paper when you sense that anything you say can be used against you, and that the moves that got you an A in one course may earn you a C and a dirty look in the next.

One of the oddest things about the university is that it calls itself a "community of scholars," yet it organizes itself in a way that conceals the intellectual links of that community from those who don't already see them. I trace this oddity to what I call the course fetish, the assumption that the natural unit of instruction is the autonomous course, one not in direct dialogue with other courses. The classes being taught at any moment on a campus represent rich potential conversations between scholars and across disciplines. But since these conversations are experienced as a series of monologues, the possible links are apparent only to the minority of students who can connect disparate ideas on their own.

No educator would think of deliberately creating a system designed to keep students dependent on their teachers. Yet this is precisely the effect of the course fetish, which systematically deprives students of a connected view of the universe of scholarship, thus reinforcing their dependency on individual teachers to make sense of it for them.

Traditionally, it has been difficult to link courses without cumbersome administrative red tape, prohibitively expensive team teaching, or the return to a rigid core curriculum that would deny teachers and students a diversity of choice in what is taught and studied. A promising alternative, however, is suggested by a new book entitled *Learning Communities* by Faith Gabelnick, Jean MacGregor, Roberta S. Matthews, and Barbara Leigh Smith (Jossey-Bass, 1990), which advocates taking advantage of the common themes and issues that already exist across different courses and disciplines. Courses in philosophy, literature, and political science, for example, can be linked around the theme of the debate over objectivity that my student saw only in confusing glimpses. The very conflicts in the university over such issues of common concern become the principles of connection and coherence.

The authors of *Learning Communities* describe numerous colleges and universities around the country that are connecting diverse courses through discussions of common themes. Sample themes include "Science, Technology, and Human Values," which links science and humanities courses through discussion of important ethical questions; "Law in Nature, Society, and Language," which connects courses in management, philosophy, and speech through examination of legal issues; and "The American Myth of Success," which links courses in management, composition, and film through critiques and defenses of American individualism.

The formats for learning communities range from a model in which all students register for the same cluster of courses to one in which students in several courses meet together periodically during the semester to discuss a common text. If the same text—Orwell's *1984*, say—is assigned at the same point in the semester in particular literature, philosophy, and political-science courses, students have a basis for joint discussions, which can then be built upon when each course reconvenes separately.

Ms. Gabelnick and her colleagues believe that the richer and more continuous intellectual discussion that learning communities create makes students more independent and motivated. Faculty members in these programs feel that a higher proportion of students identify with intellectual roles, so that teachers are able to "demand more . . . and get more in terms of student perseverance and quality of performance." And far from being effective only in small colleges, as one might expect, they say learning communities have proven "particularly valuable in large institutions and commuter campuses, where close personal contacts and community making are problematic at best."

Learning Communities does not mention any campuses at which courses are linked around the recent much-publicized conflicts over multiculturalism and what texts to include in the humanities canon. But one program that aims to make educational use of this conflict is underway at Syracuse University, a new major in English and Textual Studies. It replaces a major in English based on "traditional pluralism"—in which different viewpoints are represented separately—with a framework in which each position "acknowledges its allied or contestatory relation to other positions," according to the English department's description of the new major. Steven Mailloux, the department chair who led the installation of the new program, says the goal is a curriculum in which even those teachers who choose not to enter the departmental debate and prefer to "just teach the books" can be "read" by the students as taking a particular position in the debate, as in fact they do.

How will this happen? One device that has been used in several of these programs and that may be tried at Syracuse is the academic conference or symposium. At almost every campus, a rich extracurricular array of conferences, lectures and performances runs throughout the academic year, and these events often speak directly to the concerns of the courses being given at the same time. Yet rarely are these events synchronized with the courses, something that would give the courses a common reference point without the need for exhausting faculty meetings and complicated administrative machinery.

For example, two or three teachers (in the same or in different departments) who will be teaching the same text in a coming semester could organize their own trans-course symposium to compare their different approaches, to clarify disputed issues, or just to stir things up a bit. A department's or a college's whole semester might even be organized around a broad issue such as "Challenges to Traditional Culture" or "Is Scholarship Political?" so that current debates over the politicization of academic work would get some much-needed discussion from all the fields that have a stake in them across the humanities and sciences.

Thinking of an academic semester as a set of thematically focused events through which courses connect seems more imaginative and intellectually stimulating than conceiving it as just a bunch of more or less valuable courses that (yawn) "cover" a spectrum of fields. To combat the deadly syndrome in which teachers talk only to other teachers and students remain passive spectators, students could be assigned varying roles in such a conference, ranging from writing papers about it afterwards, to giving some of the papers and responses, to eventually organizing and running similar events themselves (see the more extended discussion of this idea on pp. 38–40 above and in Chapter 9 of *Beyond the Culture Wars*).

I observed a very successful student-run conference on Darwin and *Genesis* in a new freshman seminar—supported by the National Endowment for the Humanities—at the University of North Carolina at Greensboro (entitled "Teaching the Canon and the Conflicts"). What impressed me was not just the high quality of the student-run discussion and the high proportion of students who took an active part, but the way students took responsibility for the discussion rather than waiting for cues from their professors. The Butler University English department has held a student-run conference for several years, and students in an Arizona University English course recently did a conference on Joseph Conrad's *Heart of Darkness*.

Turning courses into conversations in this way does not mean adding yet another task for already overburdened teachers, but taking advantage of the missed opportunities for dialogue that are already latent in what they do every day. In the long run, such an innovation figures to make teaching less rather than more arduous, since it gives teachers a set of reference points outside their own classroom. Being able to say to my class, "the objection to relativism, as you saw in Professor X's talk yesterday . . . ," relieves me of having to redefine the issue and enables me to play off what my colleague has said.

When I urge these ideas, I am sometimes told that academic conflicts have become so polarized and acrimonious that one cannot imagine professors' agreeing to put their courses into dialogue with one another. But the logic of this objection is circular: We are said to be too far apart to have a discussion, but since there's no discussion, we all grow even farther apart. The objection reflects a greater concern for the faculty's sensibilities than for the students' intellectual progress. We faculty members don't assume immunity from the disagreements of our colleagues when we publish our work or present it at conferences. It's only in the classroom that such immunity seems normal, a kind of extension of academic freedom.

But if it is true that students need to experience an intellectual conversation to be able eventually to join it, then we cannot responsibly refuse to represent that conversation in a more connected way. We hear a lot from progressive educators today about "empowering" students to become independent critical thinkers. But real empowerment means giving students a chance to become members of the academic intellectual community; this in turn means representing that community to students as a community, not a series of disconnected courses, however excellent.

II. Commentaries and Critiques

Theory, the Canon, and the Politics of Curricular Reform: A Response to Gerald Graff

Carl Freedman

Of the various courses I regularly teach at my own university, my personal favorite, probably, is a seminar called Critical Practice. It is intended mainly for first-year graduate students, and aims to provide an introduction to the institutions of professional literary study in America today and an overview of the most currently prominent theories of critical methodology. Such a course is obviously susceptible to a variety of approaches, and it is easy to think of dozens—perhaps hundreds—of texts that might appropriately be assigned. But invariably the first text I do assign is Gerald Graff's *Professing Literature: An Institutional History*. I assign it partly because I think that those aspiring to enter our profession should be acquainted with a basic narrative of its history, but also because Graff's book (despite the modesty of its tone) raises a number of general theoretical issues with which my students and I wrestle throughout the semester, in authors from Cleanth Brooks to Elaine Showalter, from T.S. Eliot to Foucault, from Lacan and Derrida to Bakhtin and Raymond Williams. No text, obviously, can say everything that one might ideally wish to be said in the first assignment for such a course, but I consider that *Professing Literature* provides as solid an introduction to the profession of literature as any week's worth of reading that one could suggest.

I begin with this personal detail in order to give some very definite weight to what otherwise might be (wrongly) taken as a mere gesture of academic *politesse*: namely, my acknowledgment that Graff's ongoing historical and theoretical analyses of our profession—above all, I think, in *Professing Literature* but also in the three closely allied essays under review here and in other works as well—constitute one of the more valuable projects, intellectually and politically, in the American academy today. Among those of us who "profess literature," very few—I myself would name Terry Eagleton, Richard Ohmann, and Edward Said—have contributed more to the understanding of the profession itself and of the ways that our interpretations of literary texts are connected to the particular institutions in which those interpretations take place. Since what follows will be largely critical, I want to make my appreciation of Graff's work and my sense of indebtedness to him explicit at the outset.

To a certain extent, Graff's virtues are the unglamorous but not-to-be-despised virtues of centrism. This is not, however, to say that he has maintained an Olympian or neutral stance toward the two major forms of critical insurgency that have reshaped the American literary academy and helped to embroil it in controversy (often overtly political controversy) for the past fifteen to twenty years. I mean, on the one hand, the advent of "theory" in its current sense—which might be more precisely defined as the remaking of critical methodology in the light of the major conceptual innovations of Continental modernity, perhaps most notably the problematics of Marx, Nietzsche, Freud, and Saussure as these have joined with and reconfigured the traditions of German philosophical aesthetics and the French human sciences—and, on the other hand, the expansion of the academic canon beyond the form in which it had stabilized by the 1960s, in particular so as to include more works by female, African-American, and postcolonial writers, as well as works from various forms of mass and popular culture. In both cases, Graff's loyalties are clearly with the progressives. He considers the (partial) victories of the two related insurgencies to be changes for the better, and understands that reactionary rollback is probably impossible as well as certainly undesirable. At the same time, however, he has avoided close identification with any particular school on the progressive side; and he has tried to articulate the issues at stake in longer (if not, as we shall see, necessarily wider) historical perspective than most of the participants in the controversy have attempted. He coolly insists that the actual achievements of theory and canon revision are more limited and ambiguous than zealous progressives often suppose, but also more limited and ambiguous than they need be. He is even not wholly without sympathy for the rearguard traditionalist opposition: not so much because he shares any of their positive views, but because they do, in his opinion, have a real point when they identify inconsistencies and fragmentation in the profession of literature today.

Here we come to what is, I think, the central argument in Graff's entire project, one that he has reiterated, with variations, in work after work. Graff's originality is to have raised, from the Left, an issue normally voiced only by the Right: namely, the *incoherence* of literary study today. There is no general agreement on *which* texts it is most important to study or *how* they should be read. What Graff terms the field-coverage model assures that courses are taught in isolation from one another, with students left to make what connections they can, and that hiring practices discriminate against candidates with area specialities already "represented" by faculty in place. It is not only (to pick up one of Graff's illustrations) that one professor may consider it obvious that "Dover Beach" is an articulation of universal human problems, while another professor considers it just as obvious that the same poem is a nasty bit of phallocratic propaganda. It is also that the radical differences between these two viewpoints are more often assumed than actually argued; and, when they *are* argued, it is usually far from the classroom, in learned journals and professional conferences to which very few undergraduates and by no means all graduate students have access. The right-wing response, of course, is to bemoan the disappearance of a common culture with shared humanistic values, and to suggest that it might be possible to reimpose such a consensus, if only the "tenured radicals" on the faculty could somehow be purged and the unpleasant interlopers into the curriculum, from Lacan to Alice Walker, could somehow be made to go back to wherever they came from. But such a putsch is unlikely, and Graff, of course, would have no sympathy for it in any case. His own call is quite different: it is for coherence *without* consensus.

This is, I think, a most original, provocative concept, though familiar by now to Graff's regular readers. It is, in effect, a dialectical approach (though Graff himself does not employ this vocabulary), for it amounts to finding the solution to a problem in what had seemed to be the primary *obstacle* to solution. Graff points out that not only liberal-democratic pluralism and diversity but also fundamental disagreement simply *are* the givens of our profession today. Therefore, he argues, let us *use* our situation instead of vainly lamenting it or trying to conjure it out of sight. If we cannot agree on what or how we should be teaching our students, we can and should let our students in on the arguments. A "dialogical" pedagogy would not only represent an improvement in honesty and rigor but probably in excitement too. We neither can nor should resolve the debates over the canon before drawing up a curriculum; on the contrary, those debates need to be made *part of* the curriculum, so that students can consider the issues and draw their own conclusions. Theorists need to be *more* theoretical, in the sense of understanding that the traditional institutions in which we work have powerful theoretical implications and are in urgent need of retheorization; otherwise, theory is likely to become just another "field," and even in its most radical versions will probably follow the progression from "rags to riches to routine" that has been the fate of such earlier critical insurgencies as positivistic literary history and New Criticism. But a genuinely dialogical curriculum—concretized through such specific innovations as more interdisciplinary work under such rubrics as Cultural Studies, required theory courses, more collective teaching, groups of courses systematically coordinated both within and among various departments, and even the thematization of whole semesters—will allow us to practice, in actual pedagogy, the virtues of dialectical conversation that normally we only preach to fellow professionals.

It sounds good. Indeed, though Graff never, I think, puts the matter exactly this way, the general implication of his suggestions for curricular reform is that *everyone* would win.

Students would be incomparably better educated. Instead of being left to wonder how Professor X's deconstructive-feminist approach to the Victorian novel could possibly be related to Professor Y's Christian-humanist readings of Sidney and Spenser, they would attain some real grasp of literary studies as a whole—not as an imaginary harmonious unity but as a real contested terrain, structured by exciting contradictions and disagreements. Proponents of the current critical insurgencies would resist marginalization in ghettos called Women's Studies or Critical Theory; instead, they could enact their values of diversity and self-reflexivity within the curriculum itself, and so give their radicalism an institutional as well as a textual reality. Even conservative traditionalists, it can be argued, would come out ahead. Though they would undoubtedly prefer *no* theory in the curriculum and *no* debate over the canon in the first place, those are probably not real options; and they might well be more interesting to their students, their colleagues, and themselves if they functioned as engaged participants in vital debates rather than as pedantic dinosaurs or unbalanced eccentrics.

So what's wrong with everybody's winning? In those terms, of course, nothing at all. Graff's general argument seems to me wholly cogent, and his specific proposals for reform are all quite worthy. If some group of literature departments—or, better, some entire division of humanities and social sciences—were to give Graff carte blanche to remake a curriculum, the result would doubtless be an excellent place to work and one where I personally would feel engaged and happy. Indeed, it is, in a sense, the very unassailability of Graff's program that arouses suspicion. For whenever one is presented with a set of proposed reforms, it is, I think, always worthwhile to ask not only whether they would actually improve matters—as Graff's reforms, in my view, certainly would—but why a situation that needs improvement should exist in the first place. The answer may sometimes lie partly in historical accident and bureaucratic inertia, and both factors have certainly been at work in the formation of the American academic literary profession. But since—as Graff himself has convincingly shown—the profession for nearly the entirety of its fully professionalized existence has always resisted the kind of program that Graff proposes, and has instead taken refuge in the fragmentation of field coverage, then we are bound to suspect more powerful factors at work also. After all, if Graff's proposals are as compelling as I believe them to be, why have they not already been adopted almost everywhere? If his curriculum is truly one in which everyone would be a winner, why has "everyone" been so slow to respond? To deal with questions of this sort requires us to move beyond the conceptual space that Graff's own argument occupies.

We might, for example, consider a category, already mentioned in passing, that has recently become rather prominent in Graff's work and that, indeed, seems to sum up a great deal of what he values in his preferred curriculum: the dialogic. Now, although Graff acknowledges him only in a fleeting and somewhat misleading fashion, this term is indissolubly associated with the work of Mikhail Bakhtin, arguably the most widely productive influence on American criticism and theory during the past decade. For Bakhtin, language and literature are inescapably dialogic—that is, they are defined by a plurality of competing voices—because they refract (*not* reflect) a radically heterogeneous and conflictive material social reality. Bakhtin criticizes the Saussurian notion of the linguistic sign (in terms that interestingly parallel but are finally rather different from Derrida's), because Saussure assumes a stable correspondence between signifier and signified that is guaranteed by uncontroversial social convention. The Bakhtinian sign, by contrast, is a multiaccentual site of ideological *contestation*, with relations between signifier and signified very much up for grabs (see Volosinov 1986, especially 9–106). Similarly, a work of literature for Bakhtin is a site of numerous contesting voices, each with its own ideological and social resonances, many of which are finally irreconcilable to one another; the novel is Bakhtin's privileged literary genre because it stages the dialogic *agon* in the most various and radical ways (see Bakhtin 1981, especially 259–422). Bakhtinian dialogics, accordingly—whether it takes place on the level of the individual sign or the thousand-page novel—is in crucial ways very unlike the discussion that normally takes place when professors and students of differing viewpoints meet in the academy. For Bakhtin, what is at stake is not just plurality, but *struggle*; not just disagreement, but *war*—war, as one might say, continued by other (linguistic and literary) means and defined by the major fault lines of an oppressive society, including class, of course, but also the lines of nation, ethnicity, race, gender, religion, occupation, and other social divisions. In Bakhtin's framework, heterogeneous voices in dialogic contention with one another cannot be reduced to differing "opinions," but involve objective differences of material social interest. In other words, the dialogic is, for Bakhtin, a matter of *power*—a category whose general absence in Graff's version of dialogics is particularly surprising in one who has clearly been productively influenced by not only Bakhtin but Foucault as well.

The point here is not simply that the classroom, whether traditional or Graffian, is, as an unfortunate nominee to the U.S. Supreme Court once put it, a place where no one can get hurt—or, we might add, at least a place where people do not get hurt nearly so badly as they do in sweatshops or in strikes, on plantations or in civil wars. What is more important is to understand that, in appropriating Bakhtin's category, Graff has quietly severed the link—indeed, the entire network of links—that for Bakhtin connects the dialogic as such to the life-and-death struggles that define the history of oppressive societies. Like Walter Benjamin (see Benjamin, 256), Bakhtin understands every document—whether an "isolated" sign such as *Christ*, *nigger*, *justice*, or *rape*, or the entirety of *The Brothers Karamazov*—to be deeply embedded, precisely in its dialogic character, in the barbarism and struggles against barbarism of particular times and places. But for Graff, the dialogic curriculum would seem to operate almost entirely apart from such gritty unpleasantries. It would almost seem to exist in the kind of pure, autonomous intellectual ether whose illusory existence has, at least since Plato, ever and inevitably exercised such a powerful attraction for the professional intelligentsia. The problem, then, is not that, relatively speaking, nobody gets hurt in a classroom—a fact hardly to be regretted, after all. It is rather that, for Graff, the classroom does not seem to be related in any very important and interesting ways to those places where people *do* get hurt all the time—places, after all, that abound in the society and the world where Graff and the rest of us profess literature.

Indeed, one of the curious shortcomings of *Professing Literature* is the way that its admirably long historical perspective narrows considerably as the diachronic narrative progresses. The earlier chapters tend to be fairly well informed by a sense of how the academy and literary study functioned within the structures and processes of American society as a whole. Considering the state of culture during the Gilded Age, for instance, Graff demonstrates how, in America, culture in even the most conservative, traditional, canonical sense has been unable to enjoy the kind of cozy, harmonious relationship with the real centers of social power that has widely obtained in Europe—an extremely important insight, which, unfortunately, nearly all participants in the canon debates have, for different reasons, found it polemically convenient to ignore. But as the narrative enters the twentieth century and especially as it approaches the present—with which Graff's shorter works on the profession of literature are almost exclusively concerned—this kind of analysis dwindles nearly to the vanishing point. It is illuminating, in this context, to contrast Graff with the colleagues to whom I compared him at the beginning of this essay. For, very different as their own contributions to the study of the profession have been, what Eagleton, Ohmann, and Said share with one another, but not with Graff, is a close attention to some of the different ways that the academy in general and the literary academy in particular currently help to reproduce—but also potentially to resist—the relations of oppression that govern the society at large. Throughout most of *Literary Theory* and in the later pages of *The Function of Criticism,* Eagleton shows how the major forms of modern criticism have assisted the flight from historicity that has proved so attractive to a bourgeois ruling elite unable to come to terms with the contradictions and limits of its own historical role. In his pioneering *English in America: A Radical View of the Profession* and in some of the essays collected in *Politics of Letters,* Ohmann demonstrates how the teaching of composition and literature has often functioned so as to encourage the mental habits appropriate to a fairly docile white-collar work force employed by the ruling military-industrial complex. Said, in his equally pioneering *Orientalism*, as well as in its sequel, *The Question of Palestine*, and in some parts of *The World, the Text, and the Critic*, exhibits, often in immense detail, the deep involvement of academic scholarship with the formation and perpetuation of state worship—arguably the most widespread public ideology in America today. Of course, the concerns of Eagleton, Ohmann, and Said are urgently political as well as analytic: for to demonstrate how our profession can and does give aid and comfort to oppression is also to suggest—sometimes implicitly, sometimes explicitly—how it might, at least to some modest extent, do the opposite.

Graff does not share—at least not overtly—this kind of concern. Yet his analysis of the profession could certainly be extended so as to attempt the sort of concrete historicization that he himself, at least when considering the present, generally declines. There is hardly space to make such a serious attempt here. But, since I have criticized what seems to me a serious absence in Graff's work, it is only fair to offer at least some idea as to how that lack might be made good.

The most fruitful approach, I think, would be to question whether the traditional field-coverage curriculum, which forms the chief object of Graff's critique, is really held in place by nothing more than administrative convenience. That is the explanation Graff stresses, and no one with even the slightest experience of academic administration will fail to appreciate its genuine force. But much more, I believe, is at work also. I have elsewhere tried to analyze the role played by *empiricism*, especially in its positivistic versions, in the formation and deformation of our profession (see the articles listed below); and it seems to me that this category is again pertinent. Once (when oriented primarily in opposition to theological dogmatism) a relatively progressive epistemology, empiricism has long served a mainly conservative social function: its mechanistic dichotomy between subject and object encourages a contemplative, nontransformative version of knowledge, while its bias for atomistic data over conceptual critique makes it difficult to theorize the social field as a total, mutable entity. It is therefore not difficult to understand why empiricism should be the dominant epistemological ideology of our conservative bourgeois society, nor is it surprising to find that empiricist assumptions silently govern most of our academic and especially curricular institutions. Field coverage may indeed make everyday life easier for deans and department chairs; but, more importantly, its tendency to isolate courses and professors from each other also provides powerful institutional impetus to the fragmentation of knowledge itself. What might be taken as a total object of investigation (in the manner, for instance, attempted by some of the work done under the name of Cultural Studies) instead tends to be splintered into a multitude of discretely contemplated monographic "specialities," mastery of one or more of which becomes a necessary badge of professional legitimacy. The powerful social forces making for the epistemological hegemony of empiricism are thus at work against the kind of dialogical curriculum that Graff would substitute for field coverage. To be sure, theory and canon revision have both made important challenges to the empiricist conservatism of our curricula. Theory, in nearly all of its varieties, enjoys nonempiricist intellectual roots, most frequently in the critical philosophy of Kant and the idealist or materialist dialectics of Hegel and Marx. And expanding the canon not only tends to display cultural formations as historical totalities rather than as sets of isolated "masterpieces," but also frequently packs an even more directly political charge by calling attention to literary production from areas of the most wretched victimization by global capital. Indeed, it is, in some ways, surprising that theory and canon revision have enjoyed what limited success they have had. But it is not surprising at all—and no mere matter of bureaucratic convenience—that empiricist conservatism has enjoyed considerable (though by no means total) success in blunting their radical impulses by transforming theory and canon revision from total political challenges to safe, containable "fields." Indeed, such domestication is in many ways in the interests of the insurgents themselves as individuals: it may well be more pleasant, and it certainly seems (by prevailing positivistic criteria) more scholarly, to advertise the internal complexity of one's own "field"—Lacanian psychoanalysis, say, or African-American literature—than to appear to run amok throughout the curriculum. It ought not to be forgotten that if, as insurgencies, theory and canon revision are both late outriders of the radical energies of the sixties and early seventies, they have both been institutionalized in their current academic form during the implacably conservative Age of Reagan—a designation that may serve as convenient shorthand for what Graff's dialogical curriculum is *really* up against.

There is obviously a great deal more that could be considered in the attempt to concretize Graff's analysis of our profession today. We could, for example, try to chip away at the wall of separation that Graff erects throughout his argument between professing literature and professing (or instructing) composition. Though the former is of course an important object of study in itself, certain distortions result when its analytic separation from the latter is too stark. It is not just that one could, I think, read the entirety of Graff's excellently researched narrative history without quite realizing the extent to which the growth of English departments has been dependent on the centrality accorded English composition by the general undergraduate curriculum of the modern American university. Even more important is to understand the conservative tug that composition—as the most instrumental, the most corporately respected, and therefore the most heavily and conservatively policed area of English or literary studies—exercises on the profession as a whole. In the bulk of higher-educational contexts (though largely excluding the most elite institutions), composition tends to enjoy a unique halo within English departments. Those professors who run composition programs and devise composition pedagogies are often among the best paid and most upwardly mobile members of the profession, while their colleagues in other fields nod reverently at department meetings when composition is mentioned. On the other hand, most of the actual teaching is done by the least secure and thus most easily controlled faculty available— graduate students, instructors, and perhaps untenured assistant professors. Of course, teaching composition is usually considered drudgery. But it is so considered mainly because composition pedagogy is so thoroughly policed, and because composition is saturated in hegemonic empiricist assumptions— sometimes, indeed, almost to the point of apparent mindlessness—more than any other area of the literary profession (see Ohmann 1976, 93–206, and Freedman 1981). Its prestige and even (insofar as nonliterary sections within the academy and social power centers beyond it are concerned) *centrality* to the profession are thus by no means politically innocent. Given the enormous weight of composition programs, staging a dialogical curriculum in the same department offers problems of somewhat the same sort as staging Woodstock next to the Pentagon.

I have scarcely begun to analyze the filiations between the literary academy as Graff so valuably describes it and the larger society in which it functions. But I want to end, as I began, on an appreciative note. If Graff's implicit conception of the literary academy as autonomous represents an absence of sufficiently concrete historical analysis—or if, in a somewhat different vocabulary, it amounts to that philosophic optical illusion known as idealism—it can also, I believe, be understood as a kind of Utopian figure. However conservative the academy in many ways is, it is nonetheless true that, like the also generally conservative church (the only other major institution in America that enjoys an institutional memory older than capitalism), the academy, emphatically including the literary academy, has been one of our few major institutions to harbor a vital tradition of social radicalism during the Reagan and post-Reagan years. It is, indeed, the sanctuary that the academy gives to *some* degree of critical social thought that accounts for the current right-wing antiacademic assault, whether in the form of hysterical vituperations against an (almost) completely imaginary university regime of "political correctness," or of what Graff himself has usefully documented to be a preposterous disinformation campaign about the canon. With such ferocious winds blowing outside the groves of academe, it is obviously tempting to take refuge in a certain institutional introversion. But it is not, I think, always necessary to resist the temptation. Imagining the academy as autonomous—so long as such imagining is understood to be a fiction or figure—may have an authentic Utopian value in allowing us some faint idea of what radically free discussion in a living intellectual and political culture would feel like. For mainstream political and journalistic discourse in America today is, insofar as basic issues are concerned, more ossified, narrow, and conservative than at any time in at least four decades, perhaps longer. At such a historical moment, the extent of free, radical debate still permitted within the academy may micrologically figure a revitalized public sphere in somewhat the same way that, for example, the affective and intellectual exploits of Henry James's wealthy aristocrats can be read as providing a partial, distorted, but extremely valuable figure of how a society freed from material necessity might occupy itself. The dialogical curriculum for which Graff calls cannot really be disconnected from the increasingly mean, hopeless society beyond; but occasional imagining of such autonomy may teach its own valuable lessons in the struggle against meanness and hopelessness. It is thus characteristic of Graff's importance that, even at those points in his work where one disagrees, the issues with which it moves us to grapple are fundamental.

WORKS CITED

Bakhtin, M.M. *The Dialogic Imagination*. Ed. Michael Holquist. Tr. Caryl Emerson and Michael Holquist. Austin: University of Texas Press, 1981.

Benjamin, Walter. *Illuminations*. Ed. Hannah Arendt. Tr. Harry Zohn. New York: Schocken, 1969.

Eagleton, Terry. *The Function of Criticism: From "The Spectator" to Post-Structuralism*. London: Verso, 1984.

———. *Literary Theory: An Introduction*. Minneapolis: University of Minnesota Press, 1983.

Freedman, Carl. "Marxist Theory, Radical Pedagogy, and the Reification of Thought." *College English*, Vol. 49, No. 1 (January 1987): 70–82.

———. "Writing, Ideology, and Politics: Orwell's 'Politics and the English Language' and English Composition." *College English*, Vol. 43, No. 4 (April 1981): 327–340.

Graff, Gerald. *Professing Literature: An Institutional History*. Chicago: University of Chicago Press, 1987.

Ohmann, Richard. *English in America: A Radical View of the Profession.* New York: Oxford University Press, 1976.

————. *Politics of Letters.* Middletown, CT: Wesleyan University Press, 1987.

Said, Edward. *Orientalism.* New York: Pantheon, 1978.

————. *The Question of Palestine.* New York: Times Books, 1979.

————. *The World, the Text, and the Critic.* Cambridge, MA: Harvard University Press, 1983.

Volosinov, V.N. *Marxism and the Philosophy of Language.* Tr. Ladislav Matejka and I.R. Titunik. Cambridge, MA: Harvard University Press, 1986. [This work is generally considered to have been actually authored by Bakhtin.]

Establishing *A Way* in a World of Conflicts

Harold Fromm

Over the past fifteen years or so, Gerald Graff has served as a sober conscience for literary theory, a discipline often inclined to postmodern tricksiness and meretricious displays of sophistry masquerading as ethical highmindedness. Graff's austere integrity has functioned as a badly needed corrective to the commodification of culture against which "oppositional" theorists rail even as they themselves exemplify this self-same vice in their "race for theory" (to use Barbara Christian's expression). As the Spartan Ralph Nader of literary theory, Graff has embodied many of the virtues he esteems, so that if one were inclined to be a follower of gurus at all in this age of unbelief (an age nonetheless fatuously credulous of mountebank metaphysics), Graff would seem to be one of the few to be taken seriously.

Although Graff began to make his reputation in the seventies as a rebellious young, albeit somewhat liberal-conservative, Turk—a period culminating in his influential book *Literature against Itself* (whose oppositional mentality he now seems to be repudiating or historicizing)—his success in the academy has gradually subsumed him into the prevailing world of literary theory as one of its most serious, intellectually committed spokespersons. To sum up in as few words as possible, he has moved from an earlier "oppositional liberalism" into a sort of "domesticated radicalism" that in reality is the New Conservatism of today's academic literary Establishment. Thus, by one of the ironies of finite existence in human culture (where no matter how open-minded you strive to be, you have to be one thing or another, and where consequently there is no way to avoid being kicked in the butt for being the wrong thing), he is now one of our leading Establishment patriarchs. Since Graff claims to be an enemy of patriarchal hegemony, this transformation (or the fact that some people see it as such) can only be a source for him of exquisite pain and a sense of betrayal.

Because Graff has always been an unusually selfless person, gladly writing detailed commentaries on other people's manuscripts, helping students and younger faculty to pursue their careers, and performing multiple tasks to aid our profession, and because his whole sensibility has always been focussed upon the "intellectual thing" in itself, rather than personalities and fashions, his recent move into pedagogy from "theory" has to be seen as one more example of his service-oriented character, his aim to make the world a better place, his continued belief in some sort of truth and virtue in an age where fifteen minutes of fame—but preferably half an hour—is one of the more potent desiderata.

Yet there is nevertheless cause for alarm, for in an imperfect world purity often breeds impurity, utopian schemes have a way of backfiring (consider the sorry case of Conrad's Mr. Kurtz, whose grim history has recently been taken up as a Graffian exemplum), and the turn to pedagogical idealism can sometimes become the last infirmity of a noble mind. This turn, as seen in Graff's essays, "Taking Cover in Coverage," "Other Voices, Other Rooms: Organizing and Teaching the Humanities Conflict," and "How Curricular Disconnection Disempowers Students," is an offshoot of the research he did for his 1987 book *Professing Literature: An Institutional History*, in addition to the large number of talks and papers he has delivered around the country on the programmatic subject of "teaching the conflicts." Over a period of more than seven years during which these discourses were generated, the central ideas have developed and changed, but the consistent heart of the matter appears to be Graff's belief that departments of literature in American universities have dealt with innovations and changes in critical, historical, and canonical aspects of literary study by simply incorporating them into new, independent, autonomous courses that will "cover" the most prevalent interests without causing open conflict. This accretion of specialist fiefdoms ruled by professors unbeholden to their colleagues or to the structure of their departments is seen by Graff as a malaise detracting from literary studies in contemporary American higher education, "which has neglected traditional theoretical questions about the ends and social functions of literature and criticism" ("Taking Cover" [TC]). The "incoherence" and messiness of the period and genre distinctions that now compartmentalize course offerings need to be replaced with a more conscious and structurally apparent organization of literary study that would acknowledge, says Graff, that *everything* is ultimately based on a theory, even the apparent negligence that characterizes the current arrangement.

In his earliest treatment of this matter, Graff portrays the average undergraduate as a somewhat dazed, simpleminded innocent, staggering aimlessly from class to class while his various instructors spout incompatible dogma which the student is afraid, or too naive, to question. Although "the coverage model solved the problem of how to make the university open to innovation and diverse viewpoints without incurring paralyzing conflicts" (TC), the very suppression of such conflicts, according to Graff, contributes to student confusion because typical undergraduates see only parts of the whole picture of a profession in turmoil, parts that look arid and irrelevant. "Vigorous controversy did [sometimes] arise," Graff admits, "but usually only behind the scenes of education . . . where students derived little benefit from it" (TC). Because the conflicts were not publicly aired, the fiction of a coherent set of humanist beliefs and traditions could be peddled to both students and the population at large, a set of beliefs increasingly espoused by the political right in their attacks against the left-generated disarray in higher education. And because no consensus can be reached in a discipline characterized by conflict, the discipline is also marked by incoherence. But, Graff asks, "Must we have consensus to have coherence?" (TC) His reply is that the lack of consensus is itself the theoretical issue that would provide coherence to literature departments if it were exploited as a subject for public scrutiny and debate.

In essence, Graff dislikes the idea that theory is being incorporated as just one more specialty to be "covered" inside and ignored outside the theory classroom. Instead of incorporation, he wants theory to become the "Master Discourse" (an idea that he intends, but a phrase that he demurs to use) that would, in effect, organize the literature department into a cultural studies department dominated by theory.

A few years later, in his "Other Voices" article, Graff is more ready to concede that "the conflicts" are getting pretty obvious, "openly taught in courses like women's studies, post-colonialism, cultural materialism," and elsewhere. Nor are undergraduates perceived to be quite as bovine as before. Now they "probably noticed discrepancies . . . but they were too polite to mention them"! Instead of raising challenges, these "polite" students resolve conflict by humoring their professors, giving them what they want—in a word, doing what students have always done to professors, even if Graff implies that there is something uniquely new in this response.

In "How Curricular Disconnection Disempowers Students," Graff expresses interest in "learning communities" where symposia, coordinated course offerings, shared themes, and the like would force students and faculty to come together to air important ideas and social issues rather than simply read in isolation. The suggestions made here are sensible and worthwhile, though nothing about them can be seen as earthshaking or unprecedented. Practices of this kind have been employed for years, albeit in more limited amounts than Graff would like. But there is no reason why more of them could not be included in almost any existing curriculum, adding richness and variety. What this program fails to acknowledge, however, is that the principal task in the teaching of humanities subjects to undergraduates is simply to get students to read a massive number of books, not only for "their own sake" but to provide foundations of knowledge on which to base future opinions—what we normally mean by "education." It is during these youthful, elastic, and formative years that reading, absorbing, and thinking are easiest to do and, indeed, produce their most powerful effect. So for students to spend large blocks of this precious time arguing about current issues on the basis of very thin and extremely contemporary (i.e., trendy) knowledge could ultimately be intellectually crippling—impoverishing the storehouse of ideas upon which intelligent adult life is constructed. (Most people do not find themselves reading Plato or Machiavelli at age 50, though they may very well read Toni Morrison.) It is, after all, a common complaint that today's students know little or nothing about eras before 1945, getting most of their information about life and culture through *now*-oriented TV. Since one of the classical functions of education is to go against the grain of the student's narrow upbringing—a technique heavily dependent on reading—excessive emphasis on the contemporary (i.e., today's "conflicts") will only reinforce the misconception that reality began just after World War II.

As one views and reviews the arguments about teaching the conflicts in these three essays and the latter half of *Professing Literature*, one is persistently struck by their weakness, even as they are modified into newer but equally tendentious versions (presumably in response to criticisms raised at conferences and in published replies). Their rationales depend on imperceptive and "polite" students, theory-starved faculty members who need to attend conferences for relief from their respectfully zombified clientele or their professionally incommunicado colleagues, and conflict taking place behind (but also *not* behind) the scenes. A special weakness is Graff's failure to acknowledge the casebooks that have been classroom staples for the past thirty years—collections of critical essays on *The Catcher in the Rye, Huckleberry Finn*, and practically anything else you would like, as well as Routledge's "Critical Heritage" series and the "Twentieth Century Views" from Prentice Hall, all serving to foreground the "conflict" that has always existed between competing interpretations of literature and culture and between professors conducting their own classes (a conflict that only the dullest of students could fail to observe, a conflict that is life itself). The best-edited of these did not fail to point out the "political" (as we now call it) underpinnings of critical conflicts, whether the conservatism of T.S. Eliot and T.E. Hulme or the radicalism of Leslie Fiedler, the psychoanalytic predisposition of the earlier

Frederick Crews or the myth-dependency of G. Wilson Knight. Books such as Morris Weitz's *Hamlet and the Philosophy of Literary Criticism* (which I myself used as a text when I taught history of criticism in the early seventies) explicitly addressed this multiplicity, if not in precisely today's heated terms. But these terms are becoming increasingly explicit both inside and outside the classroom, as Graff gradually concedes in his later writings.

These weaknesses, as far as I can see, are the result of Graff's own hidden political agenda (perhaps even hidden from him, though I would think he finds the charge familiar enough by now) and his wish for theory to achieve the status of Master Discourse in the humanist academy, a wish that is repeatedly presented by means of key words: "organize" (as in "Other Voices, Other Rooms: Organizing and Teaching the Humanities Conflict," and "The question is how the many different kinds of things professors do may be so organized as to begin providing a context for one another and take on a measure of corporate existence in the eyes of the world" [*Professing Literature* 251]); "connected" (as in "How Curricular Disconnection Disempowers Students"); "focused" (as in "But the university *has* failed so far to make a focused curriculum out of its contentiousness" ["Other Voices" (OV)]); "programmed" (as in "Individual teaching is arguably the least promising place to start in transforming education, since it is the aspect of the system that is most subject to idiosyncrasies of talent and inclination and thus least amenable to being programmed" [OV]); "thematize" (as in "The idea is to *thematize the semester*" [OV]); and so on. Although Graff might very well reply there is no favored *doctrine* he is trying to "program," that it is just the *discourse of conflict* that he wants to "institute," I have to admit that I wouldn't be able to believe it, for the evidence to the contrary is too strong.

To begin with, apart from the particular documents in question, Graff's general political position is well known to anyone who has read his recent writings or heard him deliver papers at the Modern Language Association meetings and elsewhere: it is the position of leftist orthodoxy or what is nowadays called "political correctness." This is at present the dominant position in the humanist academy, animating its de facto Establishment, not necessarily through the sheer number of people who espouse it but through the powers that operate university presses, determine the nature of textbooks, establish the contents of graduate education at the most influential universities (the ones that in turn determine what books are read by graduate and undergraduate students everywhere and what sort of teachers they will become, even if what filters down to the hinterlands takes many years). Graff is by no means shy in pushing this agenda—and to suppose that he is not hegemonizing one would have to be even more naive than his putatively glazed and insulated undergraduates. Although Graff may say that his program is not prescriptive, in reality it bears more than a passing resemblance to the aborted program at the University of Texas that attempted to use a collection of civil rights cases about race and gender as a textbook in the required freshman composition course, while claiming complete neutrality.

If there were any doubt about this, a reading of the "Other Voices" essay would certainly dispel it. The essay begins with an imagined quarrel between an Older Male Professor and a Young Female Professor over the relative merits of Arnold's "Dover Beach." The OMP extols the poem as a great masterpiece of the Western tradition and the YFP denounces it as an example of male phallocentric hegemony. Although in truth both of these characters come off as thoroughgoing jerks, the YFP is clearly the intended hero. And if we happened to miss that fact, Graff obligingly informs us that "there is no question of occupying a neutral position here: in my view, the shift from the traditionalist to the revisionist view of culture is very much a change for the better." Again, Graff might very well counter that while he is avowedly on the side of the YFP, he is neutral as far as the idea of teaching and debating the conflicts is concerned. That is, while owning up to his own political views, he could say that his interest in debate is not to push these views but simply to legitimize culturally diverse literary studies through a more open public discourse. But is it really possible to believe such a distinction? The obvious purpose of the imagined conflict between OMP and YFP is to embarrass OMP and push him to the margins (but given that he's such an idiot, he *deserves* to be

pushed to the margins, along with YFP). Yet one is not sure why
Graff wants to bother doing even that, since he acknowledges
that the proportions of older male professors who resemble OMP
"may be smaller now that a generation of teachers has entered
the university for whom terms like 'dialogical,' 'rhetoric,'
'interdisciplinary,' 'conversation,' and 'public sphere' pack a
positive charge" (in essence, conceding my argument above
about the composition of the current Establishment). And it will
be even smaller when the generation of which OMP is a part has
vanished from the university, by which time there will be a new
YFP (or more likely a YMP or a YGP [young gay professor]) to
denounce the old YFP as a reactionary fossil.

As things turn out, this concession about the changing
proportions of with-it faculty undercuts and renders irrelevant
much of Graff's argument about the need to foreground the
conflicts. Now that the ideological mix is increasingly weighted
towards a politically correct *mentalité*, humanities students going
from class to class are seeing the conflicts in action as part of
their normal daily academic lives, conflicts that—if anything—
are bound to peak and then decrease as political correctness
takes on the monolithic character of an Althusserian state-
supported ideology (or are "chosen" ideologies exempted from
this fate?). Granted, their professors are not actively arguing
with each other face to face; nonetheless, these conflicting
viewpoints are being expressed and absorbed throughout a
student's typical day. Why is it necessary to assume, as Graff's
argument keeps doing, that the students are vacuous, insensitive
nonentities, too thickheaded to notice what is before their very
eyes unless they are pedagogically bombarded with operatic
supertitles? Unless, of course, there is an urgent lesson that must
not be left to chance.

Graff's earlier professed aim to make literary theory
intelligible to lay persons also turns out to be far from
disinterested and by no means to be taken at face value. In the
1986 essay "Taking Cover," he writes: "But here is another
misconception—that theory is necessarily obscure, technical and
abstruse, and therefore too advanced or esoteric for the average
college or high school student of literature. This belief fails to
recognize that all teaching involves popularization. . . ." In 1987,

in *Professing Literature*, he remarks, "Literary theory only exemplifies to a heightened degree the tendency of all professional literary fields to define their interests parochially and to close ranks against outsiders. . . . The controversies of theorists are only the latest in a long line of professional disputes whose potential cultural relevance has remained invisible to outsiders" (152). He goes on to recommend that theory come "to the forefront where outsiders might have a chance to learn from it" (254).

Yet what is it that happens when "outsiders" presume to have noncanonical opinions about deconstruction and other theoretical matters that are taken as the proprietary province of the vanguard university literature department? And who exactly is an "outsider," anyway? In the case of William Bennett (whom Graff regularly criticizes), I might concede that not only is he in some respects an outsider but an outsider whose opinions about intellectual affairs I can generally do without (though even he can sometimes say valid things). But more instructive is the discourse about knownothings and outsiders that Graff pursued in a fairly highbrow radio symposium about deconstruction that was broadcast on August 21, 1991, on WBEZ in Chicago. Sounding like an august patriarch of the French Academy denouncing uneducated *canaille*, Graff repeatedly described hostile criticisms of Derrida as "pretty bizarre" and writers such as David Lehman as "totally ignorant." Lehman's book, *Signs of the Times: Deconstruction and the Fall of Paul de Man*, while not successful in establishing any connection between de Man's infamous life and the doctrines of deconstruction (as he intended), was an extremely sensitive ethical evaluation of the self-protective mendacities that are widespread in the "radical" academy. Lehman, however, far from being a "totally ignorant" outsider, has a Ph.D. in English from Columbia and taught for a few years at Hamilton College, although he did not end up as a career academic. He knows the canonical deconstructive texts quite well, if not as a priestly specialist, and refers to many of them in concrete detail; so if Graff really believes that literary theory is not "too advanced or esoteric for the average college or high school student of literature," then it is surely "pretty bizarre" that he should find David Lehman "totally ignorant."

Yet it's not only "outsiders" that Graff regards as outsiders, but insiders as well: in the notes to "Other Voices" he attacks Robert Alter, Denis Donoghue, Roger Shattuck, Christopher Clausen, and others for their objections to the hegemony of literary theory, and elsewhere he attacks plenty of other dissenters (whose opinions I don't necessarily agree with). I have no a priori objection to attacking people—I do it all the time. One begins to fear, however, that what Graff really wants is not conversation or diversity, but *absolute conformance and identity*. If he feels that so many of these academics and public intellectuals are unable to understand theoretical ideas with any precision, what can he really expect from students and "outsiders," despite his claim that theory is not too "advanced or esoteric" for *their* mental powers? Easy for students but impossible for David Lehman and Robert Alter?

The upshot for me is that Graff has gradually evolved from a free-spirited but basically judicious and benign oppositional critic to a paradigmatic hegemonic professional, an agent of the "thought police," an equal but opposite double of William Bennett, zealously guarding and aggrandizing his turf (recall "the tendency of all professional literary fields to define their interests parochially and to close ranks against outsiders" [*Professing Literature* 252]) while turning everything around him into demonizing adversarial politics. Not content merely to do his thing in a specialist or generalist niche, he seems to want total institutional control over the operation of literary studies in the academy, not only as chief choreographer but as Zen master, allowing only the most pious and unquestioning acolytes unobstructed access to The Way. The method for doing this would be a rigidly defined professional elite (Graff and his friends) that determines "the conflicts" to be promulgated while proscribing as "ignorant" and "bizarre" any deviation from the orthodox party line, any stumbling in the recitation of the authorized litany, but at the same time employing the rhetoric of populism and of solicitude for lay "outsiders," not to mention timorously "polite" students. The buzzwords may be dialogics, conflict, conversation, and public sphere, but the operants are elitism, professionalism, and rigid, repressive orthodoxy. As for the fungal messiness of the institution of literature, better an unholy mess than a holier-than-thou hierophancy.

Rhetorically Covering Conflict: Gerald Graff as Curricular Rhetorician

Steven Mailloux

> Since some groups and interests are inevitably excluded
> from any institutional conversation, the metaphor of
> "conversation" or "dialogue" is often justly criticized as an
> ideological mystification. But if some groups must be
> excluded or marginalized, an organization that
> foregrounds difference and conflict would promise to give
> the more arbitrary exclusions and marginalizations a
> better chance than they now have of coming to light and
> becoming an explicit theme of discussion. Conversation,
> then, becomes a less politically suspect trope the more the
> conversation thematizes its own exclusions.
> —Gerald Graff, "Other Voices, Other Rooms"

In *Professing Literature,* Gerald Graff presents academic literary
studies with a valuable rhetorical history of its past disciplinary
life. With his proposal to "teach the conflicts," Graff advocates a
rhetorical solution to the discipline's present curricular
problems. In both cases, he uses tropes of "debate," "conversation," and "dialogue" to help us rethink our understanding of
institutional practices and structures. This rhetorical vocabulary
could become even more useful if it were foregrounded as a
topic within Graff's proposals for curricular reform. Indeed, I
believe Graff would increase his persuasiveness if he combined
"teaching the conflicts" and its dialogic structure with an explicit
thematizing of "cultural rhetoric" both as a name for that

structure and as a recurring topic within the curriculum it organizes.

In this essay, my ultimate purpose is to suggest that the study of cultural rhetoric offers a useful framework for reconceptualizing not only literary studies but also the human sciences more generally. To make my case, and show its relation to Graff's proposals, I will first argue that Graff's model of "teaching the conflicts" is not just incidentally rhetorical in its tropology and argumentation. I will do this by commenting on bits of Graff's rhetoric and using some of it to redescribe one recent attempt at curricular reform, the new major in English and Textual Studies (ETS) at Syracuse University. My rhetorical reading of Graff's vocabulary and its juxtaposition to this new major will clarify both the utility of Graff's proposed framework and the advantages of thematizing its rhetoricity. Finally, I will promote a more rhetoricized version of Graff's model as one specific way of institutionalizing a college-wide reorganization of the humanities and social sciences under the the rubric of "cultural rhetoric studies."

Graff himself makes some suggestive comments about the relation of his model to the Syracuse ETS major. Remarking in "Other Voices, Other Rooms" that "knowledge and culture now look less like a unified package, capable of being formalized in a list of great books or cultural literacy facts, and more like a set of unruly and conflicted social practices," Graff notes that "departmental and curricular structure continues to express an earlier positivist-humanist paradigm" that fails to recognize these recent transformations in the shape of knowledge and culture or even acknowledge that there is a deep and widespread conflict between the old structures and the new assumptions. "This very conflict and the need to work through it," Graff argues, "demands a model of the curriculum that is neither a cafeteria counter nor a core, but something more like a conversation." He then cites the Syracuse ETS major as one example of this model of curricular conversation about the conflicts.

One of the most admirable characteristics of Graff's model is its oft-stated goal of helping students "become interested participants in the cultural conversation" over our society's aesthetic, ethical, and political values. Teaching the conflicts within the university is a way of introducing students into "the intellectual vocabularies" in which those conflicts are carried on, and a curricular structure aimed at enhancing such "academic literacy" must work against "a disjunctive curriculum in which students encounter each course as an isolated unit" and instead put each course into a "conversational relation to other courses and discourses."

Though the privileged trope of its self-descriptions tends to be that of contestation rather than conversation, the Syracuse ETS curriculum shares many of the rhetorical goals of teaching the conflicts. It attempts to introduce students into a vocabulary which will help them enter into debates over such topics as canon reform, cultural heritage, aesthetic value, political ideology, multiculturalism, and other topics of intense controversy within English studies and higher education more generally. The introductory course—ETS 141: Reading and Interpretation—attempts to initiate students into the basic theoretical vocabulary of the major, especially semiotics and discourse analysis. In the words of the college catalogue, ETS 141 involves "the reading of literary and nonliterary texts" and "juxtaposes language as a system of differences to language in its concrete social and historical uses." This first course provides a basis for further work in textual studies and makes it easier for students to use the curricular structure or grid to read the differences that matter most among the courses offered in the department. In Graff's more rhetorical terms, the grid can be used to place the various courses into "conversational relation." (See the Appendix for an overview of the ETS structure and its twenty-seven new categories of courses organized under three modes of inquiry—historical, theoretical, and political.)

From Graff's perspective, one of the advantages of the ETS major must surely be that the new curricular structure highlights the differences between the old model of literary historical coverage and the newer projects of critical theory and cultural critique. It does this, for example, by placing the traditional literary history courses under one subcategory of the historical mode of inquiry rather than using literary historical coverage as the overarching frame for all the courses. By resituating traditional courses in this way, the curricular structure creates a "conversation" among diverse ways of reading and talking about literary and nonliterary texts. In this curriculum in any given semester, "Shakespeare" might appear as a subtitle for several different courses, such as ETS 411, Studies in Literary History to 1800; ETS 343, Introduction to Cultural Theories of Representation; and ETS 491, Studies in Feminisms. What gets foregrounded in such contrasting uses of Shakespearean texts are the distinctive modes of inquiry or critical perspectives and the interpretive and often political stakes in reading texts differently. The point of such a curriculum, Graff notes in "How Curricular Disconnection Disempowers Students," is to replace "a major based on 'traditional pluralism'—in which different viewpoints are represented separately—with a framework in which each position 'acknowledges its allied or contestatory relation to other positions.'" Again, "allied or contestatory" here might be read in rhetorical terms, for certainly the relations aimed at are those of direct and indirect dialogue, just the kind of "dialogic curriculum" that Graff advocates.[1]

Though Graff's rhetorical explanations of his conflict model can be used to read the ETS major more rhetorically than it reads itself, what I really want to emphasize is how his proposal to teach the conflicts might benefit from making its rhetoricity a more public part of its self-descriptions. But certainly by this time my reader must be asking, "Why all this harping on 'rhetoric?' Why, after all, should we emphasize the rhetorical nature of Graff's proposals?"

Graff helps me begin my answer to these questions when, at the end of "Taking Cover in Coverage," he recommends that "the university subsume literary studies under cultural studies." I would like to suggest, in turn, that cultural studies become *cultural rhetoric studies* and that Graff's teaching the conflicts model could become one influential way of institutionalizing such a disciplinary reorganization.

I see several reasons for adopting the study of cultural rhetoric as a means for rethinking literary studies specifically and the humanities and interpretive social sciences more generally. Simply put, the study of cultural rhetoric has significant relations to several emergent proposals for changing the practices and structures of the human sciences: (1) it has important intellectual connections with the cultural studies movement, transdisciplinary inquiry, and interdisciplinary projects like feminist, African-American, and postcolonial studies; (2) it has pedagogical connections to such proposals as Graff's "teaching the conflicts" model; and (3) it has institutional connections to composition as a discipline. Let me elaborate briefly on each of these points.

Cultural studies has become the most influential new alternative to literary studies as a paradigm for English departments. Some departments have explicitly embraced cultural studies in the titles of their new graduate programs, and many others have incorporated cultural studies arguments into their proposals for revising their curricula. Even more pervasive are the number of published attempts to promote a redefinition of traditional literary studies as a study of cultural texts more generally. There is continuing debate about the definition and purpose of cultural studies,[2] but most of its advocates within English departments propose expanding the study of literature into an investigation of many kinds of cultural productions, including noncanonical literature, nonliterary written texts, and other media such as film and television. Advocates also promote an analysis of the relations among these different cultural practices and the sociopolitical formations in which both their objects of study and the studies themselves are situated.

I propose that we take an explicitly rhetorical slant on this emergent field of cultural studies. As I have argued elsewhere, such a slant would begin by conceptualizing the object of study—culture—as "the network of rhetorical practices that are extensions and manipulations of other practices—social, political, and economic."[3] A study of cultural rhetoric would attempt to read the tropes, arguments, and narratives of its object texts (whether literary or nonliterary) within their sociopolitical contexts of cultural production and reception. Such an enterprise might figure its work as investigating the rhetorical dynamics of cultural conversations at particular historical moments, through certain institutions, within specific material circumstances.

This rhetorical enterprise would necessarily be inter-disciplinary, strategically borrowing from many different subdisciplines focused on interpretation, communication, and symbol-using broadly defined. The study of cultural rhetoric would also be transdisciplinary, investigating the conditions, purposes, activities, and results of the disciplinary production of knowledge, especially within academic institutions such as the U.S. university. Thus, the study of cultural rhetoric would link up with two currently growing fields within the human sciences: the rhetoric of inquiry movement and the study of professionalized disciplines' histories and contemporary organization.[4]

A politicized study of cultural rhetoric would also need to relate its agenda to work in such fields as feminist, African-American, and postcolonial studies. We might begin by defining cultural rhetoric more specifically as "the political effectivity of trope and argument in culture" (Mailloux, *Rhetorical Power* xii, 59) and thus build into cultural rhetoric study from the very start an investigation of political questions, such as those involving the ideological production of communal solidarity and conflict and the symbolic mechanisms of domination and resistance within a multicultural society. I believe that rhetorical study generally should reclaim its (often ignored) political heritage and should install a concern with power into its project from the beginning rather than tagging it on at the end as an afterthought.[5] Michel Foucault's genealogical work is especially helpful in theorizing rhetoric politically right now. Let me give just one example.

In answering the question "What happens when individuals exert (as they say) power over others?" Foucault in a late essay distinguishes three kinds of relationships: objective capacities, power relations, and relationships of communication. By "objective capacities" he means power over things, abilities to "modify, use, consume, or destroy them . . . a power which stems from aptitudes directly inherent in the body or relayed by external instruments." Foucault distinguishes this form of power from the one with which he is most directly concerned: power that "brings into play relations between individuals (or between groups)." The exercise of this power is "always a way of acting upon an acting subject or acting subjects by virtue of their acting or being capable of action." Foucault then differentiates these power relations from relationships of communication "which transmit information by means of a language, a system of signs, or any other symbolic medium" (Foucault, "Subject and Power" 217–20). In another place, he describes this relationship more satisfactorily as involving "technologies of sign systems which permit us to use signs, meanings, symbols, or signification" (Foucault, "Technologies of the Self" 18).

Foucault does not mean to define these three kinds of relationships as separate domains, for in his view the three "always overlap." For example, he says that "communicating is always a certain way of acting upon another person or persons," and "the production and circulation of elements of meaning can have as their objective or as their consequence certain results in the realm of power." The study of cultural rhetoric might elaborate theoretically and illustrate historically exactly how relations of power and communication overlap. Indeed, my earlier definition of cultural rhetoric could easily be rewritten in Foucauldian terms: cultural rhetoric involves power relations that "pass through systems of communication."[6]

Foucault's rhetoric (like that of Graff's model and the Syracuse ETS major) tends to privilege the trope of "conflict" in its theoretical and historical work. Further rhetorical use of the Foucauldian vocabulary should probably be balanced by figurings of rhetorical exchanges or cultural conversations in terms of more collaborative or cooperative metaphors (see Mailloux, *Rhetorical Power* 146–47). Still, rhetorical conflict, especially in times of historical crisis, seems much more pervasive than rhetorical cooperation. The battle metaphor— especially in its masculinist forms—might be somewhat overused at the present moment in critical theory, but it does usefully convey a sense of the many tensions and conflicts in various contemporary cultural sites. Not the least important of these sites is U.S. higher education.

These academic conflicts are most evident in debates over curriculum reform and pedagogical practices. Again, the study of cultural rhetoric gives us some helpful hints in thinking about these issues. Rhetoric provides a way of analyzing the controversies within contemporary "culture wars" and curriculum debates. But more important, perhaps, are the possible rhetorical "solutions" to those conflicts, such as Graff's dialogic curricular proposals. As I have already noted, Graff suggests that since English studies no longer has a generally stable consensus on some of its most basic issues of canon, methodology, curriculum, and pedagogy, perhaps the best mode of disciplinary organization is to thematize the conflicts. As Graff and William E. Cain put it, "the best solution to the conflicts over the canon, the curriculum, and the culture is to teach them. Teach the conflicts themselves." They go on to argue that the "classes conducted in the university at any moment make up a potentially coherent conversation, but it is not experienced *as* a conversation by most students, who encounter its different voices in separation from one another. . . . If the academic conversation were made less disjunctive and more coherent, we suspect that more students would see the point of acquiring the information needed to participate in it" (Graff and Cain, "Peace Plan" 311). Whatever the validity of the authors' hopefulness, they are certainly persuasive when they claim that a curriculum that explicitly relates the different, conflicting voices to each other will have a better chance of achieving the end they seek: curricular effectiveness through student understanding. Teaching the conflicts as a model for curricular and pedagogical reform would be a definite improvement over the disorganized practices and contradictory structures on the current academic scene. What I would like to emphasize here is that these descriptions of Graff's conflict model already exemplify one very rhetorical way of framing and addressing problems in curriculum and pedagogy. Adding to Graff's proposal an explicitly self-conscious rhetorical vocabulary might further promote a new effective collaboration within a discipline lacking consensus on important topics and goals.[7]

All the connections sketched so far provide reasons for institutionalizing the study of cultural rhetoric by name. A reform of English departments along the lines proposed would most likely require a major rethinking of the relation of English studies to other disciplines in the human sciences, and such a rethinking could lead to very different institutional structures than those presently governing the academic study of the humanities and the social sciences, again as Graff has suggested in the case of his own curricular proposals. However, what I am most interested in pursuing here is still another reason for English departments to adopt cultural rhetoric study as a new framework: the connection of cultural rhetoric to the discipline of composition.

English departments and composition programs have much to gain intellectually and politically by working as institutional allies within American universities. However, to accomplish this alliance in the nineties, these two changing disciplines must work out their agendas in view of each other. The best, and perhaps the only, way for this to be done is through the development of local institutional agreements among groups in literary studies, composition, ESL, cultural studies, literary theory, linguistics, creative writing, and other fractions of traditional English departments. No national, discipline-wide solution seems possible at the present moment. Furthermore, these local agreements and alliances must be rhetorically negotiated in full awareness of the controversial history of the relation between traditional English departments and their composition programs. In light of that often regrettable institutional past, I would like to suggest the following: literature faculty throughout the country should reconceptualize their English curricula *not* in their own terms (literary history, cultural studies, critical theory, or whatever) and then ask their understandably suspicious composition colleagues to join up. Rather, English departments should adopt a term traditionally associated with composition study and use that concept as a way of rethinking their own theories, practices, and structures. Of course, the term I suggest that English departments adopt is the term "rhetoric." More specifically, the notion of "cultural rhetoric" could be used as a means to renegotiate the relationship between English departments and composition programs as well as their joint relation to other disciplines throughout the university.[8]

Though Graff's model of teaching the conflicts is not the only structure available for organizing the study of cultural rhetoric, it is, as I've tried to show throughout this essay, one proposal that is especially compatible with a rhetorical vocabulary and framework. Thus, cultural rhetoric study might find teaching the conflicts a useful strategy for accomplishing its own dialogic purposes. But Graff's model itself would also benefit from a cultural rhetoric focus. Indeed, by explicitly emphasizing the rhetorical in its self-descriptions, Graff could more easily incorporate into his model composition research and teaching, to which he has given less prominence than literary studies in his histories and curricular proposals. In any case, I propose this essay as another episode in a curricular conversation between teaching the conflicts and rhetoricizing cultural studies, a conversation that Gerald Graff has already so helpfully initiated.

Appendix

Major in English and Textual Studies, Syracuse University[9]

Lower-Division Requirements

    ETS 141   Reading and Interpretation I: From Language to Discourse

    ETS 214   Reading and Interpretation II: Practices of Reading

Upper-Division Requirements

Courses are divided into three groups, according to whether their mode of inquiry or conceptual orientation is primarily historical, theoretical, or political. Students are required to take two courses from one of these groups, two courses from a second group, and one course from a third group. The three remaining courses are major electives, which can come from any of the three groups or from among other courses not included in any group, for example, creative writing workshops or upper-level composition studios.

Historical inquiries assume that texts bear meaning as they are produced and read in specific historical formations. Courses taught under this rubric will study, for example, periods and periodization, reception aesthetics, modes of historical inquiry, and specific histories of genres.

Theoretical inquiries, instead of taking the possibility of textual meaning for granted, investigate the conditions under which texts can be said to bear meaning, as well as the questions of whether and how such meaning can become available to a reader. They include courses in psychoanalysis, deconstruction, hermeneutics, rhetoric, and poetics.

Political inquiries assume that texts are bearers of political meaning; that is, they mediate power relations. Courses taught under this rubric will focus, for example, on the politics of canon formation, the writings of "marginal groups," and the institutional mediation of reading and writing, and include courses in modes of ideology critique, Marxism, cultural rhetoric, and materialist feminism.

In the following list, fifty-four courses are represented. The 300–level number in each pair represents an "Introduction to" course while the 400–level number represents a "Studies in" course. For example, under the "Rhetoric" division of the general "Theory Group" courses, there is a listing "362/462 Hermeneutics," which stands for two courses: "362 Introduction to Hermeneutics" and "462 Studies in Hermeneutics."

HISTORY GROUP

   I. Literary Histories
      311/411 Literary History to 1800
      312/412 Literary History, 1700 to Contemporary
      313/413 Periodization and Chronology

   II. Histories of Symbolic Forms
      321/421 History of Forms
      322/422 History of Ideas
      323/423 History of Myths

   III. Discursive Histories
      331/431 Discourses
      332/432 Reception Aesthetics
      333/433 Language

THEORY GROUP

  I. Theories of Representation
    341/441 Psychological Theories of Representation
    342/442 Semiotic Theories of Representation
    343/443 Cultural Theories of Representation
  II. Poetics and Formal Analysis
    351/451 Theory of Genre
    352/452 Theory of Forms
    353/453 Style and Language
  III. Rhetoric
    361/461 Tropes and Figures
    362/462 Hermeneutics
    363/463 Discourse Analysis

POLITICS GROUP

  I. Culture, Power, Knowledge
    371/471 Ideology
    372/472 Canons
    373/473 Institutions
  II. Resistance and Power
    381/481 Race and Discourse
    382/482 Imperialism and Nationalism
    383/483 Class, Culture, and the Power of Discourse
  III. Gender and Sexualities
    391/491 Feminisms
    392/492 Gender Studies
    393/493 Sexualities

NOTES

    1. It should be noted that this rhetorical reading of Syracuse's ETS major goes somewhat against the grain of its institutional history. That is, the Syracuse English faculty did not accept "rhetoric" as an organizing term for their innovative curricular reforms when they

produced them in 1986–89. For one narrative about how and why this happened, see Mailloux, "Rhetoric Returns to Syracuse." For two other, very different stories about the ETS major, see Cohan et al.; and Morton and Zavarzadeh, "Theory Pedagogy Politics."

2. For discussion and bibliography, see Grossberg, Nelson, and Treichler.

3. Mailloux, *Rhetorical Power* 165. Also see Mailloux, "Rhetorical Hermeneutics Revisited" 234–35.

4. On the former, see Nelson, Megill, and McCloskey; and Simons. For examples of the latter within English studies, see Graff, *Professing Literature*; Berlin; and Shumway.

5. T.V. Reed calls such work "radical rhetorical studies" and provides a useful list of examples, most of which I would include on any list of my own (Reed 174, n. 5).

6. Foucault, "The Subject and Power" 217–18. For other attempts to adapt Foucault's work to rhetorical studies, see Blair; Foss and Gill; Foss, Foss, and Trapp, ch. 8; Cooper; Mailloux, *Rhetorical Power*, ch. 4 and 5; and Mailloux, "Rhetorical Use."

7. For other curricular proposals that give a central role to rhetoric, see Waller; and Culler. Also see Lanham; Winterowd 323–53; Booth, "Revival of Rhetoric" and "Mere Rhetoric"; and Bialostosky, "Dialogics" and "Liberal Education." For a critique of rhetorical studies as curricular framework, see Morton and Zavarzadeh, "(Post)modern Critical Theory" 54–55.

8. This last paragraph has been adapted from Mailloux, "Rhetoric Returns to Syracuse."

9. Information taken from *The English Newsletter: Undergraduate News from the English Department, Syracuse University*, 1, no. 1 (March 1990) and no. 2 (November 1990).

WORKS CITED

Berlin, James. *Rhetoric and Reality: Writing Instruction in American Colleges, 1900–1985*. Carbondale: Southern Illinois University Press, 1987.

Bialostosky, Don. "Dialogics as an Art of Discourse in Literary Criticism." *PMLA* 101 (October 1986): 788–97.

———. "Liberal Education and the English Department: Or, English as a Trivial Pursuit." In Lunsford, Moglen, and Slevin. 97–100.

Blair, Carole. "The Statement: Foundation of Foucault's Historical Criticism." *Western Journal of Speech Communication* 51 (Fall 1987): 364–383.

Booth, Wayne. "Mere Rhetoric, Rhetorology, and the Search for a Common Learning" (1981). Rpt. in his *The Vocation of a Teacher: Rhetorical Occasions, 1967–1988*. Chicago: University of Chicago Press, 1988. 105–28.

———. "The Revival of Rhetoric" (1965). Rpt. in his *Don't Try to Reason with Me: Essays and Ironies for a Credulous Age*. Chicago: University of Chicago Press, 1970. 35–46.

Cohan, Steven, John W. Crowley, Jean E. Howard, Veronica Kelly, Steven Mailloux, Stephen Melville, Felicity Nussbaum, Bill Readings, Bennet Schaber, Linda Shires, and Thomas Yingling. "Not a Good Idea: A New Curriculum at Syracuse." Unpublished essay, December 1987.

Cooper, Martha. "Reconceptualizing Ideology According to the Relationship Between Rhetoric and Knowledge/Power." In *Rhetoric and Ideology: Compositions and Criticisms of Power*. Ed. Charles W. Kneupper. Arlington, TX: Rhetoric Society of America, 1989. 30–41.

Culler, Jonathan. "Imagining Changes." In Lunsford, Moglen, and Slevin. 79–83.

Foss, Sonja K., and Ann Gill. "Michel Foucault's Theory of Rhetoric as Epistemic." *Western Journal of Speech Communication* 51 (Fall 1987): 384–401.

Foss, Sonja K., Karen A. Foss, and Robert Trapp. *Contemporary Perspectives on Rhetoric*. 2nd ed. Prospect Heights, IL.: Waveland Press, 1991.

Foucault, Michel. "The Subject and Power." In Hubert L. Dreyfus and Paul Rabinow. *Michel Foucault: Beyond Structuralism and Hermeneutics*. 2nd ed. Chicago: University of Chicago Press, 1983. 208–26.

———. "Technologies of the Self." In *Technologies of the Self: A Seminar with Michel Foucault*. Eds. Luther H. Martin, Huck Gutman, and Patrick H. Hutton. Amherst: University of Massachusetts Press, 1988. 16–40.

Graff, Gerald. *Professing Literature: An Institutional History.* Chicago: University of Chicago Press, 1987.

Graff, Gerald, and William E. Cain. "Peace Plan for the Canon Wars." *The Nation,* 6 March 1989: 310–11.

Grossberg, Lawrence, Cary Nelson, and Paula Treichler, eds. *Cultural Studies.* New York: Routledge, 1992.

Lanham, Richard A. *Literacy and the Survival of Humanism.* New Haven: Yale University Press, 1983.

Lunsford, Andrea, Helene Moglen, and James F. Slevin, eds. *The Future of Doctoral Studies in English.* New York: MLA, 1989.

Mailloux, Steven. "Rhetoric Returns to Syracuse: Curricular Reform in English Studies." In *English Studies/Culture Studies: Institutionalizing Dissent.* Eds. Nancy Ruff and Isaiah Smithson. Urbana: University of Illinois Press, forthcoming.

———. "Rhetorical Hermeneutics Revisited." *Text and Performance Quarterly* 11 (July 1991): 233–48.

———. *Rhetorical Power.* Ithaca, NY: Cornell University Press, 1989.

———. "The Rhetorical Use and Abuse of Fiction: Eating Books in Nineteenth-Century America." *boundary 2,* 17 (Spring 1990): 133–57.

Morton, Donald, and Mas'ud Zavarzadeh. "(Post)modern Critical Theory and the Articulations of Critical Pedagogies." *College Literature* 17 (October 1990): 51–63.

———. "Theory Pedagogy Politics: The Crisis of 'The Subject' in the Humanities." In *Texts for Change: Theory/Pedagogy/Politics.* Eds. Donald Morton and Mas'ud Zavarzadeh. Urbana: University of Illinois Press, 1991. 1–32.

Nelson, John S., Allan Megill, and Donald N. McCloskey, eds. *The Rhetoric of the Human Sciences: Language and Argument in Scholarship and Public Affairs.* Madison: University of Wisconsin Press, 1987.

Reed, T.V. *Fifteen Jugglers, Five Believers: Literary Politics and the Poetics of American Social Movements.* Berkeley: University of California Press, 1992.

Shumway, David, ed. "Episodes in the History of Criticism and Theory: Papers from the Fourth Annual Meeting of the GRIP Project." *Poetics Today* 9, no. 4 (1988).

Simons, Herbert W., ed. *The Rhetorical Turn: Invention and Persuasion in the Conduct of Inquiry.* Chicago: University of Chicago Press, 1990.

Waller, Gary. "Working within the Paradigm Shift: Post-Structuralism in the Undergraduate Curriculum." *ADE Bulletin* 81 (Fall 1985): 5–12.

Winterowd, W. Ross. *Composition/Rhetoric: A Synthesis.* Carbondale: Southern Illinois University Press, 1986.

Composing Conflicts: A Writing Teacher's Perspective

John Schilb

Having taught writing in English departments for several years, I share Gerald Graff's view of them. When I talk with colleagues in literature, as well as with other writing teachers, I sense that English faculty often hold different beliefs on important matters. Just as often, they resist acknowledging and negotiating these differences in public. Graff is right to urge that they make such conflicts explicit and productive for their classes.

Yet even though Graff's curricular framework has merits, at least two problems can arise if and when English departments implement it. First, a department may use Graff's model to keep focusing on literature courses, thus perpetuating the traditional neglect of composition in English studies. Second, the department may also continue to marginalize its students, producing a situation that Graff briefly alludes to in "Other Voices, Other Rooms." If faculty get preoccupied with their own conflicts, they may indeed wind up "inflicting new kinds of boredom and alienation on students," making them feel that the most impassioned academic disputes are merely academic.

Conflicts and Composition

When Graff first proposed a conflict-centered English curriculum, he slighted the potential role of writing teachers in it. His 1987 book *Professing Literature* barely mentions them before moving to its title subject. When the book concludes by suggesting that English departments address their internal differences, it continues to focus on issues in literary analysis. Similarly, in the 1986 paper included here ("Taking Cover in Coverage"), Graff seems to equate English studies with the study of literature. Inevitably such moves have antagonized some people in composition. They have excoriated Graff for neglecting their very presence in English departments, let alone their perspectives on them (e.g., Friend).

Still, those who teach composition in English departments should consider even Graff's mid-1980s writing potentially useful for them. Take the case of his book. Often the priorities of writing teachers get ignored because colleagues assume literature courses are the fixed and indisputable center of the English curriculum. Graff's book can help challenge this attitude, for it shows that "professing literature" has been a historically contingent and conflicted enterprise. At any rate, Graff has demonstrated significantly greater interest in composition since then. For one thing, he has acquainted himself more with the field's scholarship; note that "Other Voices" cites Patricia Bizzell and David Bartholomae. Moreover, for the last three years, he has given papers at the annual meeting of the Conference on College Composition and Communication (CCCC). Actually, Graff is now one of the very few literary theorists who have regularly attended this event. In each of his CCCC presentations, he has called for English departments to extend his curricular model by considering how the teaching of writing differs from the teaching of literature.

In a 1989 article, I recommended similar broadening of his plan. More precisely, I suggested that teachers of literature and teachers of writing collectively examine their various stances on the subject of "rhetoric." As Graff indicates in "Other Voices," this term has become central again for a number of English faculty. Terry Eagleton spurred many to consider it when he climaxed his 1983 book *Literary Theory* by urging that literary study be replaced with the study of rhetoric. During the 1987 Modern Language Association (MLA) conference on English doctoral programs, numerous speakers invoked the word as a possible rubric for the profession's future (e.g., Bialostosky, Booth, Culler, Lanham, Lauer and Lunsford, and Waller). Nevertheless, even those who now champion "rhetoric" in English departments fail to agree on its meaning and scope. Not everyone would associate it, as Eagleton does, with concern for the socialist benefits of discourse. Whereas composition theory tends to follow Aristotle, linking rhetoric with persuasion, poststructuralist literary theory has often followed Paul de Man, seeing rhetoric as the destabilizing interplay of tropes. Therefore, in my article I envisioned an English department whose members explore together "(1) the differences *between* rhetoric and other forms of inquiry, (2) the differences *within* the history of rhetoric, and (3) the institutional pressures that affect theoretical decisions—including the official goals of individual courses, the role of the overall department in the college's curriculum, the declared mission of the college, and larger social conditions" (437–38).

This kind of English curriculum can still serve as a pragmatic compromise for writing teachers. It offers them the possibility of a greater voice in departmental affairs without assuming that teachers of literature will immediately share their beliefs. This Graff-inspired scheme does, however, ask English departments to respect composition more than they usually have. At present, many still regard it as the basest form of intellectual labor, suitable only for graduate students or for a permanent reserve force of part-timers. Admittedly, in a number of places, the same faculty teach composition and literature. Often enough, though, they see writing instruction as a grim departure from their true calling. The department that maintains this sort of view will have difficulty engaging all of its staff and courses in the collective inquiry that Graff recommends. Although his curriculum allows for disagreement, it grants at least provisional equality to the various subjects that have comprised English studies, and composition has certainly been one.

English departments will give composition equal status only when they confront certain oppositions that have bolstered their contempt for it. Robert Scholes identifies and deconstructs some of these in his book *Textual Power* (5–9). He observes that English departments look down on composition because they arbitrarily prize "literature" over "nonliterature" and consumption of texts over production of them. Composition also suffers, he notes, because such departments falsely separate the academy from "the real world." More precisely, they assume that their influence on society is at best indirect, so they suspect that all a composition student can write is "pseudo-nonliterature."

Another dichotomy often leads English departments to privilege literary study over composition: scholarship versus teaching. Traditionally, universities have emphasized published research over pedagogical expertise. Increasingly, undergraduate colleges are tempted to do so. As much as any other discipline, English has perpetuated this hierarchy of values. Although they may actually work hard at their own teaching, literature specialists have often considered their publishing records more important. Following this line of thought, they denigrate composition in part because they associate it with "mere" pedagogy. To be sure, composition specialists do concern themselves primarily with issues and methods of writing instruction. But their colleagues in literature need to recognize that teaching writing can be just as valuable as churning out traditional scholarship. Besides helping students write—no small achievement in itself—the composition classroom can produce, test, ponder, and revise theories of discourse, interpretation, and cultural analysis. Perhaps more writing teachers should publish the results of such inquiry, but many spend all their time and energy coping with the working conditions that English departments impose on them, including low salaries and large classes. When they can write about their teaching, their departments often see their books and articles as inherently less interesting than analyses of literary texts.

This situation may be changing. When he first published "Other Voices," Graff accomplished much in suggesting that articles about curriculum and pedagogy belonged in journals like *New Literary History*. As I have noted, his citing composition scholars there was also auspicious. So, too, is the new series of volumes in composition studies published by the MLA, long a fortress of literature specialists. But unless individual English departments consider their own composition teaching as an intellectual endeavor—and unless they challenge the other polarities identified by Scholes—they will, again, limit their ability to adopt Graff's model.

The Role of Students

Like any curriculum, Graff's conflict-centered one must constantly recognize two principles articulated by Alexander Astin, a veteran educational researcher: "First, the amount of student learning and personal development associated with any educational program is directly proportional to the quality and quantity of student involvement in that program. And second, the effectiveness of any educational policy or practice is directly related to the capacity of that policy or practice to increase student involvement" (36). Astin's remarks may seem so commonsensical as to verge on platitude. But he makes this argument because curriculum planners have often focused more on specifying, organizing, and reifying subject matter than on motivating students. A department that sets out to use Graff's model can lapse into this trap. It can get so caught up in fashioning a curriculum out of its staff members' conflicts that it forgets once more to make student involvement its ultimate goal.

Graff does indicate that students need opportunities to practice the rhetorics of the academy themselves. He does not seem to assume that they can learn these discourses just by watching their teachers deploy them—in other words, through sheer osmosis. Certainly he wants students to participate in the various activities that he recommends. When he proposes a department-wide discussion in "Other Voices," he declares it a matter "of crucial importance" for him "that students not remain in a passive relation to this symposium." In his "Curricular Disconnection" piece, he praises a conference that students organized for a seminar on "Teaching the Canon and the Conflicts."

I would emphasize even more than Graff does, however, the necessity of involving students in such departmental events. More specifically, a department using his model needs to do something that he does not explicitly call for: invite students to bring up what *they* see as issues in their everyday lives, instead of simply making them deal with those that their teachers deem important. A department that focuses solely on its faculty's disputes can easily discourage students by mistakenly assuming that they will agree—or can be forced to agree—with their teachers' sense of what the "hot" issues are. Even if OMP and YFP publicly debate whether "Dover Beach" is phallocentric, students may have trouble understanding why Arnold's poem is worth analyzing; the argument may still leave them feeling that English studies is a darkling plain. Conversely, Graff's curriculum may enlighten and energize students if it explicitly allows them to analyze their daily concerns.

Once invited to do this, students may even desirably transform the rhetorics of the academy. These rhetorics are, in fact, hardly beyond criticism, as the very conflicts cited by Graff demonstrate. Purveyors of academic "theory-talk" should keep in mind that it risks becoming insular, abstract, and overblown when it tries to avoid being contaminated by students' worldviews. If forced to confront their perspectives as potentially legitimate forms of "theory," academic discourse might very well become more conceptually rigorous, as well as more responsive to society at large. At its best, then, college is a place where students and faculty teach each other.

Regrettably, the academy has often failed not only to motivate students, but also to appreciate how they can challenge its parochialism. Along with other disciplines, English has opposed Wise Teacher to Ignorant Pupil. English departments scorn composition partly because they see it as grappling with the limited intelligence of first-year students.

Given this history, questions need to be raised about some of Graff's phrasing in his essays here. Occasionally he makes statements that can justify faculty who would keep dismissing students' concerns, even if he himself would actually protest their doing so.

Recent developments in composition theory provide a useful context for this issue. Recall that Graff cites Patricia Bizzell and David Bartholomae. In the 1980s, they and other composition theorists like Kenneth Bruffee and Elaine Maimon pushed the field to reinterpret students' problems with academic discourse. Instead of attributing such difficulties to a basic lack of intelligence, they argued that students were often just inexperienced with the discursive practices of academic disciplines. According to the title of a Bizzell review article, teaching writing meant "initiating" students into these practices, and that was best accomplished by introducing students to specific disciplinary conventions instead of one generic model of *the* composing process. Graff promotes a similar theory; "Other Voices" frequently refers to "initiating" students into academic discourse.

This "social constructionist" perspective on academic writing has helped composition teachers. Above all, it has made them much more aware of differences among the various "discourse communities" that comprise the academy. Yet, as Bizzell ("Marxist Ideas") and other commentators have lately observed, "initiation" theory threatens to constrain and underestimate students once again. As Susan Wall and Nicholas Coles point out, it often fails to conceive "the relationship between a student's discourse and that of the academy . . . as dialectical, [as] a two-way process of interaction that will, if it succeeds, necessarily involve teachers and students in the re-formation of both discourses" (235). Unwittingly or not, some of Graff's language suggests how the idea of "initiating" students can fall short of this ideal.

Like certain advocates of "initiation" theory, Graff shifts back and forth between an anthropological view of the academy (it is just one "discourse community" within society) and an honorific view of it (it is distinctly superior to students' "discourse communities"). Consider his ambiguous use of the

word "culture" in "Other Voices." Sometimes Graff applies it to
the world beyond the academy, indicating that college is just
one part of that world: Arnold's poem may or may not become "*a
live issue* in the culture again"; the whole society is
"increasingly being forced to come to terms with cultural
difference"; colleges are now seeking faculties that are "far
more representative of the diversity of culture than in the
past." At other times, however, he links "culture" specifically
with the academy and suggests that a college education should
provide students access to it as a definite good. For example, he
invokes "academic culture," "intellectual culture," "academic
intellectual culture," and the "revisionist culture" that certain
faculty prize. Either or both senses of the term may be at work
when Graff suggests that "the aim is to help students become
interested participants in the present cultural conversation." At
this point in the essay, Graff might have acknowledged that
students are *already* "interested participants" in certain
"cultural conversations," and that faculty have to take *those*
seriously if they are to help students understand the relevance
of academic "theory-talk."

A similarly troubling passage appears in "Taking Cover,"
where Graff asserts that "the established [literature]
curriculum" leaves "average-to-poor" students without "conceptual contexts that make it possible to integrate perceptions and
generalize from them." While a curriculum should try to make
its theoretical framework(s) explicit, even "average-to-poor"
students in traditional English departments are not as
cognitively deficient as Graff makes them out to be. They are
always contextualizing, integrating, and generalizing from
their school experiences, even if *their* frameworks are not what
educators had in mind. Faculty have to understand and
provisionally value *those* frameworks if the curriculum is truly
going to connect students' lives with theirs.

As Tom Fox observes, part of the problem with
"initiation" theory is that it risks "overstating the differences
between academic discourse and students' discourse, especially
by attributing the differences to linguistic habits or cognitive
conventions" (70–71). Paradoxically, faculty have to view
students as being close enough to the academic world so that

they can appreciate the distinct perspectives they offer it. Although students often do have trouble reading and writing in the academy, treating them as thoroughly remote from it deters them from seeing how their experiences can serve as resources for their education and as challenges to conventional academic wisdom. Critiquing Bartholomae's work, Wall and Coles suggest that "initiation" theory in general seems "to rest on a rather thin conception of student culture, of the material of their lives as this can be brought to bear on the development of a critical academic stance" (235). Their awareness of this shortcoming leads Wall and Coles to criticize in particular "initation" theorists' habit of referring to students as "outsiders" and as visitors to a foreign country (244).

Unfortunately, Graff relies on this language as well. At the conclusion of "Other Voices," he suggests that many students are "outsiders" to the academic community, and he goes so far as to claim that "most Americans ... do not speak the language of academic intellectual culture because they do not feel themselves part of the country in which the language is spoken." Earlier in the essay, he makes similarly questionable declarations about students' distance from the academy, suggesting that even after years of high school they stand remote from "academic literacy *as such*" and *"the life of books* itself." Although Graff may believe that at these moments he is criticizing the academy, not students themselves, his descriptions of them fail to indicate ways they might actually contribute to their own education and teach faculty something as well.

If pressed, almost all faculty can recall times when students did enhance their courses by injecting personal experiences or concerns. I immediately think of something that occurred one day in a writing course I taught recently. We had spent a number of classes discussing the extent to which the term "community" fit human relationships in general and, more specifically, the relationship that a writer seeks to establish with a reader. On this particular day, I wanted to discuss papers that the students had written about their efforts to join certain "communities" in their hometowns. Two of the women students, however, could not stop talking about the night before. They had stayed in one of the campus computer rooms until two o'clock, "meeting" students from other colleges by exchanging anonymous messages with them via electronic mail. As they described the evening, they acknowledged that it had not been unusual for them: they had routinely engaged in such e-mail "conversations," and so had many of their friends. The two women were pleased that the e-mail network had enabled them to make risk-free contact with new people. They could, if they wished, deceive their correspondents and avoid face-to-face encounters with them. At the same time, they worried that they were getting downright obsessed with this activity, and they suspected that some of their correspondents were deceiving *them*.

The rest of the class was immediately gripped by what these women reported. At first, I worried that their story would pull us away from the "real" material of the course. Gradually, though, I saw that their personal concerns nicely expanded our analysis of "community." For them, computer networks seemed to encourage new forms of "community" while undercutting the mutual trust that the word has traditionally indicated. If I had not allowed them to bring up their experiences, I would not have understood how even on our campus, new technology may transform everyday forms of collective life. As they discussed how and why they were driven to e-mail, these particular students also made me realize that our campus presently failed to offer them sufficient "community" feeling. Overall, what I might have dismissed as a digression from our topic actually contributed fresh insights and details to it. Without the women's testimonies, I suspect that I would have kept the discussion fairly abstract, and surely the class would have been less engaged in it.

Several years ago at Denison University, a colleague and I built an entire course around particular student concerns. Denison requires all students to take a course in women's or minority studies. Members of the school's many fraternities and sororities have always been suspicious of this requirement, seeing it as a feminist, left-wing assault on the Greek system's power and values. My colleague and I decided, therefore, to develop an interdisciplinary women's studies course that would address these students' anxieties while satisfying the requirement. Our main title for it was "The Idea of Fraternity and Sorority," which indicates the central role that discussions of the Greek system played in it. On the basis of this title alone, over 150 students enrolled. The class included die-hard defenders of the system as well as students bent on abolishing it.

Our subtitle for the course was "Groups of Men and Women in America." As these words suggest, we tried to establish a broad context for the students' local issues. Throughout the course, we encouraged them to relate their experiences with Denison's fraternities and sororities. At the same time, we encouraged them to historicize these organizations by looking at the values, structures, and effects of other more or less single-sex groups, ranging from the nineteenth-century suffrage movement to modern-day corporate firms. The result was a constant dialectic: the class shuttled back and forth between immediate campus matters and historical events, between dispassionate analyses of familiar institutions and heated debates about their ultimate merits.

This course might, I think, serve as a model for a conflict-centered English curriculum. Admittedly, this was a single course, whereas Graff wants interlinked courses and even departmental conferences. Yet our topic enabled students to articulate and explore conflicts among their world views. Far from dominating the course, we as teachers found ourselves in constant debate with the students as well as with our ten teaching assistants. The course also drew upon a range of disciplinary perspectives, especially since we invited faculty from various departments to speak about their own experiences with single-sex groups. Most important, the course thoroughly engaged students, even if their involvement sometimes took the form of anger.

English faculty might believe that its topic would never be appropriate for a course or conference in *their* department. But certainly this subject can bring conflicts in English studies together with the conflicts that students experience. "The Idea of Fraternity and Sorority" could actually serve as a very good focus for debates about the literary canon. Is *Moby-Dick* somehow universal, or does it remain embedded in the life and concerns of specifically male groups? Does Charlotte Perkins Gilman's feminist utopia *Herland* merit the regard of literature specialists for its affirmation of female solidarity? What should they now think of the nineteenth-century women's groups who studied American literature, and how should they view the predominantly male professoriate that later made it a full-fledged academic subject? To what extent has the distinction between "literature" and "nonliterature" reflected the interests of men?

As I argued earlier, any English department using Graff's conflict model should address issues of writing instruction. If it focused on "The Idea of Fraternity and Sorority," the department might ponder questions like the following: When is it fair to say that a writer is assuming a single-sex audience rather than a heterogenous one? When, if ever, is it all right for a writer to address just his or her own sex? What sorts of rhetoric do single-sex organizations use to justify themselves? Do women's writing groups have the same values and purposes as men's? Why has the composition labor force been predominantly female? Moreover, students as well as faculty can draft and circulate position papers on all of the issues that the department considers.

I cite "The Idea of Fraternity and Sorority" as simply one example of a topic that might bridge students' conflicts and faculty's. For particular English departments, other topics would better suit this purpose. To determine what subjects would engage its own students, the department might poll them both formally and informally. It might still take note of OMP and YMP's argument in the faculty lounge as it starts to redesign its curriculum along the lines that Graff suggests. But the department might also begin by heeding *students'* conversations in *their* campus lounges. The potential for exciting conflicts lies just as much in these other voices, these other rooms.

WORKS CITED

Astin, Alexander W. "Involvement: The Cornerstone of Excellence." *Change* 17.4 (1985): 35–39.

Bialostosky, Don H. "Liberal Education and the English Department: Or, English as a Trivial Pursuit." Lunsford, Moglen, and Slevin 97–100.

Bizzell, Patricia. "College Composition: Initiation into the Academic Discourse Community." *Curriculum Inquiry* 12 (1982): 191–207.

———. "Marxist Ideas in Composition Studies." *Contending With Words: Composition and Rhetoric in a Postmodern Age.* Eds. Patricia Harkin and John Schilb. New York: MLA, 1991. 52–68.

Booth, Wayne. "Reversing the Downward Spiral: Or, What Is the Graduate Program *For?*" Lunsford, Moglen, and Slevin 3–8.

Culler, Jonathan. "Imagining Changes." Lunsford, Moglen, and Slevin 79–83.

Eagleton, Terry. *Literary Theory: An Introduction.* Minneapolis: University of Minnesota Press, 1983.

Fox, Tom. "Basic Writing as Cultural Conflict." *Journal of Education* 172.1 (1990): 65–83.

Friend, Christy. "The Excluded Conflict: The Marginalization of Composition and Rhetoric Studies in Graff's *Professing Literature.*" *College English* 54 (1992): 276–86.

Graff, Gerald. *Professing Literature: An Institutional History.* Chicago: University of Chicago Press, 1987.

Harkin, Patricia, and John Schilb, eds. *Contending With Words: Composition and Rhetoric in a Postmodern Age.* New York: MLA, 1991.

Lanham, Richard A. "Convergent Pressures: Social, Technological, Theoretical." Lunsford, Moglen, and Slevin 73–78.

Lauer, Janice M., and Andrea Lunsford. "The Place of Rhetoric and Composition in Doctoral Studies." Lunsford, Moglen, and Slevin 106–10.

Lunsford, Andrea, Helene Moglen, and James F. Slevin, eds. *The Future of Doctoral Studies in English.* New York: MLA, 1989.

Schilb, John. "Composition and Poststructuralism: A Tale of Two Conferences." *College Composition and Communication* 40 (1989): 422–43.

Scholes, Robert. *Textual Power: Literary Theory and the Teaching of English.* New Haven, CT: Yale University Press, 1985.

Wall, Susan, and Nicholas Coles. "Reading Basic Writing: Alternatives to a Pedagogy of Accommodation." *The Politics of Writing Instruction: Postsecondary.* Eds. Richard Bullock and John Trimbur. Portsmouth, NH: Heinemann—Boynton/Cook, 1991. 227–46.

Waller, Gary. "Polylogue: Reading, Writing, and the Structure of Doctoral Study." Lunsford, Moglen, and Slevin 111–20.

Graff's Project and the Teaching of Writing

Andrea A. Lunsford
Suellynn Duffey

Scholars in composition and rhetoric have not unanimously embraced Gerald Graff's curricular and pedagogical reforms in English studies; on the contrary, several have been overtly critical of his project. Those critics of Graff's proposal to "teach the conflicts" most often base their objections on two not unrelated elements of his work. Christy Friend articulates one point of view when she argues that Graff's plan ignores writing and the teaching of writing—just as *Professing Literature* does not deal with the place of rhetoric and composition in the emerging discipline of English studies. By this omission, Graff loses an opportunity to consider one major conflict in English studies or to engage the conflicts surrounding this departmental "other." As Friend's reading makes clear, Graff's plan rests on a curriculum that stresses reading in general and the reading of literary texts in particular, a curriculum that inevitably casts writing into the role of secondary or marginalized other.

A second and related criticism of Graff's proposal objects to its focus on the agonism implied in "teaching the conflicts." Such an agonistic emphasis on conflict, debate, and dialectic highlights the way the academy has tended to represent teaching and learning as combative. In focusing on conflict, Graff simply perpetuates such a view of learning. In response to this aspect of Graff's work, Dale M. Bauer calls for a dialogic classroom, noting that an agonistic epistemology and its related pedagogies are not inviting ones for many students, particularly for women and quite probably for other marginalized groups as well.

We take the point of these criticisms, and yet we believe that Graff's project entails two very important moves for members of the academy interested in rhetoric and composition. His focus on pedagogy and curricula—and his refusal to view them as somehow beneath our attention—is to our minds one entirely salutary effect of his work. In addition, Graff's championing of theory, his willingness to examine the ideological stakes in all educational practices, and his insistence that students understand the implications of theoretical stances all open a space in which to recast the role of students and the metadiscursive practices such a role entails. These important moves may have been obscured for some readers, however, by competing visions of the classroom which exist side by side in Graff's work.

Let us take, as a first instance, the vision of the classroom as a battleground. As noted above, agonism reveals itself in the many conflictual and warlike images and metaphors Graff often favors. Debates among speakers or visitors are said to be "face-to-face showdowns" ("Conflicts"); teachers are engaged in "the culture war" or may "lose the war" ("Other Voices"); "hostile agendas" ("Conflicts") and "conflict" abound ("Other Voices"). And yet, concurrent with this agonism, Graff presents an alternate though somewhat less explicit vision. In describing current curricular needs, Graff illustrates, almost simultaneously, both a conflictual vision and a communal one as well:

> Knowledge and culture now look less like a unified package, capable of being formalized in a list of great books or cultural literacy facts, and more like a set of *unruly and conflicted* social practices. . . . This very *conflict* . . . demands a model of the curriculum that is neither a cafeteria counter nor a core, but something more like a *conversation*. ("Other Voices"; emphasis ours)

In fact, in this same essay, Graff's view of the classroom invokes a concept of conversation at least partially in accord with dialogism and the "connected" epistemology described by Mary Belenky and her colleagues in *Women's Ways of Knowing* and explored by many compositionists interested in the concept of the classroom as a discourse community (Bartholomae, Bizzell). In Graff's words, "the classroom is the 'country' that mediates between the foreign languages of intellectual culture . . . and the students," a place that is, ideally, an "intellectual community" ("Other Voices"). While a conversation and a community may or may not be conflictual, the image Graff creates through these terms much more strongly implies a continuing dialogue in which viewpoints do not so much oppose one another dialectically as weave recursively in and out, moving each other along into uncharted territory and new knowledge.

Specifically in response to Bauer's call for a dialogic classroom, Graff clearly acknowledges one of the advantages of such a classroom: "questions that challenge or redefine the premises of the discussion would not arise in one class only to be abruptly dropped in the next" ("Other Voices"). And yet, Graff eventually rejects dialogism—and he does so on pragmatic grounds. He explains: "I doubt whether 'the classroom' can become effectively dialogic as long as it is not itself in dialogue with other classrooms" ("Other Voices"). In this discussion, however, Graff imagines a dialogic classroom in only *one way;* he clearly suggests that the most sophisticated and challenging questions would be asked only by faculty of one another, not by students of each other or of their instructors. Graff argues that the "inevitable inequalities of authority in the pedagogical situation" work against a fully dialogic classroom. Certainly, power inequalities significantly affect classroom discourse, but Graff's position fails, we believe, to allow students to assume roles that are not somehow radically subordinate to the teacher's. This position also fails to account for the ways in which both students and teachers can negotiate classroom power relationships—and it fails to give students credit for their ability to assume "authority" when they are allowed to do so.

Just as dual images of classrooms emerge in Graff's work, so also competing images of teachers and students appear superimposed on one another. One image represents the teacher as a performer who enacts the conflicts for the supposed instruction and delight of undergraduate students. Such a view of teachers correspondingly casts students in the role of observers, "readers" of the dialectic/debate being carried on before them as well as readers of the texts around which that debate takes place.[1] As readers, students fall into the role of receivers of canonical information or of supercompetitors in a kind of academic sweepstakes in which the prize goes to those who can best imitate the teacher/performer. Privileging the professor as theorizer and primary knower parallels the privileging of literature, the secondary role falling, inevitably in each case, to students and writing.

In contrast to this view of students and teachers, however, is another competing representation. In one of the main pedagogical options Graff offers, the multicourse symposium, he argues that in order for such a symposium to work "it would be of crucial importance that students not remain in a *passive* relation to [it]. . . . The point would be not just to expose students *passively* to the interplay of diverse discourses, but to help them gain control of these discourses by experiencing them as part of the social practices of a community rather than in closed classrooms" ("Other Voices"; emphasis ours). In this passage, Graff emphasizes students as (active) "writers" of texts rather than or in addition to (passive) "readers" or observers alone. He also wishes to embed these roles in a social context, although this aspect of his proposal is not fully developed.

Because we have profited from studying Graff's work and because we find his proposals important and provocative, we have puzzled over these competing images and the tension they create in our reading of Graff's work. And the more we puzzle over these tensions, the more they seem to us to reflect competing definitions of what constitutes literacy and literate practice. Just as theory is imbricated in the roles we allow students to assume, so is a definition of literacy imbricated in how and what we teach and in the goals we seek to accomplish. But literacy is far from monolithic.

For many members of the public—and for members of the academy as well—literacy signifies elementary, basic decoding skills. Such a view of literacy embraces what historians refer to as the "signature" stage of literacy, in which signing one's name demonstrates literacy; the "recitation" stage, in which decoding and memorizing signify literacy; and the "comprehension" stage, in which understanding unfamiliar material in a fairly literal way comprises literacy (Kintgen, Kroll, and Rose, xiv). If students are to become competent but fairly docile workers in an industrial or cultural assembly line, or if they are to be measured on how well they know 5,000 facts about a supposed common culture, then such a reductive view of literacy is efficient, even necessary. But students today need more complex literacies, literacies that call for the ability to analyze unfamiliar material with comprehension and to draw valid inferences from that material.

Lauren and David Resnick argue that such a "high literacy standard is a relatively recent one as applied to the population at large and that much of our present difficulty in meeting the literacy standard we are setting for ourselves can be attributed to the relatively rapid extension to large populations of educational criteria that were once applied to only a limited elite" (191). The Resnicks further demonstrate that "the standards currently applied to mass literacy have been with us for at most three generations" (191). While the standard for mass literacy may have coincided with the advanced literacy described above, the new standard has not entirely superseded earlier, simplistic ones. Witness, for example, the widespread adulation of rote memorization—in the popularity of TV game shows that reward recalling trivial information and in the fear that using calculators in school will damage children's memories or even their mental acuity.

We agree with the Resnicks' analysis, but we wish to push it a bit further. Our own experience suggests that in spite of a kind of national longing for simple definitions of literacy we are already well beyond what the Resnicks and other historians of literacy identify as an "analysis" stage. In fact, we find Graff's focus on theory and its accompanying metadiscursive practices suggestive of a vision of literacy that goes well beyond analysis, one based on generation rather than recovery or consumption of knowledge, on production rather than recitation of discourse and knowledge.[2] Yet this view is more often implicit than explicit in Graff's work, and it often competes with the more reductive view of literacy described above.

When Graff focuses on students as decoders of texts, observers of debates, or even imitators of disciplinary conventions, for instance, he evokes the traditional view of literacy as one of the "basic skills." Often, however, Graff offers a much more complex and compelling view of literacy as those acts of mind through which students create their own knowledge and examine that knowledge critically, a kind of "hyper-literacy" that goes beyond simple or even analytic literacy. In other words, by "teaching the conflicts," by placing different theoretical perspectives alongside one another, Graff creates in part the circumstances necessary for students to become hyper-literate—to become theorizers of their own learning. Contrastive and comparative points of view (the conflicts) supply information for students to analyze and on which to build theoretical stances.

And yet merely placing these views side by side will not allow students to engage with them as fully as Graff wishes, will not ensure the metadiscursive theorizing nor the social context that Graff's reforms implicitly call for. In short, it seems entirely likely that students could sit in a class based on theorizing about the conflicts and enact reductive versions of literacy—by memorizing, taking notes, imitating the teacher, and offering up all of the above on examinations. That way lies not reform, not revolution, but merely a rearranging of the status quo.

In the spirit of resisting rather than reproducing the status quo, we wish to take up what we see as the implicit challenge of Graff's richer and more complex invocation of what literacy can and should be by reimagining both the students' role—as cooperative builders of theory, interpretive frameworks, and strategies for engaging or even transforming canonical information—and, correspondingly, the teachers' role—as senior but by no means sole experts in a collaborative undertaking. We wish to do so, however, in concrete rather than abstract terms by focusing on a particular pedagogical project, one which we hope embodies Graff's theoretical aims while going beyond his proposals. In particular, we wish to enact a pedagogy considerably different from the one Graff imagines, a pedagogy that rewrites students' and teachers' roles, as we have just said, and that recasts the social context of the classroom and the sites and means of instruction. Such a pedagogy addresses a multitude of conflicts—in competing definitions of literacy; in institutionally constructed hierarchies of reading and writing, literature and composition, students and teachers; and in interactions between ethnic, gender, and other diverse groups. But it does so dialogically, not conflictually.

Our project takes place in first-year writing classes, a perhaps unlikely site for the advanced metadiscursive and theoretical practices both we and Graff advocate. And yet, these classes create scenes of social interaction where intellectual interchange is the defining activity, and they involve complex structures which ensure the expression of diverse experiences and theoretical perspectives. Perhaps most importantly, they open the doors of the classroom not only to other classrooms but to spaces outside the classroom and the academy as well.

Instead of focusing on literary works as texts, students in these first-year writing courses study the cultural or language practices of different groups. Whatever their specific project, the students work to define the uses of language in the group they study and to induce definitions of literacy characteristic of that group, ones they can then compare to definitions of literacy embedded in works such as Maya Angelou's *Heart of a Woman*, E.D. Hirsch's *Cultural Literacy*, or Mike Rose's *Lives on the Boundary*. These competing definitions of literacy enact one major conflict in the field and engage students in sorting out such definitions for themselves. In the focus on literacy, these classes might be said to be organized "thematically," as Graff calls for ("Other Voices"), and to offer texts "not only for their instrinsic value but for their usefulness in illustrating exemplary problems and issues" ("Taking Cover"). Pairing such works as *Heart of a Woman* and *Cultural Literacy* also invites students to explore the traditional hierarchical dichotomy between literary and nonliterary texts, thus introducing another set of conflicts characteristic of English studies. These conflicts are not introduced, however, as conflicts per se, but rather as the natural outgrowth of the tasks students have set for themselves, all in an atmosphere that is collaborative and, we hope, dialogic.

In preparation for their more abstract theoretical undertakings, the students actively engage in concrete ones.

They investigate literacy and community in their own lives—through writing assignments, class discussion, and small-group work as well as through reading. They conduct field work (inside and outside of class) and collect data about the cultural and literate practices of various communities to which they have access—student or faculty governance bodies, sports teams, religious organizations, employees at campus or local job sites, dormitory groups, and so forth. They analyze and interpret their data, build taxonomies to serve as frameworks for the data, write "ethnographic" reports, and present their findings to class, using both verbal and visual media. These projects inevitably engage students in sorting out conflicting claims, in examining multiple perspectives on an issue, and in finding a way to situate themselves in these ongoing discussions. Thus the projects provide students with specific and concrete experiences of the issues addressed more abstractly in readings and in some class discussions. Throughout the term-long inquiry, students work from familiar to more distant subject matter and from the concrete to the abstract and back again. The assignments work recursively: themes turn backward and forward upon themselves, and reading and writing assignments all speak to one another as the information students generate from their own and others' lives shapes the direction of the class assignments, discussions, and theoretical analyses.

Class discussions do not so much "cover" an issue the teacher has established as they dialogically "cover" themes: corollaries to and qualifications of previous discussions, matters that arise because of the students' own insights and questions. In class discussions, the teacher is often silent, listening to points the students make or asking questions to facilitate further inquiry. Because students are often the real experts on the information collected, it having been brought from sources the teacher does not know, the teacher becomes a co-constructor in the process of interpreting information and adjudicating conflicting claims. With flexible questioning, attentive listening, thoughtful probing, and the very hard work of keeping quiet more often than most of us are comfortable doing, the teacher joins the students in bringing forth the theoretical issues and competing claims inherent in the information and data under discussion.

As active producers rather than consumers of knowledge and as the major sources of data in the course, students bring to the classroom an even greater diversity of information and issues than does the simple addition of a traditional faculty member (as in team or parallel teaching). By recasting the student into the role of active learner, we increase the possible diversity of points of view and enable students, in very concrete ways, to experience the "interplay of diverse discourses" and to "gain control of these discourses by experiencing them as part of the social practices of a [real] community" ("Other Voices"), the community of their peers.

To further complicate and enrich perspectives, we invite additional points of view into these first-year classes by attaching advanced undergraduate "consultants" to them. These undergraduates meet weekly with small groups of first-year students, respond to assignments, contribute their own writing for discussion, and facilitate group interaction. The groups address course problems—for example, how to understand and interpret assignments, how to work to understand diverse points of view, how to give good advice for revision. As a result, the first-year students have many "teachers" (their classmates, their undergraduate consultants, their instructors, and those in the language communities they are studying), and they regularly articulate and negotiate among all the different perspectives these "teachers" present. The students perform, on multiple levels and on multiple occasions—in fact almost daily—the metadiscursive practices of higher-order literacy and of theorizing that Graff advocates. In these richly structured ways, we aim to achieve many of the same ends Graff strives for by team teaching and course pairings—but all without combativeness or an overt focus on conflict.

Probably our most unusual attempt to realize Graff's goals is a pairing project we have not yet mentioned—the linking of marginalized students (basic writers) with academically privileged students (honors students) to follow the same curriculum and to work in groups with one another on common tasks. This pairing takes place in the first-year required English course described above. While the thematic inquiry remains the same, the difference is this: classes meet in adjacent computer classrooms with a sliding door between. When the door opens, as it regularly does, the two classes are one; the students from each class mix in small groups and in whole class discussion with one another. In addition to representing students and teachers as co-constructors of knowledge, asking students to engage in the practices of hyper-literacy, and constructing classrooms dialogically, these paired classes draw attention to the particular institutional structures that have placed students in them in the first place.

The pairing, easy to arrange administratively, thus opens to question the institutional structures that "write" basic writers and honors students as intrinsically different from each other—one group deficient, the other able. In the course of defining literacy for themselves, of describing their own literate histories and their experiences with competing views of literacy, and of discussing them in class, students run head-on into the ways in which they have been labeled (or constructed) by the university, by writers like Hirsch and Rose, and by larger social institutions such as university placement systems. Without necessarily invoking Foucault or other poststructuralist theorizers, students come to articulate and theorize about what they have long known in their bones: if the schools have labeled them—as "good learners," "advanced," or "gifted," or as "remedial," "slow learners," or "vocational"—these labels have consequences that create a reality for students. Such a realization stands in stark contrast to the competing message that students often get: that they can achieve anything they aim at through perseverance, rugged individualism, and faith in the American way. Here then is yet another set of conflicts experienced in a classroom where students work collaboratively to explore the consequences of such conflicts in their own lives. As Graff recognizes, when we "apply theory within the existing structure but . . . fail to make a theoretical examination of the structure itself," we limit theory to its "instrumental uses" and reforms are truncated ("Taking Cover").[3] Perhaps because he has not focused on composition and rhetoric, however, Graff has overlooked this sort of opportunity to call into question an aspect of departmental—or institutional—structure, the very embodiment, in Graff's view, of (literacy) theory.

Our experience with these pairings of honors and basic writing students has been intriguing and highly instructive. We have indeed been able to observe some differences in the ways in which these two groups of students approach and carry out reading and writing tasks. We have also been able to observe how well both groups respond to a common syllabus and how many literate practices these groups share. As one honors student remarked to us about halfway through the paired course experience, "One thing I've learned so far is that everyone in this class is smart. And everyone in here is streetwise. But do we ever come from different streets! And the university gives us different names because of these streets" (Payne). Thus do concepts of institutional hierarchy and social stereotyping come to life in this particular class.

In every case, we have found these first-year classes to be sites for intellectually and theoretically exciting work. Our teachers think so; our students—like the one quoted above—certainly think so. As another first-year student wrote in his final course evaluation, "When I talked to friends at other colleges who were also taking classes similar to this one, such as anthropology, I could talk to them about it mainly because we were learning the same things. I was lucky, though. I actually had the opportunity to go out and do the field work and my friends didn't. I think I got a lot more out of this class than my friends did. All they did was read and get tested; I actually performed what I was learning and that is a lot more effective" (Pojednic).

Equally instructive are the responses of the advanced undergraduate students who serve as consultants in the courses. Invited to attend a handful of the first-year classes in order to familiarize themselves with the curricula, the pedagogy, and the nontraditional course atmosphere, these consultants routinely find themselves so interested that they attend classes far more than the required number of times—to watch, for example, the students' progress toward a cultural literacy debate and to witness its culmination. Because their advanced English course is attached to the first-year course and because of the content, pedagogies, and student-teacher roles in both classes, the consultants also experience different discourses and varying perspectives at work in a social milieu. Opening the doors of the advanced English classroom into the world of practice—and the complications practice always offers theory—provides a powerful and exciting experience that the undergraduate consultants invariably remark on.

Our goal in these brief remarks has been, in the spirit of dialogue and cooperation, to bring what we know about contemporary literacy studies, and about writing and the teaching of writing, to bear on the model Graff proposes. What emerges, in part, is a course that focuses not on reading *or* writing but on critical inquiry; that views students not as absorbers of information or mimics of their teachers but as theorizers in their own rights; that views teachers not as transmitters of information or combatants but as senior colleagues in a common endeavor. One effect of such a course, as we hope we have suggested, is to challenge hierarchies of all kinds: between teachers and students, literature and composition, academic structures and workplace expectations, institutional demands and individual aspirations. In challenging these hierarchies in our first-year writing classes, students and teachers enact a pedagogy that offers an opportunity to go beyond studying the conflicts, a pedagogy that has the potential to do more than rearrange the status quo. It is a pedagogy, we argue, that is worthy of Graff's curricular reforms.

NOTES

1. We do not mean to suggest that reading is a passive act; too much research—and our own experience—argues for the ways in which reading demands constructive acts of mind. But insofar as the student becomes an observer—of teacher debates or even of texts—reading in its broadest sense is not as active and constructive as we would like it to be.

2. In "The Fourth Vision: Literate Language at Work" and elsewhere, Shirley Brice Heath articulates a similarly complex view of literacy, focusing particularly on the student's role as theorizer.

3. Although Graff here was referring to how to "integrate theory into individual classrooms," we believe that his point is more generally applicable.

WORKS CITED

Angelou, Maya. *The Heart of a Woman*. New York: Random House, 1991.

Bartholomae, David. "Inventing the University." *Perspectives on Literacy.* Eds. Eugene Kintgen, Barry Kroll, and Mike Rose. Carbondale: Southern Illinois University Press, 1988: 273–285.

Bauer, Dale M. "The Other 'F' Word: The Feminist in the Classroom." *College English* 52 (1990): 385–396.

Belenky, Mary Field, et al. *Women's Ways of Knowing.* New York: Basic, 1986.

Bizzell, Patricia. "What Happens When Basic Writers Come to College." *College Composition and Communication* 37 (1986): 294–301.

Friend, Christy. "The Excluded Conflict: The Marginalization of Composition and Rhetoric Studies in Graff's *Professing Literature*." *College English* 54 (1992): 276–286.

Foucault, Michel. *Discipline and Punish*. Trans. Alan Sheridan. New York: Vantage, 1979.

Graff, Gerald. "Colleges Are Depriving Students of a Connected View of Scholarship." *The Chronicle of Higher Education* (1991): A48.

———. "Conflicts Over the Curriculum Are Here to Stay; They Should Be Made Educationally Productive." *The Chronicle of Higher Education* 34 (1988): A48.

———. "Other Voices, Other Rooms: Organizing and Teaching the Humanities Conflict." *New Literary History* 21 (1990): 817–839.

———. *Professing Literature: An Institutional History*. Chicago: University of Chicago Press, 1987.

———. "Taking Cover in Coverage." *Profession 86* (1986): 41–46.

Heath, Shirley Brice. "The Fourth Vision: Literate Language at Work."
    The Right to Literacy. Eds. Andrea A. Lunsford, Helene Moglen,
    and James Slevin. New York: MLA, 1990.

Hirsch, E.D. *Cultural Literacy: What Every American Needs to Know*.
    Boston: Houghton Mifflin, 1987.

Kintgen, Eugene R., Barry M. Kroll, and Mike Rose, eds. *Perspectives on
    Literacy*. Carbondale: Southern Illinois University Press, 1988.

Payne, Rosemary. Private conversation with Andrea A. Lunsford. Ohio
    State University, May 1991.

Pojednic, Chris. English 110W Evaluation. Ohio State University,
    December 1991.

Resnick, Daniel P., and Lauren B. Resnick. "The Nature of Literacy."
    Perspectives on Literacy. Eds. Eugene Kingten, Barry Kroll, and
    Mike Rose. 190–202.

Rose, Mike. *Lives on the Boundary: The Struggles and Achievements of
    America's Underprepared*. New York: Free Press, 1989.

Graffian Relevance in a Millennium of Retrenchment: Views from Several Places at the Table (or Ambiguity and Its Discontents)

Deborah H. Holdstein

In my title, I allude, of course, to Gerald Graff's assertion in *Professing Literature* that critical theory risks being marginalized in departments of English, that it risks its rightful "place at the table" at which the primary discourse of the disciplines within English occurs: ". . . we can expect literary theory to be defused not by being repressed but by being accepted and quietly assimilated . . . where it ceases to be a bother" (249). In fact, once it becomes part and parcel of a "department's table of areas," literary theory might become, Graff fears, "a private enclave in which theorists speak only to one another" (Graff 1987, 251 Holdstein 36).

Many in other fields within English studies might find this theory-based angst a bit surprising, possibly a bit precious: after all, composition is perhaps the most truly marginalized subject and faculty within English departments, more often than not supporting through freshman-level courses and rather heavy courseloads the relatively light—or so it seems—on-campus requirements of those in more anointed areas (and, most particularly, those in literary theory). Moreover, many in composition might legitimately rail against Professor Graff's having ignored completely the subject and political football of composition in *Professing Literature*, a slight compounded when one considers that the title itself belies a book about the profession as a whole and, with added irony, features a professional endorsement from the eminent Wallace Douglas, a specialist in Wordsworth turned composition scholar, whose contributions to the field of writing in the 1960s remain essential to this day. Yet aspects of Graff's work offer the opportunity to demonstrate that the best theory can be and should be emphatically practical. At least on the face of it, much of Graff's theory seems to reinforce the hierarchy of that which is and isn't valued in English studies. Yet we can, indeed, capture and rehabilitate it. Taking Graff's lead in letting students ". . . in on whatever matters of principle are at issue to them" (251–52), we can, in this case, *carpe* theory to benefit the existing literature or composition curriculum at a time when any change that has a cost (and, alas, I do literally refer to dollars here) might prove professionally suicidal during an era of program elimination, faculty/position cutbacks, and increasing teaching loads at the university level.

I come to this essay from several places at the table of English studies, debunking once and for all the myth that it is impossible to be in several places at once: as director of a writing program at a state-supported commuter institution that serves a population of adult learners, a program housed in a division of humanities and social sciences; as the coordinator of the English program (literature and composition) within that same division; as a faculty member/quasi-administrator putting out (or starting) brushfires related to program integrity, faculty empowerment, the university administration, and the most academically sound ways to serve our students; as a literature Ph.D. "converted" postdoctorate to composition studies; as a teacher of composition and literature; and, not insignificantly, as an undergraduate student in the Northwestern University Department of English during the early years of Gerald Graff's influence on that campus.

As is the case at virtually every academic institution across the United States, our institution is in crisis: generally, because of the budget; specifically, for English, because of threatened elimination of our M.A. in English (so that faculty resources might be reallocated to the B.A. without adding new staff), gradual administrative dismantling of composition-informed decisions regarding assessment, and overburdened faculty trying to serve our excellent, overwhelmingly committed students in an academically sound manner despite dwindling resources and none with which to recruit new colleagues. Moreover, English (the B.A. and M.A. programs) now finds itself "up for program review," in the lingo of our state institution. This activity requires that my colleagues and I write extensive, thorough, lengthy documents for the state board regarding each of our programs and respond in detail to a stock set of questions (not always suited to the purposes and activities of English). Certainly others experience at their institutions a similar rhetorical challenge. For us, the challenge seems acute: while facing the threat to the M.A., we need to replace faculty who have retired or found new positions; and while we want to change aspects of our curriculum, we cannot do so without additional resources. Most frightening, however, is that once-sacred assurances and assumptions no longer hold: we cannot assume that English studies find themselves universally regarded as the heart and soul of curricular offerings at any institution of higher education. Its historic stature no longer serves as leverage for effective argument in curricular rebuilding, in assuming influence on academic values, or in the inherent salience of its offerings, even in successful programs.

While debilitating, however, crises in institutions also provide the opportunity for Professor Graff's proposals—at least some of them—to be realized, offering the occasion to reconsider and revitalize. Yet more often than not, change must grow from positions of strength in a department; many of Graff's suggestions don't take into account the near-laughability of any proposal in these times (at most institutions) for bottom-up change, particularly in English—again, hardly perceived as the cash crop on the mechanized farm. Here, then, I will wear my teacher hat as I sit at a relatively undistinguished locus at the end of the table and ask the following: as teachers, what kinds of changes can we make in our courses, if not in our entire curriculum, to begin to implement Graff's most useful ideas? In what ways might we heighten the embedded nature of the curriculum's commitment to make our students think and write well, first about texts (their own and others'), then about any other discipline within the institution? Might these changes seem alien to students or indeed help them integrate their learning into other courses? Will these course-level changes seem like a lone experiment venturing into the never-never land of theory, or harbor another approach that ultimately enhances good pedagogy?

Several years ago, I had the pleasure of responding to Graff's essay describing the banter between the Old Male Professor (OMP) and the Young Female Professor (YFP) at a conference sponsored by the Illinois Humanities Council. It was for my remarks during that occasion that I thought to test one aspect of Graff's ideas in the classroom: in this case, in the second semester of our English literature survey. As serendipity would have it, we were studying "Dover Beach," the subject of the initial OMP/YFP debate. In fact, I thanked Professor Graff for being foremost among those who help theory to "'break out,' like those ubiquitous fights at hockey games" (1990, 1). Careful to choose a metaphor from one of the noncanonical sports (the canonized metaphor is, of course, baseball, with football running a close second), I suggested that "if theory is the fight, and literature and whatever we usually teach is the hockey game, then we might extend the old joke that says, 'I was at a fight and a hockey game broke out' to describe how I put Professor Graff's thoughts to the test in my survey class just two days ago" (1990, 1).

Despite the (slightly) limited nature of this "test"—one discussion revolving around one relatively short text during one 75-minute session of one class during one semester at a state institution—I am willing to assert both the good news and the bad (which is also good) with regard to pedagogy: first, that our discussion of Graff's "Dover Beach" debate indicated to me that theory in this instance had empowered and authorized my students; and second, that formalizing the importance of conflict as a precursor to intellectual development and effective argument raised interesting questions that seem to affirm the centrality of English studies to work in other disciplines.

Since the student population at my institution is not only older (with the average age hovering around 33, although we have several M.A. students in their 60s) but also culturally diverse, the issues of gender and "whose culture?" become important and significant, particularly for the juniors and seniors. In my Fall 1990 survey course, I read sections aloud of what was then a working paper by Professor Graff; the students, again, had come prepared, having read "Dover Beach." To a great extent, they had already been primed for several of the issues I raised in conjunction with Graff's essay because of my own commitments and the ways in which I teach (and my running commentaries on the recent changes in and additions to the *Norton Anthology of English Literature*). After a rather dramatic reading of parts of Graff's text, I explained additional facets of the debate to the class. The group—about fifteen students—was unanimous in declaring that, yes, Graff's paper and the arguments it helped to reveal about goings-on in the profession were galvanizing, enlivening, and stimulating. Quite satisfying to me was that discussing OMP and YFP helped them to make connections not only between theory and their reading, but among other contexts about the poet himself. One student, Mickey, commented that this seemed to her the perfect example of what Arnold had meant by "culture" (and we discussed the frequent misunderstanding of that term): an open-minded intelligence, the ability to learn and to see things in a variety of contexts from a diverse set of perspectives. And besides, she noted, ". . . why couldn't OMP and YPF both be right? Why couldn't 'Dover Beach' represent the finest that a certain kind of poetry could offer" because of qualities that were still admirable yet worthy of criticism, qualities that straddled that fence between OMP and YFP?

Having obligingly read the introductions to both the Victorian era and Arnold himself in the *Norton*, the students saw the OMP/YFP debate openly and simply—as nothing radically theoretical or indeed radical, just another context for their discussion of the poem, but an *interesting* one. One student said that she was "satisfied" with having an awareness of these debates, that to her it was "just another context for the poem, you know, like why the speaker suffers from such loss of faith," or Ruskin's oppressive dictum regarding the qualities of a perfect woman in the Victorian era, or the cultural and social information about the industrial world of nineteenth-century England. Another student commented that, to her, there was a certain timelessness about the poem, that is, the disheartened intellectual turning to his (and she added "or her") lover for comfort from the emptiness of the world—and that in fact (taking on YFP), "it's the man in the poem who suffers" because he has been part and parcel of that dominant, phallocentric ideology that precludes his realizing that "nothing is more fragile than love and relationships."

Another student wondered why we as professors would even wonder whether or not to introduce theory and conflicts about theory in the undergraduate climate of the basic survey course. She noted that we can understand a poem in terms of the times in which it was written, with Arnold a full-fledged member of a dominant culture at a time when many things might have been questioned, but patriarchy and ideology (at least as we approach it now) weren't among them. "No matter how many OMPs there are," she announced, "they won't be here forever." Literature and civilization—and she even explicitly said "theory"—keep evolving. She concluded her remarks by saying that the canon could be expanded just as we expand our ways of talking about it: that, in fact, we should just accept the fact that it's a "moving target."

Not surprisingly, my heart leapt up when the discussion encouraged connections among other works we'd read: students mused, wondered, posited in ways they hadn't before considered. One found that discussing this conflict made him think about whether or not Browning—and he meant Elizabeth, not Robert—could have written a poem like "Dover Beach," bringing us however briefly into discussion about women's ways of writing and feminist/feminine discourse. (Lest you think I edit student comments towards perfection, let me note that this is the same student who said that he "loved talking to 'girl' English majors," but that he wouldn't want to marry one. Sigh.)

Gerald Graff's work triumphs in this instance when he tells us that students have a problem with not with "what is assigned to be read but how it is to be read." Theory proved essential here with "how it is to be read," or at least in helping us arrive at the contexts that served us well for our discussion. Theory supported well students' concerns not only about ways of under-standing the poem but also about understanding themselves and their "entitlement" to read and critique literature, canonized or otherwise, which to many of my students seems like the most distant of high culture. In this regard, we touched on the notion of "who determines what high culture is, anyway?" Obviously, we do; if the *Norton* excerpts Alice Walker, then we are in the presence of de facto high culture, and, as Graff points out, the text presents the same problems of interpretation and approach as any other. But in addition to a careful and close reading of the poem, aspects of theory "up front" helped students to understand, helped them to formulate their own perfectly valid relationships to the text, and helped them to make connections among the other things they had read.

And therein lies part of the flip side—in my view, the most productive side of all this. After I read Graff's paper in class and began our response-discussion, I realized anew, as we all must now and then, the accurate sense of Pope's warning against "a little learning." Certainly the students were prepared to argue their points of view—and the theory debate gave them ammunition—but they assumed that the positions of OMP and of YFP in particular were monolithic. I labored carefully to explain that many feminist critic-theorists wouldn't agree with YFP's response, that feminism itself encompasses a wide range of perspectives, and so on. In fact, I mentioned in class an anecdote about a colleague, a feminist theorist and editor, who responded to Graff's YFP with, "God, I think YFP needs to go out in the hall and have a Kool-Aid." The issue shifts, then, to encompass not only theory but the embarrassing banalities of practice, the kinds of questions that make me groan when others ask them. These kinds of concerns often seem to surface— stupidly and illegally, I always think—when colleagues in other disciplines moan about having to incorporate writing into their courses as the result of a "writing across the disciplines" effort. And yet my complaint offers a "theory" version of theirs: when I have between 2:00 and 3:15 P.M., twice a week, to expand the canon, put theory in front of the desk instead of in its usual, covert, allegedly "nonexistent" place in class, then how much theory? Is it enough to say in this survey class, "well, guys, y'see, there are many permutations of feminist theory, so don't take this as an all-encompassing perspective," leave it at that, and make sure to spread more seed (as it were) in later courses?

More interesting to me, however, was the ongoing "problem"—read the "intellectual training ground"—of ambiguity, and my students' discomfort with it. Certainly most who major in English reject pseudoscientific notions of "accuracy" and the need to quantify everything, even texts. And yet students often want one singly held view of the definite, canonized texts of literature; they want us to tell them what is the best, the most wonderful, the most worthy, even across cultures. They believe that true critics should be able to identify these universals, that the decisions should be final, immutable. They suspect that the dispute illustrates that we don't *really* know what we are talking about, but that there is an ultimate truth and that it will prevail. The need for certainty transcends race, gender, and class, when students want to be let into the "community of interpreters," whatever in this case that might be. But when we teach Walker, for instance, we by implication tell our students that her work is part of the canon, that it's important. By raising the issue of theory and the conflicts among us, do we do students an intellectual disservice by suggesting that there are those who think Walker doesn't belong, or shouldn't, or who have the (irrational) fear that Walker might— gasp—replace Hawthorne as class time becomes short while ethnic, racial, and class consciousness is ever high?

No. We balance that out by allowing our students *the necessity, the intellectual importance of frustration by ambiguity.* And it appears that the debates can in fact help students begin to approach any text that they perceive as unapproachable, whether it's Poe or Arnold or Baraka or Shange. In their fear of ambiguity, among other fears, our students retain the remnants of the new criticism with which we and they were schooled to approach literature; as a result, they ironically and yet naturally want that same elusive certainty and authority so desperately sought by the speaker in "Dover Beach."

Certainly any discussion of the debates and any stress on the virtues of ambiguity must not neglect the importance of our students' being able to take a stand—to risk judgment, to come to a strong, arguably acceptable interpretation, say, of a poem. One might posit that Graff's proposals overemphasize debate and discussion, underrating the crucial step of coming to that kind of resolution. I suspect that Graff would applaud a reminder about the importance of taking a stand, but could argue that allowing for debate about the "debates" in class demands that students assume positions and argue them as part of this theory-practice exercise. As I found during my own class discussion, students used theory and the professional debate about theory as other contexts by which to interpret the poem, not as ends in themselves.

How do we extend our desire to "let students in" to the conflicts among specialists in composition studies? How might discussion with our students help formulate for ourselves those areas that actually merit debate—most specifically, public debate?

As director of a writing program, I can easily extend to composition the notion of ambiguity brought on by my classroom discussion of the canon debates and the ways in which students approach any text. I think here of the desire for absolute certainty in the ways we read or in what we read when we participate in or spearhead writing assessment programs at the university level. Although theory tells us that writing is a recursive, nonlinear process, unique to the individual, we allow legislators and school districts to banish the notion of what has been called "at-onceness" in writing and in texts for the sake of .9 reader reliability, for a false public God of formulaic, statistical "perfection" (Holdstein forthcoming). When we test for competency in writing we are asked, despite the ways in which we teach process, for instance, to find a single truth about a student's text. While we can argue effectively for the importance of any student's being able to write a short sample in a relatively short period of time, however, we do not debate about what the testing means, allowing instead a myth of the impossible: value-free assessment, or statistically "reliable" instruments instead of open discussion that admits that there is no "perfect" testing of writing as there might be, say, of algebra. More often than not, a person who scores exams, it is perceived, should know exactly what good writing looks like according to divine, canonically inspired criteria, and then be able to judge it precisely as would the person next to her.

As with the canon of literary texts, it appears that we need to be concerned more with the ways in which we approach what we read, both as students and as teachers. If the "canon debates" in theory can initiate lively discussions in our classes as we examine texts—as it seemed in my representative sample of one class—and if open hockey games make literature and the experience of the reader important and edifying, then the Graff experiment is worthy of seizure and replication in other theory and other practice, highlighting and reminding us of what we always knew: that English and composition studies can provide as effectively as ever the intellectual confidence that extends to sound work in any other discipline or endeavor, and that in forms of ambiguity and open debate begin intellectual responsibility, not only for our students, but for ourselves.

WORKS CITED

Graff, Gerald. *Professing Literature: An Institutional History.* Chicago: University of Chicago Press, 1987.

Holdstein, Deborah H. "Response to Gerald Graff," presented at conference of the Illinois Humanities Council, October 1990.

———. "A Theory of Our Own? An Introduction to Theoretical and Critical Contexts for Computers and Composition," in D. Holdstein and C. Selfe, eds., *Computers and Writing: Theory, Research, Practice.* New York: MLA, 1990.

———. "A Thwack to the Unworthy: Collaboration, Institutional Agendas, and Writing Assessment," in D. Bleich et al., *Collaboration.* Albany: State University of New York Press, forthcoming.

Conflict, Curriculum, and Reform

Patrick J. Hill

I am delighted with this opportunity to participate in what promises to be an important national conversation. I will organize the first part of my comments on Professor Graff's work around an enumeration and commentary on what I regard as his three great and central insights. In so doing, I will link Graff's efforts to similar efforts in the so-called "learning-community movement," hoping thereby to encourage a wider dialogue about reform in and of higher education. In the second part of this paper, I will attempt to name the unshared assumptions which may have led to the significantly different emphases in Professor Graff's approach to reform and the approaches with which I have been associated. A concluding section suggests an agenda for a dovetailed approach.

I

Professor Graff begins, as does Clifford Geertz and as should we all, I believe, with the acknowledgment that diversity or multiplicity of consciousness is the hallmark of our time (Geertz 161). That diversity, of course, is not only the diversity, so obvious in academia, of disciplines, perspectives, standards, methods, goals, and ideologies, but as well the diversity of cultures, subcultures, gender, access, and socioeconomic opportunity. Graff's interpretation of diversity has two distinctive aspects: (1) he speaks with a refreshing candor frequently absent in discussions about multiculturalism in academia not just of diversity but of conflict, a conflict so pervasive as to merit the description of our times and of our "universities" in terms of "a radically dissentient climate"; but (2) unlike the work of Arthur M. Schlesinger or Allan Bloom, he laments neither the diversity nor the conflict but looks upon them as signs of vitality, as a challenge which might elicit something surely new and perhaps exciting as well. As I (paraphrasing Dewey) like to phrase it, diversity and conflict are resources for our learning, not problems to be lamented or avoided.

Those who are absorbed by the diversity and conflict of our time have been challenged by Graff's second major insight about American higher education. Like a modern-day Abailard exposing the fiction of doctrinal uniformity in twelfth-century Christianity, Graff rails against the fiction of shared purposes and values which pervades the literature and the public image of our universities and our departments. He charges not only that the conflict is pervasive in the humanities and the social sciences, but that at least some departments are reluctant, as was the medieval Church, to air their differences; and that the university as a whole, while enacting the major conflicts of our times, is systematically and structurally evading them. While there are enormous and multiple consequences to that evasion—social, political, intellectual, and pedagogical—the one of seemingly greatest interest to Graff is the loss of the opportunity to engage the student body in the exciting intellectual controversies shaking the very foundations of Western culture. To the extent that we hide these controversies from our students, I would say, or even to the extent that we lead them to believe that the "solutions" or responses which we present to them in the controlled space of our private classrooms are intellectually decisive, we are misleading and even miseducating them.

The third of Graff's great insights, the one shared by most everyone in the so-called "learning-community movement" (including its pioneering reformers, Meiklejohn and Tussman),[1] identifies the origin of the ineffectiveness of the curriculum, including its incapacity to tap the pedagogical potential of conflict, in the near-total reliance upon the self-standing three-credit course as the fundamental unit or building block of an undergraduate's education. This mode of academic organization—what Graff calls the "disjunctive curriculum"—privatizes teaching and learning, courts unintelligibility by isolating instruction and inquiry from the larger, complementary and conflictual contexts which give them meaning, and privileges monologue over the kind of intellectual conversations out of which social and political accord (not to say "agreement") is presumed to flow in a democracy. Graff therefore applauds the now familiar innovations of the learning-community movement, such as the linking of courses and the thematized semester. He also highlights creative departmental and interdepartmental innovations which bring isolated courses into conversation in regular colloquia or conference-like arrangements which become part of a revised curriculum still based primarily on the (now) semiautonomous three-credit departmental course. To the extent that Graff is successful, it should be noted, in actually basing these linkages on the deepest of our intellectual conflicts, he will be accomplishing something infrequently accomplished or even attempted in many of the learning-community experiments which, for complicated reasons, become too interdependent to function with the truly major disagreements of most concern to Graff.[2]

II

My assessment of Graff's work, as would be the case in my assessment of any reform effort, is a contextual one: I assess it relative to its diagnosis of higher education's problems and relative to the goals it pursues. As a social philosopher and a long-time participant in educational reforms, I also compare his diagnosis with other diagnoses and thereby raise less contextual questions about the appropriateness or helpfulness of Graff's focus relative to other highly desirable reforms in higher education.

As I read Graff, there are one or two dominant purposes in his work and several subdominant ones. The dominant ones concern the evasion of intellectual conflict and the consequent waste of pedagogical opportunity. Relative to these purposes, I wish to do nothing but echo and applaud Graff's work.

There are several major differences between Graff's approach to the reform of higher education and my own. The origin of those differences, and perhaps the partial explanation as well of why he is teaching at the University of Chicago and I have spent the greater part of the past fifteen years in the administration of alternative educational experiments at publicly funded institutions, relates centrally to our differing diagnoses of the major ills of higher education in America and to our differing readings of the conflicts it faces. I have been concerned with (1) the radically mismatched or conflicting expectations of our faculty and our new student bodies; (2) the intolerable consequences engendered by that conflict: among other things, passivity, lowered self-esteem, extraordinary waste of talent and energy, and anti-intellectualism; and (3) the broad policy-level changes in the society, our educational institutions, and the whole curriculum which might render possible the kind of educational effectiveness which our increasingly complex, globally interdependent, and multicultural democracy so desperately needs. I believe, as explained in what follows, that Professor Graff, with significant consequences, is focused elsewhere. Additionally, I have been absorbed with (1) the major conflicts of our society and our world (e.g., racial, economic, gender, and environmental); (2) the subtle and not so subtle ways in which higher education is complicitous with the dominant side in those conflicts; and (3) the policy-level changes necessary to make higher education at least less complicitous with if not outrightly involved in challenging the whole society to change. Graff, while not evidencing any belief that higher education is a moral oasis in an otherwise racist, sexist, and classist society, is focused on the academic reflections of those conflicts within higher education—mostly within the humanities—as presently constituted; and he asks how the curriculum might be differently structured to address those conflicts.

From my point of view, the differing purposes and emphases result in a mischaracterization and consequent understatement on Graff's part of the magnitude and pervasiveness of three major conflicts in American higher education: those between students and faculty, those among the faculty (and also their administrators) in the different divisions of the university, and those between the university and the larger society. Our differing purposes and emphases, I wish to stress, are at least theoretically compatible. Graff might well reply to the observations which follow, and I would agree, that one has to begin somewhere. I am not saying that the more comprehensive agenda I have pursued is necessarily more valuable.

Let me now attempt to name and comment upon what I judge to be the three assumptions of Professor Graff's which I do not share and which I believe to be at least a partial explanation of our differing approaches to reform. If I am wrong in characterizing his assumptions, he will of course correct me. If I am right, we can then talk further about the origins and consequences of these unshared assumptions. Given the nature of Graff's work, we should hardly be reluctant to air our differences.

First of all, Graff seems to assume that the institutionally legitimated activities of the faculty, aside from the cover-up of pervasive conflict among themselves, are basically sound and more or less worthy of imitation by our students. Somewhat to his credit, Graff's reforms are not "student-centered," meaning that they don't begin by assuming that characteristics of the current student body semiautomatically imply needed changes in faculty behavior or institutional practice. Indeed, a major point of Graff's recommended reforms is to immerse or acculturate students into the exciting but currently hidden activity of the faculty pretty much just as it is. My reform activities, while also not accurately describable as student-centered, have been based on a very different assumption; namely, that the expectations of the faculty and the students as to the purpose of an undergraduate education are at the deepest levels mismatched; and that in a democratic (not to mention a postmodern) society, we ought not to be presuming that the expectations of the newer (not to say "younger") generation should carry little to no weight in determining the priorities of the institution of higher education.[3]

The reforms I initiated in the learning-community movement included, among several structural reforms, a new kind of teaching professional, a so-called "Master Learner," a highly respected teacher and scholar who *mediated* between the expectations of faculty and students, legitimating what was worthwhile in the expectations of each and hence challenging the accustomed behavior of the other. Third-generation spin-offs of the experiment, misreading what was presumed in the innovation at Stony Brook (if not at Rollins and College Park and elsewhere) to be a conflictual context, eliminated the Master Learner and what was described by an outside evaluator as her/his frequently "searing feedback" to both faculty and students, thereby reducing the open-ended experiment to that of "an improved delivery system" for the presumedly healthy and benevolent system. Graff's proposed reforms, like those halfhearted imitations of the original learning-community experiments, ignore—or, more carefully, *fail to make visible and legitimate*—those un-articulated conflicts between faculty and students which might make the system more effective for a vastly larger number of students, both those currently within the system and those currently excluded. Graff assumes that the direction of significant reform moves in just one direction; namely, making the students more appreciative of and able to participate in the exciting intellectual life—the currently hidden intellectual life—of the faculty.[4]

I am deeply appreciative, as I hope my previous work has demonstrated, of the educational impact of vital communities per se. My appreciation of such communities diminishes, however, when there exist no built-in processes or mechanisms whereby the goals, focus, and procedures of the community might be peacefully changed in the light of the experience and expectations of the next generation of participants.

Graff has focused his reform efforts in such a way that it is possible to read him as believing that the atomistic three-credit course is the major or sole cause of the noninteraction among our conflicted faculty or (worse yet) the sole cause of higher education's most serious problems. He does not emphasize how that noninteraction is fundamental to the operation of the university and deeply attractive—academically, psychologically and politically attractive—to many of its members.

Graff, I know, is aware that the current organization of our colleges and universities reflects a particular understanding of the nature of knowledge and of knowledge-seeking, which understanding of course oozes with hidden but highly controversial judgments about the nature and relationship of the faculties in the various academic divisions and departments. These hidden controversies surface annually in barely public budget-hearings and sporadically in the nonpublic classrooms of the professors. For the most part, however, these hidden conflicts sedimented in the departments and "divisions" of our institutions (why not call them "walls" or "boundaries"?) manifest themselves in the lives of the faculty not only in noninteraction with but outright disinterest in or disdain for what goes on in the rest of the so-called "university." Administrators in charge of the heating system or the distribution of travel funds can see the whole faculty as involved in a single universe of activity; and physicists may occasionally acknowledge the existence of the English department in their misdirected complaints about the writing skills of their students. But neither those physicists nor many of their colleagues in the sciences or any division of the college are sitting around complaining about their inability to do their own work because their students have read either too little Chaucer or too few writers of color. (The reverse pattern, of course, holds true as well.) For the most part, the independence and noninteraction among the faculties have no perceived consequences for them.

Graff, I repeat, seems as aware as anyone of the speciousness of the so-called "university" or "academic community," though his focus on the comparatively insular conflicts in the humanities makes these other hidden conflicts less prominent than they would need to be in a more comprehensive reform agenda. His analysis tends to downplay or minimize the deeply political-economic attractiveness of the hierarchies and pecking orders built into the very conception of the modern university. And as significantly for the wider viability of his innovations, he seems to underestimate the extraordinary attractiveness of the present nondialogical curriculum to the academic psyche, especially the male academic psyche.

This last-mentioned point deserves elaboration. Within the walls of the privatized three-credit course, the professor constructs and controls an entire mini-world. In research-oriented colleges, that mini-world is often constructed to overlap substantially with his or her research program, on the basis of which comes professional prestige, tenure, promotions, and monetary rewards. In that mini-world, the professor controls if not creates the language, the criteria of importance and even of meaning, the rules, and the terms of interaction. While the most flagrant misuses of power in the classroom have been curtailed, it is still true, I believe, to describe the professor in the privatized classroom in the phrase which Richard Sennett somewhere employed to describe the relationship of medical doctors to their patients: they are like "little gods."

It may be necessary in these times to acknowledge that being a "god" of any size or sort is not entirely negative: the worlds created in the space of the privatized classroom often reflect extraordinary creativity, commitment, generosity, and the highest levels of personal integrity; and further, there is ample opportunity (within the rules constructed by the professor) to give free rein to the considerable inclinations for assistance and nurturance possessed by many if not most of those attracted to the teaching profession. But among the things not especially attractive to "little gods" is to have their authority questioned or undermined. Still worse is to have that authority questioned in public. And perhaps worst of all—but at the same time more respectable as a reaction reflecting both academic and personal integrity—is to see one's students "taken in" by some alternative approach to the subject matter (or to intellectual life in general) which one simply cannot respect. To paraphrase what I heard a highly respected biologist say in a frank assessment of a proposed linkage of his courses with courses in other divisions, "It is not just that I, as an intellectually and ethically committed scientist, may after many years of advanced study have dismissed such alternative approaches in my own life and in my courses as uninteresting, or misleading, or not what is truly important when you come right down to it. But if such alternative approaches are to be legitimated in the academy, if we are being asked to subtract time from our own already overloaded courses to create credit-bearing forums in which young professors in the humanities repeat tiresome, uninformed, moralistic critiques of science and technology, then much of what I have been doing with my professional life and much if not all of what I am trying to teach my students is not only relativized in its worth—which would be bad enough—but it is demeaned. Why should I, as a tenured and professionally honored academic, let this Philistine nose under the tent of respected scholarship?"

The difficulty of instituting reforms of the sort proposed by Graff and (more so) by myself may be illustrated by an analogy which I have frequently found both instructive and comforting. Such reforms are up against similar obstacles as are the ecologically imperative ideas of car pooling or mass transit: no one whom I know doubts the importance of these ideas, but the option of driving one's own car on one's own schedule in comfortable solitude is still far more attractive to most middle-class suburbanites. Car pooling is a great idea—for the other guy: the other guy whose work and time are not quite as important as mine.

My third observation about Graff's assumptions, like the second, concerns his focus on the conflicts in the humanities (and to a lesser extent the social sciences). He seems to assume that the currently covered-up conflicts in the humanities are either intrinsically important or sufficiently reflective of the major conflicts of society that they are the ones most worthy of our attention and reform efforts. I believe that the conflicts to which Graff calls our attention are important but extremely pale or domesticated reflections of the deeper conflicts facing American and global society. We need to emphasize, I believe, the extent to which the deeper conflicts seldom surface in higher education because they are eliminated either at the door or in the vestibule, so to speak: in admissions policies, in high tuition, in weed-out grading, in privileged learning styles, in job descriptions and hiring priorities for the faculty, in tenure and promotion policies, and in marginalizing patterns of resource-allocation. All institutions of higher education in America need not feel as called upon as do many community colleges to be microcosms of their surrounding societies. But we would be seriously deceiving ourselves and our students were we to think that more public discussions of unshared estimations of, say, the novels of Momaday and Wideman in any but the most cerebral sense will introduce our students to, mirror, or contribute substantially to a resolution of the deep economic and racial conflicts in America. (Many students of color at my institution with some justification believe that the open discussion of racial conflict actually *substitutes* in the minds of many in the liberal community for the needed action.) No matter who was taking part in those discussions and no matter what was said, the discussions would be taking place for the most part within the already exclusive circle of those who for whatever reason were de facto no longer in and unlikely to return to (or enter) the worlds that Momaday and Wideman describe. Their participation in such dialogues would likely signal that they were more like the privileged insiders than not.[5]

Conclusion

The above observations are not intended to suggest that we not attend seriously and creatively to the hidden conflicts which Graff has brought to our attention. However, I do think that Graff's focus on the hidden conflicts in the humanities runs the risk of distracting attention and energy from other hidden conflicts of similar and greater pedagogical, intellectual, and sociopolitical consequence within and about the "university." I think an exclusive emphasis on Graff's reforms could focus higher education not only inwardly but on issues that primarily concern the intellectual life of the faculty (by no means an unimportant or postponable issue) at a time when, in my judgment, we need to be focused as well on (a) becoming far more effective in teaching students very different from the vast majority of our tenured faculty, (b) examining in a self-critical manner our own complicity in the (re-)segregation and polarization of American and global society, and (c) exploring new ways to involve faculty and students with the problems of our world, not just with the intellectual reflections of those problems. Persons admiring Graff's innovations and sharing some major portion of this more comprehensive agenda would, I hope, continue to work for the structural changes in departments and divisions to facilitate the dialogical curriculum which Graff has envisaged while saving energy for the more comprehensive agenda with which that curriculum might dovetail.

Among the highest priorities to be considered in an appropriately democratic fashion for inclusion on that dovetailed agenda would in my judgment be the following: (1) an all-out effort to diversify our student bodies and our tenured faculties in all divisions of the "university"; (2) a similarly serious effort to diversify the curriculum and to retrain the faculty to be responsive to the differing learning styles and expectations of our new students; (3) a reconception of the content of the mainstream curriculum and of the definition of liberal education to place diversity at the center as a resource rather than at the margin as either a dollop or a defect; (4) a fundamentally new approach to general education, one which would in its very delivery retrain our faculties and immerse our students in the actual task and practice of using our partial and conflicting disciplines and worldviews as resources for their learning and as an introduction to the kind of world in which they will live; (5) the inclusion somehow or other of the central educational concerns of the natural sciences and engineering at the core of each institution's redefined liberal and general education efforts; and (6) the creation in the short run of significant incentives (professional, monetary, and psychological) for faculty retraining and participation, and in the long run of a complementary reward system appropriate to the new kind of artist/intellec-tual/teacher/researcher/person who would emerge in such an environment.[6]

NOTES

1. Alexander Meiklejohn began his experimental programs at the University of Wisconsin in the late 1920s. They are described in his *Experimental College* and in J.W. Powell's more recent *The Alexander Meiklejohn Experimental College.* Joseph Tussman worked at Berkeley in the late 1960s and wrote the influential *Experiment at Berkeley.* His work was revived and carried on at Berkeley by Charles Muscatine in the mid-1970s.

2. See my "Communities of Learners: Curriculum as the Infrastructure of Academic Communities" in Hall and Kevles 107–134 and my "Intergenerational Communities: Partnerships in Discovery" in Jones and Smith 279–296. For an overview of the full history and variety of learning communities, see Gabelnick et al.

3. My fullest description of the mismatched expectations of faculty and students is in Hill, "The Incomplete Revolution" 424–443. The characterization of that article, though still useful in terms of its general points and broad outlines of the conflict between faculty and students, is in serious need of updating in view of subsequent research on the ways of knowing of women and persons of color and more generally of differing cognitive styles and intelligence.

4. The most complete descriptions of the role and impact of the Master Learner are in the two articles of mine cited in the second endnote.

5. N. Scott Momaday is professor of English at the University of Arizona. His most acclaimed work, I believe, is *The Way to Rainy Mountain.* John Edgar Wideman teaches at the University of Massachusetts at Amherst. His 1983 novel *Sent for You Yesterday* merited the PEN/Faulkner award for fiction. Both men are writers of color.

6. My most recent statement of a comprehensive reform program, though more focused than is my current work on issues under the internal control of just the institutions of higher education, is in Hill, "Multiculturalism" 38–47.

WORKS CITED

Bloom, Allan. *The Closing of the American Mind*. New York: Simon and Schuster, 1987.

Gabelnick, Faith, et al. *Learning Communities: Creating Connections among Students, Faculty and Disciplines*. San Francisco: Jossey-Bass, 1990.

Geertz, Clifford. "The Way We Think Now: Ethnography of Modern Thought." C. Geertz (ed.), *Local Knowledge: Further Essays in Interpretive Anthropology* . New York: Basic Books, 1983.

Hall, James W., and Kevles, Barbara L. (eds.). *In Opposition to the Core Curriculum: Alternative Models of Undergraduate Education*. Westport, CT: Greenwood Press, 1982.

Hill, Patrick J. "The Incomplete Revolution: A Reassessment of Recent Reforms in Higher Education," *Cross Currents* 24:4 (Winter, 1975).

———. "Multiculturalism: The Crucial Philosophical and Organizational Issues," *Change* 23:4 (July/August, 1991).

Jones, Richard, and Smith, Barbara (eds.). *Against the Current: Reform and Experimentation in Higher Education*. Cambridge, MA: Schenkman, 1984.

Meiklejohn, Alexander. *The Experimental College*. New York: Harper and Row, 1932.

Momaday, N. Scott. *The Way to Rainy Mountain*. Albuquerque: University of New Mexico Press, 1969.

Powell, J.W. *The Alexander Meiklejohn Experimental College*. Washington, D.C.: Seven Locks Press, 1981.

Schlesinger, Arthur M. *The Disuniting of America: Reflections on Multicultural Society*. Knoxville, TN: Whittle Books, 1991.

Tussman, Joseph. *Experiment at Berkeley*. London: Oxford University Press, 1969.

Wideman, John Edgar. *Sent for You Yesterday*. New York: Vintage Books, 1983.

Intellectual Engagement in the Introductory Classroom*

Timothy D. Johnston

It is almost a platitude of the academic enterprise that scholarship and teaching are closely entwined. Most institutions of higher learning require their teachers also to be scholars, in part because we believe that active scholarship produces better teaching. Not only do scholars know more about their disciplines than nonscholars, they are also in vigorous, critical engagement with what they know and it is this engagement that generates the intellectual vitality that characterizes university teaching at its best. The vitality that scholarship produces can make a university education an intellectually transforming experience for our students, but only if we teach in such a way as to draw them into the enterprise to which we, as scholars and researchers, devote our professional lives.

The problem, as Professor Graff sees it in the essays reprinted here, is that we typically make little effort to draw students, especially beginning students, into the scholarly enterprise. As a result, they remain detached spectators, often somewhat bemused, if not altogether alienated, by academic discourse. Graff is not, I think, suggesting that our task should be to teach undergraduates as if they all were destined to become university professors—even at the University of Chicago, where Graff teaches, only a small fraction of undergraduates will go on to become professional scholars. His point is that just as it is scholarly engagement and debate that invigorates a discipline for *us*, so some version of that engagement can invigorate and enhance the study of the discipline for our students. Literary scholarship, as Graff points out, is filled with debate and disagreement but the way literature is taught typically affords few opportunities for students to enter into the debates, to their intellectual misfortune.

My own research and teaching is in psychology and the life sciences, but much of what Graff says about teaching literature seems to me to apply quite broadly to other academic disciplines. Although the explicit content of his essays has to do with the relation between current debates over the literary canon and the teaching of literature, underlying this is a deeper set of concerns about the relationship between scholarship and undergraduate teaching. I want to address four such concerns, illustrating my discussion by reference to psychology, and to science in general, to indicate their broader relevance. My attention will focus especially on these issues as they pertain to introductory teaching—on the question of how Graff's arguments and suggestions might serve to improve the ways in which we introduce students (especially freshmen) to intellectual inquiry and academic discourse.

Three of the four questions I shall raise are these:

- What can we do to help our undergraduate students reach an integrated understanding of the disciplines we teach them?
- How can we introduce the debates that engage scholars and researchers into the undergraduate classroom in a way that will benefit our students?
- How do we encourage students to develop the intellectual skills and inclinations that will allow them to engage in these debates themselves?

But I want to begin with a fourth question, only touched on by Graff, that also needs to be considered: What are our students like, intellectually speaking?

Students as Learners and Thinkers

Any discussion of university teaching should begin with an understanding of the people for whom it is intended—the students. Curiously, however, it is rare for faculty to pay much attention to this issue. Although we debate the curriculum (how many courses, in what disciplines, in what order), course content (what authors, texts, viewpoints), and pedagogy (lecture versus discussion, the use of writing, the role of laboratory work in science), we pay little attention to the students who will (presumably) benefit from the outcome of these debates. One reason for this is that most faculty implicitly adopt what might be called an accretionary view of teaching: the function of teaching is to add to students' initially limited knowledge of a discipline. Although this accretion may necessitate a certain amount of incidental ground-clearing (removing incorrect knowledge), it does not require much understanding of the cognitive foundation on which we build. The foundation serves only as a supporting platform, sturdier in some students than in others, on which to build. Our responsibility as teachers is to ensure that the information we provide is correct, that we break it into suitably sized pieces, and that we present the pieces in the proper sequence. If we do this, students should leave our course knowing more than they did when they entered it; if they do not, the fault is theirs, not ours.

This is a view of teaching that is strongly encouraged by the university's ideal of the faculty member as a scholar-teacher whose primary responsibility is to the discipline he teaches. As scholars, we are expected to understand the content and organization of our disciplines; as teachers, we are expected to communicate this understanding to students who lack it. But although students lack *our* kind of understanding of the disciplines we teach, they are not without *any* kind of understanding. Unless we take steps to discover what kind of understanding students bring with them, and then find ways to engage that understanding in the classroom, our teaching is unlikely to strike them very deeply. Instead, they are likely to maintain two fairly isolated kinds of understanding, one that they apply in the classroom and one that they use in the rest of their lives. To the extent this is true, our teaching fails to provide the kind of intellectual transformation that we might hope for in our students.

Students enter the introductory psychology course, for example, with almost two decades of experience in predicting, controlling, and explaining human behavior—the very topics with which the course will deal. Almost certainly this experience will have given them a substantial and quite elaborate understanding of behavior which, in many respects, will differ sharply from the understanding that the instructor wants to communicate. Unless we attempt to find out what students already understand about behavior, many of them will fail to see the relevance of what we tell them and will likely leave the course with two largely noncommunicating sets of knowledge about behavior: the one they brought with them and the one the instructor taught them. They will not truly engage with the scientific understanding that is offered them and it is unlikely to have much of an effect on their lives outside the course. They will have learned some suitable responses to the professor's questions, but that knowledge will remain separate from the well-learned beliefs that they brought to the class with them. The existence of such parallel domains of knowledge has been well documented in research on the way students learn (or, more often, do not learn) concepts in physics (Caramazza et al., 1981).

It is important, then, that we not simply tell students what *we* know about the discipline, but that we somehow bring this knowledge into contact with what they already know. This requires that we encourage them to articulate, either to themselves, to their peers, or to us, their existing knowledge so that we can present them with alternative understandings and ask them to make a reasoned choice among them.

If students are to make reasoned choices, both in their academic work and in other aspects of their life, we must help them develop the critical abilities they need to make such choices. Here again, we often overlook the radical differences between us and our students in some very fundamental intellectual skills. After several years as professional scholars, there are a number of things that we do almost without thinking about them, but which to our students are unfamiliar and difficult tasks. In the sciences, it is common to present the results of an experiment in the form of a graph that shows one variable as a function of another: the size of a population of animals as a function of the abundance of its food supply, for example. Scientists have seen so many such graphs that we read their meaning with very little effort and find them a quick and convenient way of representing often complex relationships. When I began teaching undergraduates, I frequently sketched graphs on the blackboard to summarize the results of experiments that I was explaining verbally in my lectures. Only gradually did I discover that to many of my students these graphs were about as illuminating as if I had summarized the results in Urdu. Reading a graph was a skill that I had learned very thoroughly but that my students had not learned at all—my graphs, intended to facilitate their understanding of the results I was describing, became for them yet another arcane and unfamiliar piece of knowledge that I was expecting them to master. In their minds, I was asking them to learn two things (the verbal description and the graph), rather than just one.

I have now learned to introduce students gradually to the art of reading and interpreting graphs; furthermore, the experience has alerted me to other differences between us in the way we engage the subject matter of my courses. For example, I have discovered that many students do not interpret familiar terms of basic logic in the same way that I do, which helps explain some puzzling features of their work. To the readers of this book, terms like *assumption, conclusion, inference, belief,* and *opinion* have distinct meanings and play different roles in explicating an argument. Many undergraduates, I discover, do not distinguish these terms clearly or, if they do, the distinctions they make do not conform to the ones that I make.[1] Thus, when I write on an undergraduate's paper, "I question the assumptions underlying your argument in this paragraph," we may be beginning a thoroughly frustrating exercise in mutual mis- understanding: she ends up believing that I am vague and unreasonable; I end up believing that she is inattentive, illogical, or lazy. The quality of the educational experience is diminished because I failed to ensure that we were operating within the same system of logic.

The Integration of Undergraduate Learning

One solution to the problem just alluded to might be to require all undergraduates to take a course in elementary logic at the start of their education, just as many institutions require a freshman course in English composition. This solution applies what Graff calls the "field-coverage model" of education. Within each discipline, we expose[2] students to a variety of specialist domains and points of view and, as Graff says, expect these "to come together in the student's mind as a coherent . . . experience." The point applies within both larger and smaller units of the institution. At the broadest level, we expect students to somehow pull together a very diverse array of the elements of their college experience into something resembling a coherent education. We expect freshman courses in English composition and mathematics to somehow infuse the skills of writing and computation into subsequent courses in specialized disciplines (though the writing-across-the-curriculum movement and kindred efforts are starting to address this problem quite seriously). More generally, we hope that by requiring students to take courses in physics, biology, literature, sociology, and a non-Western culture (among others) they will end up with an appreciation of the relationships among the different viewpoints that comprise our understanding of the physical, biological, and human dimensions of the world.

Many individual courses, the smallest institutional component of education, suffer from the field-coverage model of education as well. This problem is especially well-marked in introductory survey courses, which students typically encounter at a point in their education when they are especially ill equipped to perform much useful integration of knowledge. Introductory textbooks in many disciplines, especially my own field of psychology, are marked by a proliferation of distinct chapters through which it is extremely difficult for even an experienced reader to trace any coherent connecting theme. At best, such presentations provide a passing acquaintance with the diversity of ideas, findings, and theories that characterizes the field but leave students with only the vaguest sense of a coherent introduction. Such an approach is often defended on the grounds that students need to be exposed to a large variety of components of the discipline so that they are prepared to take more specialized advanced courses. I think most teachers of those courses would agree that we exaggerate the extent to which students retain this so-called foundational knowledge from their freshman year, so this is a somewhat strained argument. But even if it were not, there is surely a valuable alternative to be found in the direction that Graff suggests: why not show beginning students how the discipline addresses the problems and issues with which it is concerned, warts and all? Graff discusses what that might involve in the teaching of literature; let me outline a similar approach to the teaching of psychology at an introductory level.

Psychology is a peculiarly fragmented discipline in which there is very little theoretical coherence and an enormous diversity of methodological approaches. Typically, different examples are chosen to represent different theories and approaches, so the possibility that students will even discern the conflicts that exist in the field, never mind learn from them, is slim. A few years ago, I began to wonder whether it wouldn't be better to choose a single example of human behavior and illustrate the alternative theories and approaches within the discipline by showing how each of them has approached the problem of explaining that one behavior. After some experimentation, I taught an introductory psychology course called "General Psychology: Explaining Human Aggression," which showed students how psychologists have tried to explain aggression from the perspectives of physiology, genetics, development, social psychology, personality theory, and so forth. Despite the unevenness to be expected of any new course, the course did seem to accomplish two things that most introductory psychology courses do not: it clearly illustrated the way in which different psychological approaches can combine to illuminate different aspects of a problem, and it allowed students to discover some of the theoretical conflicts that make the study of psychology such an invigorating, if occasionally frustrating, enterprise.

Although this course brought some of psychology's theoretical conflicts to my students' attention, it lacked a vehicle for really engaging them in those conflicts directly. Class discussion frequently produced some interesting and vigorous disagreement among the students, but in retrospect I see that the class needed something more. One way to provide that is through student conferences, a mechanism with which we have experimented at the University of North Carolina at Greensboro in response to Graff's suggestion that we use disciplinary conflicts to enliven teaching at the undergraduate level.

Teaching by Engagement— a Freshman Seminar Program

Between 1989 and 1991, I participated in the experimental Freshman Seminar Program mentioned by Graff in one of his essays, an attempt to generate intellectual conflict as a way of teaching freshmen about different ways of interpreting the canon of Western culture. The idea was to have students in different seminar groups read some of the same texts in different contexts and then bring them together in conferences to discuss the conflicting interpretations produced by their groups' different perspectives. As might be expected, students appreciate and benefit most from a discussion of conflicting points of view if the issues at stake are familiar to them—indeed, it is often best if they are issues about which they have already formed fairly strong opinions. The conference that Graff mentions (which opposed the biblical and Darwinian accounts of the origin of humanity) drew on a dispute that was already familiar to almost every student there and about which most of them held well-established views. The reading the students had done in their seminars built on and refined their knowledge from this prior experience and the conference gave them an opportunity to articulate their positions more clearly and with better evidence.

That experience taught us something that should be fairly obvious: students will engage with a topic more thoroughly if they care about it. Many of the debates that we, as scholars, care deeply about seem simply irrelevant to our students and it is very hard to get them excited enough to want to engage with the conflicts that animate our own study of those issues. Unfortunately, in the minds of some faculty, asking the question, What do students care about? and teaching accordingly comes under the heading of pandering to student interest, rather than teaching the essential core of knowledge in the discipline. There is some justification in this and I do not advocate a wholesale replacement of traditional introductory material with the treatment of topics chosen solely because of their appeal to the average high school graduate. But in every discipline it is surely possible to select topics that connect in some way to the natural concerns of our students and that at the same time serve as vehicles to illustrate the styles of inquiry that characterize the discipline, and that erupt from time to time in disciplinary conflict.

The experimental seminar program was successful in many respects and some important lessons learned from it are now being applied to the development of a broader, and differently organized, Freshman Seminar Program at UNC Greensboro. The seminars use, if not conflicts, at least the analysis of problems and issues as a way of introducing students to the study of academic disciplines. Each seminar focuses on a problem, issue, or theme in a particular discipline and spends the semester examining that issue. The aim is to convey to students not only some of the knowledge that is fundamental to academic disciplines but also some sense of the kind of inquiry that has produced that knowledge. Issues are selected that appeal to freshman students and so help to motivate them to engage with the subject matter of the course more fully than usually occurs in the traditional introductory survey course. At their best, the seminars also can serve the integrative function discussed earlier, by using the seminar topic as a way of focussing disparate approaches within the discipline on a single concern.

Promising as it is, this is not an easy style of teaching and it requires considerable commitment on the part of the instructors.[3] We hope that the disciplinary focus of the seminars, combined with the opportunity that individual instructors have to select topics close to their own areas of research interest, will help to resolve one of the fundamental problems of the modern research university: the tension between commitment to the institution and allegiance to the discipline. Faculty in research universities typically identify primarily with their academic disciplines rather than with the institutions in which they happen to find themselves. Educational programs that do not play into that disciplinary allegiance, such as general education courses, interdisciplinary programs, and efforts such as writing-across-the-curriculum, require a special commitment that is, to some extent, at odds with the individual's professional hopes for recognition and advancement. This is not an issue, or not primarily an issue, of research versus teaching; rather it is a question of the kind of teaching that faculty see as most congenial to their development as researchers and scholars (see Boyer, 1991). Although freshman seminars cannot be taught in a way that aligns them as closely with research and scholarship as does a graduate seminar, they do offer faculty the opportunity to cast a different and perhaps broader light on their research area, to find ways of making it intelligible to a naive audience, and even to excite enough enthusiasm in some students to recruit future professionals to the discipline. Thus seminars of the kind we are developing may play more directly into the disciplinary concerns of a research faculty than do some other approaches that might be tried. How successfully they will accomplish that remains to be seen.

The Development of Intellectual Attitudes and Habits of Mind

The kind of engagement with subject matter that I have been discussing, and that the Freshman Seminar Program tries to foster, requires that students come to adopt what might be called intellectual attitudes and habits of mind. That phrase covers a lot of ground, and the ground it covers most comfortably may vary somewhat from one discipline to another, but I mean it to include, among others, such things as the critical evaluation of arguments, skepticism towards received ideas, a willingness to entertain differing interpretations of texts and other data, and the inclination to integrate new ideas with what is already known, along with the ability to write clearly, reason cogently, and argue convincingly. These are abilities that we would all like our students to have by the time they graduate and an important challenge for university education is how to foster their development.

I would argue that if we are going to develop such abilities in our students, we must start seriously during their freshman year, preferably in the first semester. The transition from high school to college is a confusing time for most students and they will respond readily to any cues that seem to provide a model for their behavior, both in and out of the classroom. I suspect (though I cannot prove) that students' attitudes towards college become established very quickly, probably during the first few months of their freshman year, and they may be relatively difficult to change thereafter. We should try to ensure that in their first semester they encounter a curriculum designed to welcome them to the intellectual culture of the university and provide them with opportunities to develop the attitudes and abilities that will allow them to participate in that culture. Of course, all university courses and curricula should have this as one of their goals, but such participatory education is often only attempted in upper-level and graduate courses. Especially in the sciences, faculty may object that only when students have learned some foundational material are they capable of the kind of advanced thinking that includes real intellectual engagement with important issues and ideas. As a result, students' first-semester coursework is likely to consist of large, impersonal lectures in survey courses, combined with a few smaller classes in "skills" courses such as English composition and elementary math. Of course, every university has its share of outstanding lecturers who can inspire enthusiasm among 500 students in an auditorium, and of dedicated teaching assistants who can use an introductory math course to arouse their students' curiosity about numbers, but such people tend to be few and far between. More commonly, students get few opportunities during their first semester to experience the kind of intellectual challenges that we would like them, eventually, to respond to with enthusiasm and meet with success.

One way to dramatically increase the level of intellectual engagement in any class (whether an introductory course or a graduate seminar) is to get students writing. Although class discussion might seem like the best way to produce engagement, because students (ideally) then speak directly to each other, writing, especially informal writing,[4] has some distinct advantages. First, it requires greater precision of thought than speaking does, because there is no immediate audience to fill in missing details, bridge gaps in logic, or request immediate clarification. Attempting the precision necessary to get anything at all down on paper soon reveals, both to the writer and to any subsequent reader, failures of understanding. Second, writing is less intimidating to most students than speaking, especially in a group whose members do not know each other well. Third, even in the largest classes, writing allows all students to experience the intellectual engagement it affords, whereas class discussion can typically involve only a few. Finally, writing provides an excellent starting point for further engagement through class discussion because each student has an opportunity to articulate some opinion or point of view before being required to submit it to scrutiny by the group. In my experience, the use of informal writing assignments is one of the best ways to stimulate a high level of spirited class discussion.

Writing alone, of course, will not foster all of the intellectual habits of mind mentioned above. The point is that we typically pay rather little attention to what *will* foster those habits in the introductory classroom, preferring to concentrate on the logic and content of what we are teaching rather than the characteristics of the people we are teaching it to. In so doing, we may be missing an important opportunity to encourage our introductory students to develop the kinds of critical, intellectual attitudes that should be the hallmark of a university-educated citizen.

Conclusion

In a recent essay in *The Atlantic Monthly*, Claude M. Steele (1992) argues persuasively that one of the most important reasons that such a high percentage of African-American students drop out of college is that they "disidentify" with the intellectual culture. That is, because colleges signal, in a variety of ways, a lack of respect for their intellectual contributions (as a race and as individuals), they see no reason to become engaged in the academic enterprise in ways that ensure success. I suspect that the same is true, to a lesser degree, for many students of all races. Introductory teaching, by stressing memorization of factual material and placing students in the anonymity of large classes, signals a lack of interest in their intellectual contributions. It encourages students to adopt a passive role in their own education and to rely on extrinsic motivation (grades and test scores) to stimulate their intellectual development. Although dropout rates are higher in some groups than others, the intellectual disengagement that results is probably quite widespread.

In the natural sciences, such disengagement is strongly suggested by Sheila Tobias's (1990) study of introductory science instruction at the college level. Tobias asked academically accomplished "informants" (graduate students and faculty in nonscientific disciplines) to take introductory courses in chemistry and physics and keep detailed records of their impressions as students in those courses. The overwhelming impression to be gained from her results is that such courses largely or completely fail to engage students' intellectual curiosity, which may account for the well-documented fact that large numbers of students leave the study of science at virtually all levels of the educational system (National Science Board, 1989). Science faculty have often believed that such attrition occurs because students find science too hard or lack adequate preparation. Tobias's results, which are reinforced by other studies, suggest that many very bright and well-prepared students may leave because they find introductory science instruction boring and so become disaffected.

The general message from both Steele and Tobias is that we must do more to engage students in the intellectual discourse of academic disciplines. Such engagement is not something that can be accomplished solely in a senior seminar or capstone course. Rather, it should be vigorously pursued from the very first week of students' freshman year, at a time when many of them are asking themselves, "What is college all about and is it the right place for me?" Doing this will require a much greater investment in freshman instruction than typically exists at most research universities, but the payoff for the remaining three years of college may well be a lower rate of attrition and more successful performance in advanced courses as students build on capabilities they are encouraged to develop in their first year. Indeed, one study shows that students who take just one small class designed to encourage participatory learning in their first year report substantially greater academic engagement and overall academic satisfaction, compared with students who take only large classes as freshmen (Light, 1992). Judicious incorporation of Graff's suggestions into the introductory classroom would begin to engage students' minds in the way we would like, and also help to develop the kinds of intellectual habits of mind they will need to benefit from that engagement, in college and throughout their lives.

NOTES

*I thank Walter H. Beale, William E. Cain, Pamela A. Mason, and Karen L. Meyers for their comments on the manuscript. The experimental Freshman Seminar Program described here was supported in part by grant EH–21005–89 from the National Endowment for the Humanities. The opinions and conclusions expressed here are those of the author and do not necessarily reflect the views of the Endowment.

1. I owe this observation to Cheryl A. Logan.

2. The metaphor of exposure is an interesting one, suggesting as it does that these domains are like diseases to which students will acquire immunity as they pass through our courses. The metaphor is reinforced by the quasi-medical terminology students and faculty sometimes adopt in talking about their courses: "I've *already had* physics"; "*Remedial* English"; "You'll *get* multivariate statistics next year"; "They'll get a *good dose* of genetics in my introductory biology course."

3. The problems of teaching freshmen, especially when such teaching involves more than simply delivering lectures, is emerging as a focus of concern in the literature on pedagogy in higher education. A good introduction is Erickson and Strommer's book, *Teaching College Freshmen* (1991).

4. "Informal writing" refers to exercises designed primarily to stimulate and focus thought rather than to permit the instructor to evaluate students' writing. Many informal writing assignments are ungraded; if they are graded, mechanical niceties such as grammar, spelling, and sentence structure are ignored. The aim of such assignments is to create an opportunity for a student to express, explore, and clarify her thoughts in words. See Emig (1977) and Fulwiler (1982).

WORKS CITED

Boyer, Ernest. *Scholarship Reconsidered: Redefining the Professoriate*. New York: Carnegie Corporation, 1991.

Caramazza, A., M. McClosky, and B. Green. "Naive Beliefs in 'Sophisticated' Subjects: Misconceptions about Trajectories of Objects." *Cognition* 9 (1981):117–123.

Emig, Janet. "Writing as a Mode of Learning." *College Composition and Communication* (28) 1977:122–128.

Erickson, Bette L., and Diane W. Strommer. *Teaching College Freshmen*. San Francisco: Jossey-Bass, 1991.

Fulwiler, Toby. "Writing: An Act of Cognition." *New Directions for Teaching and Learning: Teaching Writing in All Disciplines*. Ed. C.W. Griffin. San Francisco: Jossey-Bass, 1982. 59–65.

Light, Richard J. *The Harvard Assessment Seminars: Second Report*. Cambridge, MA: Harvard University Graduate School of Education, 1992. 50–52.

National Science Board, *Science and Engineering Indicators—1989*. Washington, DC: Government Printing Office, 1989. (NSB 89–1).

Steele, Claude M. "Race and the Schooling of Black Americans." *The Atlantic Monthly* (April 1992): 68–78.

Tobias, Sheila. *They're Not Dumb, They're Different: Stalking the Second Tier*. Tucson, AZ: Research Corporation, 1990.

The Core Course as Departmental Happening: A Modest Proposal for Integrating Public and Private Spheres

Lynette Felber

Gerald Graff's proposals for teaching the controversies of the profession offer exciting possibilities to integrate critical theory and literature, research and teaching, specialist and generalist, teacher and student—entities long considered dichotomous in English studies. His observation that "the way we organize and departmentalize literature is not only a crucial theoretical choice but one that largely determines our professional activity and the way students and the laity see it or fail to see it" ("Cover") is borne out by recent attacks on the profession by the media and the Right as well as by the various ideological divisions within it. Graff's analysis of the historical rationale behind the field coverage system of organization in "Taking Cover in Coverage" and *Professing Literature* provides us an opportunity to critique not only the way we construe ourselves but also, more fundamentally, the values of our profession. Although he mentions "the need to discuss and reflect on the values and implications" of our organization and practices, Graff gives only passing consideration to the underlying system of values that has inhibited productive dialogue between colleagues such as his archetypal OMP and YFP in "Other Voices, Other Rooms." The field coverage system is but one manifestation of a social construction we have promulgated; as such, the ideology behind the lack of dialogue Graff criticizes merits reevaluation.

To facilitate the dialogue he finds lacking under the field coverage organization, Graff proposes that the exciting conflicts we debate in the "academic conferences and symposia which so many faculty now find indispensable to our intellectual life" ("Voices") be introduced into the classroom, the multicourse symposium, and the curriculum itself. While I support such proposals, I wonder how lasting enthusiasm for these reforms will be without a more fundamental change in the values of the profession. After all, most of the proposals Graff makes were tried in the wake of student demands for relevance in the 1960s. In order to achieve any kind of lasting dialogue and reorganization, the profession must consider the implications of the activities it values and rewards. Departments must ask themselves why their faculty attend professional conferences more often than departmental colloquia. Opportunities for dialogue about the debates of our profession exist monthly or weekly—even daily—on each campus depending on the size and orientation of the institution. The obvious answer is not that faculty in a given department are unwilling to talk to each other, as the dialogue between Graff's OMP and YFP demonstrates. More indicative is the fact that professional conference participation "counts" for tenure and promotion while department conversations and colloquia do not—at least not in quantifiable ways. It is also true that junior faculty are reluctant to profess ideologies and critical biases which may be politically incorrect at their home campuses, giving the professional conference a privileged freedom of expression.

The conflicting demands of research and teaching have a problematic explanation beyond what Graff details in chapter six of *Professing Literature*, his history of the emergence of the generalist as an "academic type" in the 1870s. The terms I used in my opening paragraph to describe the dichotomies of the profession designate binary oppositions which reveal the values the profession privileges. In each case, the terms (research/ teaching, specialist/generalist) are not equivalent but hierarchical. Moreover, such terms are always gendered, as Hélène Cixous has observed; the privileged term is the one associated with the masculine ("Sorties" 91). It is significant that in criticizing the disconnection between teachers and classes in our curriculum, Graff uses the expression "privatized class-room" ("Voices"). The "privateness of academic experience" is also a key concept in the analysis which led to the Federated Learning Communities of Stony Brook, whose programs have informed Graff's thinking (Hill 135). The use of this term reveals one reason why, as Graff describes it, the autonomous instructor and classroom do not require "instructors to confer with their peers or superiors" ("Cover"). The relatively unsupervised autonomy of this private space may be contrasted to the vigorous—though not necessarily objective—peer review procedures for publication by journals and university presses. As Dale Spender points out, "private communication" does not "carry the same weight as those that have been printed" (188). The very way we construe the conflict between teaching and research and their domains, "private" classrooms and publication, suggests the gendered construction of traditionally female and male separate spheres of activity, the home and the marketplace.

At this moment the profession is in a state of flux and change; women are increasingly taking (and allowed to take) a major role in the public forums of professional conferences and publication. Curiously, however, the private (feminine) space of the classroom is still devalued. Otherwise, why would professors apply for research grants to "release" them from teaching at their "home" institutions? Why do graduate students on the job "market" aspire for positions at research rather then teaching institutions? Why is excellent teaching "awarded" (with plaques and such) while productive research is "rewarded" (with higher salaries and merit pay)? There are few, if any, grants to "release" professors from research obligations in order to reform curriculum and devote time to teaching. At this time the concept of a privileged exemption from publication is unthinkable, revealing the same gendered values which cause most part-time composition faculty, instructors or lecturers (teachers), to be female and the majority of full professors (researchers) to be male, with corresponding prestige and salaries. Although I know of no study that analyzes data in cases where tenure has been denied, I strongly suspect that it is most frequently refused on the basis of inadequate publication rather than teaching, a private activity less actively monitored and weighted.

The moral, ethical, and practical problems that continue to plague English departments—conflicts between research and teaching missions, exploitation of part-time faculty, lack of parity between male and female faculty—are intrinsically related to the curricular disjunctions Graff criticizes. His call for dialogue between classes and among students and colleagues might provide a means to challenge our privileging of authority and the public sphere. Professor Graff's proposals offer ways to remedy the problems created by the field coverage system—but only if we remedy other disjunctions in our profession. These are reasons for exploring his proposals further, and I will suggest my own adaptation of one of his reforms presently. The productive dialogue among faculty, students, and classrooms Graff advocates can be established in a lasting way *if* we revaluate activities in the "home" institution and integrate private and public spheres.

The ratio of women to men in the profession is changing, yet it is still true that some professional activities are associated with males, others with females, and as has often been noted, whatever work men do confers higher status. Statistics show that 39 percent of women faculty spend over twelve hours per week in the classroom compared to 29 percent of men, and that 33 percent of men but only 14 percent of women spend more than eight hours on research (cited in Martin 483). Elaine Martin concludes that "women faculty are more likely to spend significantly more time and effort on teaching and committee work, while men are more likely to spend more time on research and administration" (483). There is a likely correlation between these kinds of figures and the findings of the Commission on the Status of Women in the Profession, appointed by the Modern Language Association (MLA) and chaired by Florence Howe: women are clearly being *hired* in increasing numbers in the humanities, but they are not making significant gains at the upper ranks of departments.[1] While some may argue that women's entry into the profession is too recent to draw any conclusions, most departments do not seem to be making any particular effort to move women into senior positions. Since the tenure hurdle is directly related to the research hurdle, and the "percentage of tenure-track appointees with tenure is higher for men than for women" (Huber 65–66), it seems likely that the belated advancement of women in the profession is directly related to the privileging of research over teaching and our gendered construction of these activities.

Professor Graff's proposals for dialogic classrooms and curricula offer refreshing suggestions for destabilizing the hierarchy of research/teaching and public/private spheres, but we also need an accompanying formal mechanism for revaluating these activities. Otherwise, the metacourse, the coupled courses, or the "thematized semester" he proposes may become merely isolated units within a department or college in the same way the "ghettoized" theory classes Graff describes are appended onto rather than integrated into departments. We must not only change our curriculum but the way we teach and think about teaching. A major obstacle to the various kinds of dialogue Graff proposes is our attitude about professional authority. This attitude privileges the public sphere, where authority is a major criterion for success (publication), but is inherently opposed to true dialogue, characterized by egalitarian exchange. In this context, the *method* we use to teach the debate is even more important than the content of it. We must bring the advantages of the private classroom at its best—fostering community and a supportive learning environment—into the public sphere. If teaching the debates means an adversarial format, transforming the classroom into a public battle for survival of the fittest (clearly the authority), we lose rather than achieve dialogue and integration.

The example of interdisciplinary programs initiated in the early 1970s serves as a case in point. Although in some more prestigious and innovative programs, such as those Graff mentions at Evergreen, the integrated course plan *is* the liberal arts curriculum, most of these programs have faded into history as we try to "make sense of the sixties." The chief pedagogical remnant from these experiments is the team-taught class. An example of movement away from the privatized classroom, the team-taught course may reveal some fundamental obstacles—practical and attitudinal—to the dialogic classroom and curriculum. Although team-teaching can be used effectively to achieve dialogue, it requires considerable effort and commitment on the part of the instructors involved. I remember little dialogue between the professors and none among students within the two team-taught classes which I completed as a student in California in the 1970s. Because the classes each employed two professors, the enrollments were large, 60–100 perhaps, as opposed to 15–40 for the usual upper-division humanities classes at this particular state university campus. The majority of the time the professors lectured in alternation, each covering his specialty (popular-culture literature and film in one class, French symbolist poetry and art in the other). The possibilities of dialogue between professors and students were forestalled by an authoritarian teaching style necessitated by the large classes. In contrast, the smaller classes I completed with two of these professors encouraged and achieved student participation in discussion.

Graff addresses the problem of authoritarian teaching and expresses his own reservation about students being "turned off by a whole phalanx of instructors" instead of just one ("Voices"), but he neglects other underlying practical problems, particularly in this time of state budget and funding crises: overcrowded classrooms and the sheer *efficiency* of the autonomous instructor. While the time may be right, ideologically, for the kinds of changes Graff proposes, economically they may be unfeasible. The recession and university budget cuts are causing departments to tighten course offerings, moving departments away from innovative new courses and new hires to consider the need to staff "service" courses as cheaply as possible, usually with teaching assistants and part-time faculty. Administrative pressures at many universities would seem to indicate that in today's economy, dialogue must be achieved within existing courses; if we are going to teach the controversies, we will have to do double duty, as it were.

With these caveats in mind, I would like to elaborate on one of the suggestions to facilitate dialogue which Professor Graff mentions briefly in "Other Voices." The proposal for the meta- or the core course seems to me the most likely starting place for the average department (the multitude not in the very top echelon of well-endowed research institutions) in this era of budget crisis.[2] The course itself is also the logical beginning for an *integration* of private and public spheres: it is small, manageable, and can provide a supportive environment for students to develop the skills necessary to "go public." Further, most departments already have in place at the graduate level— and should have at the undergraduate level—a required course in research methodology and/or critical theory which can be modified (and elevated) to function as a core course. The current marginalized status of the methods course is seen in its lack of popularity at many institutions, and in the number of students who seek exemption from the course for a variety of reasons. The required research/theory class, although it is not a specialized class, rarely rotates among all a department's faculty. The faculty who teach such a course may be senior research faculty at some institutions but more often are the young, the untenured, or anyone with a theoretical bent.

This ugly duckling should be transformed into a core "issues" course. Drawing its topic each semester from a major controversy in the profession, the course would be organized on the model of a professional conference, the hub for department colloquia and speakers—a departmental "happening," so to speak. Such a course would *attract* students and faculty: who would seek to exempt themselves from so exciting an experience? In proposing the legitimization of the theory class, Graff argues that it be a required rather than an elective course. This principle should be applied to faculty as well: if the core course rotated among all faculty, it would be less likely to be marginalized within the department and the curriculum. Each instructor would have the privilege of choosing the semester's theme, incorporating research interests into the classroom, and serving as moderator. The role I have in mind would be akin to the conference organizer, coordinating sessions and inviting guest speakers from other campuses as well as her own. The advantage of this role, as opposed to the team-teaching model, would be that the moderator is usually the person who talks least in a professional conference session and is more liable to *facilitate* dialogue than are two instructors, who are more likely to find themselves debating each other.

At the graduate level, the core course as department happening would foster the kind of intellectual community we ourselves should be modeling for our students. Students would organize their semester's work—research and essay assignments—in preparation for a conference session, open to the public (students and faculty not enrolled in the class). The presentation of their papers would facilitate dialogue among faculty and students. Graduate students are eager to participate in activities where they can gain experience, make professional contacts, or add items—or whole new categories of items—to their vitae. The professor teaching the graduate core course could invite regional conferences—divisions of the MLA or Women's Studies conferences, for example—to coincide with the core course, providing graduate students their first opportunity not only to attend a conference but also to deliver papers. This kind of activity would demonstrate the relevance of students' seminar papers and the research methods taught, and offer the incentive of a fuller vita.

The core course is also a way to integrate emphases in large or diverse graduate programs. My home institution, New Mexico State University, offers graduate programs including the M.A. in creative writing, literature, rhetoric, or technical writing as well as the Ph.D. in rhetoric and technical communication. Although we have a required graduate methods class, it has not always succeeded in integrating our diverse emphases and meeting the needs of all the students enrolled; we also lack faculty (not surprisingly) with individual expertise in all four disciplines. Transforming this "Introduction to Graduate Studies" into the kind of conference-modeled course I have proposed would help integrate the various emphases and popularize the course among students and faculty. A special topic such as "Gender in English Studies," for example, can be approached from all disciplines: session topics might include "Fiction and Politically Correct Feminist Censorship" (creative writing), "Men in Feminist Theory" (literature), "Gender and Modes of Argumentation" (rhetoric), and "Hypertext: A Feminine Narrative?" (technical writing). This approach would build on the dialogic strength of the class as we now teach it, with faculty from various emphases taking a part as guest speakers, a variation of the "teacher swapping" Graff advocates. Reconceptualizing the course as a "happening" organized as a professional conference would increase the students' role in the course and serve as an initiation into the profession itself.

At smaller institutions the core course might be offered as a mixed undergraduate/graduate course, infusing the enthusiasm of those who have been introduced to current controversies within the profession to those who may be, as yet, uninitiated. Just as Graff warns against students' passivity while they "witness" debate between professors, however, so must a mixed-level class provide opportunities for undergraduates to participate actively in a format protected from authority—a succession of semiformal group or individual presentations, for instance. If the institution can maintain parallel courses at both graduate and undergraduate levels, the undergraduate core course offers a way to provide motivation and add excitement to a required theory and/or research class. I've found that by opening my undergrad theory course at New Mexico State with a discussion of the canon and the profession, students are much more receptive to the theoretical readings and research assignments which follow. The rationale for such a required course is much clearer to them, and they understand that they are participating in activities that are an integral part of the profession.

The current conflicts in the profession have been distorted or misconstrued by the media, yet they have succeeded in arousing the curiosity of the public in ways that discussions of structure and symbolism in *The Scarlet Letter* never could. When David Bromwich charges that teaching the conflicts is somehow self-serving, a "device of convenience worked out for scholars themselves" (555), he fails to note the *inherent* interest these issues hold for students and the general public. What Bromwich and others have viewed as a faddish curriculum which isolates students into "blocks of five or six years" only connected intellectually by "fraying ends of a half-dead quarrel" (555) is actually the means of linking these students through the ongoing debates and the critical process of examining the issues underlying their courses and curricula. While political positions may change, the conflicts themselves endure. The terms have changed—we used to argue about what was "classic"—but Samuel Johnson's and Charles-Augustin Sainte-Beuve's discussions of the canon are strikingly relevant today. Gender emerged as an issue (long before Betty Friedan wrote of it) in Aristophanes' *Lysistrata* and Sophocles' *Antigone*. Furthermore, there is a difference between teaching the conflicts and *only* teaching the conflicts, a distinction that Graff's critics seem to blur. The professor who cannot interest students in these debates has not succeeded in demonstrating their relevance—a *pedagogical* failure.

The core course fosters what Graff refers to as a "self-awareness," exposing and explaining our assumptions to students rather than assuming they will know them intuitively. Such a core course builds an ethos: it provides an opportunity for students to ask those questions that seem to have no context in a survey of British literature or an advanced course in Romantic poetry. In speculating on how his view of the history of criticism might "jibe" with those presented to his students by his colleagues, Graff claims he "had no way of knowing"; if they noted "discrepancies," his students "were too polite to mention them" ("Voices"). In a class which takes the profession and its assumptions as part of its content, however, there is a built-in context for such questions and comments. When we discuss the canon in my critical theory course, I ask students what texts they are reading and have read in classes from junior high through their current semester. This not only stimulates a lively discussion which makes the issue of canon relevant to these students, it also reveals incredible differences in students from various districts and states. I discover that many students' high school English curriculum is identical to that I experienced in a different state over twenty-five years ago—*Julius Caesar, The Scarlet Letter, Travels with Charley, Great Expectations*—while some more innovative teachers in places like Taos, New Mexico, are assigning novels I've never read. Certain departments seem to have canons of their own: Zora Neale Hurston's *Their Eyes Were Watching God* and Maxine Hong Kingston's *The Woman Warrior* are current favorites in a variety of period and genre classes in my department. These discussions provide valuable information for me in planning my own courses and texts so they will complement rather than replicate what students have studied elsewhere.

Students who have had this discussion of canon in my undergraduate research/theory course are likely to question and challenge my own authority, particularly the selection of texts, when I have them in subsequent classes, providing the kind of connection between isolated classes Graff advocates. On the first day of my Victorian novels course, for example, one of my repeat students from the undergraduate theory class asked why we were studying one more female than male novelist. The next semester in "Victorian Poetry," I was challenged for including only three female poets, providing an opportunity for a discussion which went beyond the canon to consider issues of gender, genre, and literary production in the Victorian period. By seizing opportunities to discuss issues, we can insure that our students integrate material from their various classes, making connections between periods and genres. However, the obstacle is not so much the field coverage system but an authoritarian teaching style and the lack of a context that will encourage students to ask these questions in every class. The creation of such a context can begin on the first day of class when the syllabus is presented by discussing texts that were included and excluded. Why was the Heath anthology selected for a survey course in American literature? Why was Byron or Blake omitted and Jane Austen or Dorothy Wordsworth included in a Romantics course?

The combination of a less authoritarian method of teaching and the context provided by the core course will encourage students to bring in material from other classes, integrating their courses in a personally relevant fashion. When I taught an undergraduate honors course (for mostly nonmajors) in experimental women writers last semester, one student brought in a diagram of three types of female orgasm she had studied in her human sexuality course. This not only enriched our discussion of the representation of female sexual response in *Their Eyes Were Watching God* and *The Golden Notebook*, but also opened the way for dialogue between myself and a colleague in another department. I encourage students to quote or paraphrase other professors' remarks, and if the comment or rationale does not seem clear I encourage the student to ask Professor X to clarify or explain and bring the response back to class. In this way, students function as intermediaries between classes and professors.

In order to succeed, at the graduate or undergraduate level, the core course must have a privileged status, elevating the devalued classroom by making it a public forum. The teaching of the course must be considered a plum. If the extra work and status involved in teaching and organizing the course as a "happening" were acknowledged by a reduced teaching load for that semester, or if it were considered as what it is—a valued integration of research and teaching—and rewarded by merit pay, faculty would vie for the privilege of teaching the course. Moreover, we need to find a way to count such contributions to our home campus for tenure and review as something more than the denigrated concept of service, whose status is indicated by its customary final position in the triumvirate of "research, teaching, and service" in descriptions of tenure criteria. Department heads and administrators must find a way to truly recognize and reward this kind of contribution. The term's etymology denotes serfs, servitude; its current marginalized status demeans the home institution as well as its servants and the students they serve.

Proposals such as those made in the Carnegie Foundation Report, "Scholarship Reconsidered," need to be seriously studied by all research universities. Stanford and Syracuse universities, for example, have recently been publicized for their efforts to broaden definitions of research and to revaluate teaching. The program proposed in 1991 by controversy-beleaguered former Stanford President Donald Kennedy to make incentives for teaching commensurate to those for research places the emphasis back on students, reemphasizing work with undergraduates as well as teaching and the institution itself. Kennedy has proposed "cash bonuses" and "permanent salary increases" for excellent teachers (Gordon A3, A34). Further, realizing that quantifying publications as notches on a belt privileges research at the expense of teaching rather than integrating the two, he has proposed limits on the *quantity* of articles considered for promotion and an increased consideration of textbooks as meritorious publications (Gordon A3). At Syracuse, the goal is to build a "student-centered research institution" and find ways to give teaching a "higher priority" through a new reward structure (Mooney A15, A1). These proposals do not seek to abolish research or remake the university in the image of the secondary school as some doomsayers have implied. Critics may argue that the proposals risk marginalizing research, but such a result seems unlikely as they work against the grain of current values and the competitive nature of our society—and our profession. These kinds of proposals destabilize and equalize rather than reverse current priorities and values.

For a true integration to exist, we must revalue rather than negate the positive values of the classroom as private sphere. After all, the Victorians valued the home as a refuge from the strife and chaos of the outside world; we don't want to lose a sheltered environment which encourages students to develop relationships with their peers and with their professors. Increasingly, this kind of classroom has been revalued not only by feminists such as Dale Spender and Jane Tompkins, but also by Kenneth Bruffee and Peter Elbow, who emphasize collaboration and the student-centered class. If indeed, as is often argued, integration is a higher level of human development than specialization (Appley 59–61), we want to integrate private and public spheres, teaching and research.

The lack of dialogue is, as Gerald Graff argues, a major problem in the humanities, but I am uneasy with proposals to subsume English under cultural studies or seriously tamper with field coverage. In these days of state budget crisis, suggestions to merge departments might invite administrators to replace period specialists in English studies with generalist part-timers. Graff's own history of the profession shows that the study of literature has not always been considered necessary, and he himself points out that field coverage has practical advantages—not the least of which are the variety and richness of courses we are able to offer our students. There is a new excitement these days about what goes on in the classroom. Much of it comes from the flood of recent hiring and increased faculty mobility, bringing an infusion of new ideas and energy, especially where there is a student-centered pedagogy. There are indications that the dialogue Graff proposes has already begun. Increasingly, researchers in the humanities are collaborating in essays and books. Regional conferences—those close to home—are proliferating. There is an increased interest in mentoring of junior by senior faculty and students by teachers. Activities which support dialogue already exist, but they are currently devalued. The challenge is not so much to change the curriculum as individual attitudes about which activities are most important to ourselves and our students. The values of the private sphere—community and egalitarian discussion—must be infused into the public arena. This may be even more of a challenge than drastic curricular change.

NOTES

1. A comparison of the number of women who were full professors in English shows the gain from 1977 to 1987 was minimal: from 19 to 21 percent (Huber 60).

2. The core course I propose differs significantly from that developed by the Federated Learning Communities of Stony Brook, though it could serve as an initial phase in the development of such a program. While both function to integrate other courses within a curriculum, their core course is team taught, meets only once a month, confers one unit of credit, and introduces no new material (Hill 139). The course I describe would not necessarily be part of a core curriculum, would have its own topic relevant to other courses in the department and/or college curriculum, and would meet on a regular basis for full credit.

WORKS CITED

Appley, Dee G. "Human Development and Curricular Design." *In Opposition to the Core Curriculum: Alternative Models of Undergraduate Education.* Eds. James W. Hall and Barbara L. Kevles. Westport, CT: Greenwood, 1982. 55–68.

Boyer, Ernest. *Scholarship Reconsidered: Redefining the Professoriate.* New York: Carnegie Corporation, 1991.

Bromwich, David. "The Future of Tradition: Notes on the Crisis of the Humanities." *Dissent* 36 (1989): 541–57.

Cixous, Hélène. "Sorties." *New French Feminisms: An Anthology.* Eds. Elaine Marks and Isabelle de Courtivron. New York: Schocken, 1981.

Gordon, Larry. "Stanford to Focus on Undergraduates." *Los Angeles Times* (3 Mar. 1991): A3 & A34.

Graff, Gerald. *Professing Literature: An Institutional History.* Chicago: University of Chicago Press, 1987.

Hill, Patrick J. "Medium and Message in General Education." *Liberal Education* 67 (1981): 129–45.

Huber, Bettina J. "Women in the Modern Languages, 1970–90." *Profession 90* (1990): 58–73.

Martin, Elaine. "Power and Authority in the Classroom: Sexist Stereotypes in Teaching Evaluations." *Signs* 9 (1984): 482–92.

Mooney, Carolyn J. "Syracuse Seeks a Balance Between Teaching and Research." *The Chronicle of Higher Education* (25 Mar. 1992): A1, A14–16.

Spender, Dale. "The Gatekeepers: A Feminist Critique of Academic Publishing." *Doing Feminist Research.* Ed. Helen Roberts. London: Routledge, 1981.

Invitation to an Argument: Gerald Graff's "Conflict Model" of Education*

D.G. Myers

Gerald Graff's whole theory of education rests upon a perception that was given expression in the middle of the nineteenth century by John Stuart Mill. In the first chapter of his little book *On Liberty*, Mill observes that cultural knowledge seems to prepare no one for the disappointments and misfortunes of experience. After experience we are able to recall any number of things—ethical maxims, literary parallels, historical lessons—that ought to have served as warning; never before. The "full meaning" of a cultural production, Mill concludes, simply

> *cannot* be realized until personal experience has brought it home. But much more of the meaning . . . would have been understood, and what was understood would have been far more deeply impressed on the mind, if [we] had been accustomed to hear it argued pro and con by people who did understand it. (105)

Nearly alone among recent educational theorists, Graff is trying to steer a middle course between neoconservatives' angry cries for the restoration of humanistic content and the smashing of humanistic totems on the Left. While he believes that the content of human culture only takes on "full meaning" in the context of arguments pro and con, he also knows that meaningful arguments arise only when there is a question of substance to argue *about*. It is Graff's unique perception that education, like human experience itself, might assume the form as well as content of an argument.

This, I am convinced, is the real force behind Graff's recommendation that, instead of seeking to declare a halt to the bitter conflict over the humanistic curriculum, we ought to *teach* the conflict. And I am very far from finding this an empty or unserious proposal. Our beliefs are only as strong as the reasons we can give for holding them, and it would seem to make more sense to teach students how to come up with good reasons— better examples, new perceptions, more exact discriminations— than to uphold correct beliefs. At the same time, though, I am not convinced that Graff's "conflict model" of education is the best way to pursue this goal. It may not even attain the results that Graff hopes it will. Although he says that his objective is "to help [students] gain control of [academic] discourses"—an entirely praiseworthy goal—his "conflict model" of discourse mastery may not help them do anything of the sort. I think it is important to find out. In what follows I intend to hold Graff's "conflict model" up to scrutiny. And my purpose in doing so is not to pick holes in it, but simply to determine what intensity of examination it will bear.

Graff starts from the assumption that it will be imme- diately obvious what he means by "conflict" (or "controversy" or "debate"; he uses the words interchangeably). In truth, it is far from obvious. Yet the interpretation of this notion is central to any assessment of Graff's proposals. How can we teach the conflict if we do not know what a "conflict" is?

From the beginning, Graff's model of education seems badly muddled over the notion of rational controversy. Graff appears to be snagged between two different and incompatible conceptions of the academic enterprise. On one hand he seeks to found it upon critical argument. Recent developments in the humanities, he says, have made it impossible to take cherished positions for granted any longer—they must now be *argued for*. And this is a good thing. Education is in danger of breaking down when critical argument is abandoned.

> A student today can walk from a course in which the universality of the Western literary canon is taken for granted (and therefore not stated or argued) into another

course in which it is taken for granted (and therefore not
stated or argued) that the universality of the canon has
been discredited. While this disparity can be exciting,
many students become baffled or cynical. . . .

But on the other hand, Graff subscribes to the representational model of the university, which holds that as a social and
political institution the university represents social and political
interests. Thus he defines "diversity" not in terms of arguments
that diverge when confronted by a similar intellectual obstacle,
but rather in terms of an "academic culture [that] has become
more democratic and plural in content," "more pluralistic,
multicultural, and culturally representative"; that has found
room for a "range of cultural differences," including "unrepresented groups, methodologies, and viewpoints"; an "ideological
diversity," in short. Possibly these phrases are mere shibboleths
invoked to head off politically radical objections. But the same
strain of thought shows up in Graff's words of caution that for
many students it is academic culture itself which is alienating,
"no matter which view is in charge"; that *any* literary canon
seems foreign to students, "regardless which side gets to draw
up the list."

The argumentative and representational ideals are
incompatible, because genuine arguments do not occur between
representatives of a "view" or "side." Either its representative
embraces a view in toto, in which case it contains principles that
must be installed in a place beyond argument as a necessary
condition for the integrity of the view; or the person advancing
the view explicitly accepts some principles and explicitly rejects
others, in which case it is not a settled "view" at all, but only an
argument. (It may be depicted as a view, may be hung with the
name of an "ism," by an opponent who wishes to confound or
vilify it, just as some speeches in politically radical circles of the
thirties were denounced for being "Trotskyist." But the
argumentative effect of this charge is to associate speakers by
implication with certain antipathetic positions. And if they can
dissociate themselves from these—if they can explicitly renounce
some of the principles implied by their "view"—in what regard
can they be taken as "representative" of it?) Two persons who
embark upon a genuine argument must tacitly agree to listen to

reason. They must consider each other's arguments, if only for the sake of reply; they must open themselves to being proved wrong; they must risk altering their views. And in doing this they are no longer opponents, but codeterminers of a joint hearing. They do not take sides, but cooperate in the rational evaluation of arguments. On this showing, the "conflict" (in at least one of Graff's senses) is put aside, and what remains is the serious examination of a problem of mutual concern.

There is nothing new in what I am saying. It is a familiar plea in the liberal tradition, which (as I implied by quoting Mill at the start) may be the tradition to which Graff's proposals belong. The liberal inclination is to distrust party labels. In this respect it is neatly exemplified by Cyril Fielding in *A Passage to India*, who steadfastly believes in the innocence of Aziz, the Indian who is arrested for rape. Another Indian asks him with some amazement whether he is actually on their side against his own people. Fielding avows that he is, but he is not happy to be so.

> He regretted taking sides. To slink through India unlabelled was his aim. Henceforward he would be called "anti-British," "seditious"—terms that bored him, and diminished his utility. He foresaw that besides being a tragedy, there would be a muddle; already he saw several tiresome little knots, and each time his eye returned to them, they were larger. Born in freedom, he was not afraid of the muddle, but recognized its existence. (175)

Fielding takes this step only after being warned by his colonial superior that he must "toe the line," that a man "can't run with the hare and hunt with the hounds." Although he wishes to do neither, Fielding is motivated to throw in his lot with the Indians out of a preference for fact over the emotion of the herd—the Indians have the facts on their side, while the British have the emotion. But he regrets taking sides at all, because what comes of taking sides is the making of a muddle, in which the facts slowly drop from sight.

If what Graff proposes is to exhibit the map of learning as divided into hostile camps, each of which is made up of regulars who must toe the line, the outcome is likely to be a profound intellectual muddle. For on this exhibition a camp spokesman would not be called upon to think for himself, but dutifully to recite the approved phrases. And though each camp would claim to possess the truth, from a distance their "conflict" would sound like a discord of rival claims. Because each party to a dispute is defined by its assertion of opposing versions of the truth, *neither side is equipped with any probative mechanism for evaluating the truth or falsehood of its* own *assertions.* The only testing procedure in Graff's theory is the hunt for further points of conflict.

Another possibility does suggest itself. It may just be that Graff's own thinking is split between a liberal confidence in rational persuasion and a more radical insistence upon the primacy of conflict, in which any resolution or avoidance of conflict is stubbornly regarded as the reimposition of ideological domination. Earlier in his career, the liberal streak in Graff's thinking was more pronounced. In a 1980 essay, Graff argued that the radical attack on the conventions of academic inquiry was wide of the mark. It is the *uses* to which the conventions are put, he said, and not conventions as such, that determine their political effects. Graff reminded radical educational theorists that they themselves use "conventional methods of thought and expression" in addressing problems of politics and society. "We have little choice but to try to teach the conventions we ourselves do not hesitate to use when we argue about such problems," Graff concluded, "for without the command of these conventions students are likely to be ineffectual" either in service to society or in active opposition ("The Politics of Composition," 855–56).

On this showing, education is characterized by distinctive forms of inquiry rather than sites of frequent conflict. Even earlier, in *Literature Against Itself* (1979), Graff had shown that academic inquiry is self-probing and self-correcting, because it entails a dialectical back-and-forth between *explanans* and *explanatum.* In discussing the deconstructionist view that "experience is 'always already interpreted,'" he had noted the following: "That we cannot conceive of a fact without *some* interpretive paradigm does not mean that this fact can have no independent status outside *the particular paradigm we happen to be testing at the moment*" (202). In other words, a decade ago the purpose of critical inquiry for Graff was not the wholesale adoption of an interpretive paradigm, which is the essential prerequisite for mobilizing it into "conflict" with another paradigm. Rather, the purpose of critical inquiry was the rigorous testing of facts against different possible explanations. I am not aware that Graff has retracted this earlier view.[1] In "Interpretation on Tlön" (1985) he would appear to reassert it in the teeth of counterarguments by Stanley Fish. In turning his thoughts to education recently, though, Graff seems to have dismissed from mind the probative and dialectical relationship between fact and paradigm, and has substituted in its place a shrill and rancorous conflict between paradigms.

In "Interpretation on Tlön," Graff cites work by Robert Scholes and Stephen Toulmin to distinguish between primary and secondary systems of ideas. And in terms of this distinction, academic conflicts are reserved for the upper level. Toulmin calls this the *theoretical* level of academic debate, and separates it from the more basic *disciplinary* level upon which any debate between adherents of opposing theories is founded:

> For the parties to such a debate—both those who cling to the older theory, and those who put forward a newer one—would still share some common ground: not any common body of theoretical notions, perhaps, but rather certain shared disciplinary conceptions, reflecting their collective intellectual ambitions and rational methods, selection procedures and criteria of adequacy. (79)

Graff remains conscious of this distinction, characterizing literary theory at one point as "the kind of reflective, second-order discourse about practices that is generated when a consensus that was once taken for granted in a community breaks down." But though it is pretty clear that the *theoretical* consensus has broken down within literary study and the humanities more generally, it is far from self-evident that the *disciplinary* accord has been scuttled. For if it had been, the theoretical breakdown described by Graff would not have been intelligible to those who had witnessed it. As Graff was aware a decade and less ago, theoretical debates occur between those who have already mastered a common discipline's methods, procedures, and criteria. In his more recent musings on education, though, he seems never to have asked himself whether it is possible to master first-order disciplinary conceptions through second-order theoretical debate.

I think it is improbable, and for three reasons.

First, a "conflict model" will probably not remedy the incoherence or "disjunctiveness" of the literary curriculum that, according to Graff, deprives students of a "connected view of scholarship." In reality, the conflict in literary study may be over just what constitutes a coherent understanding of literature. And thus the conflict between interpretive paradigms may not be a *cause* of incoherence, but only a *condition* of the search for coherence. The critical controversies of recent decades may indicate very little more than that literary study has begun to come into its own as a distinct and autonomous discipline of inquiry. Much modern philosophy, after all, has been an effort to specify what manner of inquiry philosophy is. In the same way, much contemporary literary thought is an undertaking to say with greater exactness than in the past what counts as literature's subject matter and special methods. It is a mistake, however, to believe that a coherent understanding of literature can ever be attained (or, as administrators like to say, "implemented") institutionally. To point out the institutional incoherence of the curriculum, as Graff repeatedly does, is to point out the unremarkable. For it can be rendered institutionally coherent only if (as Graff acknowledges) "one faction in the current disciplinary conflict can wholly liquidate its opposition. . . ." Even then, however, the resulting curriculum would be coherent only if the winning faction itself were. And how else could this be determined than by a critical inspection of its doctrines, one by one and in detail? But then it ceases to be a conflict, and becomes merely a pursuit of truth, which must be conducted in accord with common aims, methods, procedures, and criteria. Teaching the conflict would appear to lead *away* from disciplinary competence.

Second, teaching the conflict will probably not advance knowledge. Take the so-called canon wars, for instance. When conceived as a debate between antagonistic viewpoints, the very topic preassigns the roles of pro and con. What is more, those who try to advance an independent argument will be viewed suspiciously, Graff warns, "as taking a particular position in the debate, as in fact they are." In fact, it is not at all clear why taking a position is the only possible (or permitted) response to the question. If the question of the canon is merely an occasion for aligning oneself with an established position it is not really a question but a test of faith. Yet at times this is precisely how Graff appears to conceive of intellectual debate. In reply to an essay by Lorraine Clark comparing *Literature Against Itself* to Allan Bloom's *Closing of the American Mind*, Graff agrees there are points in common; but he emphasizes—and says it cannot be emphasized too strongly—that he "was coming from the political Left not the Right" (Buckley and Seaton 161). It is as if Graff were anxious about his credentials, quite apart from the propositional content of his writing.

If intellectual debate is merely an occasion to side with the angels on the Left or the Right it is difficult to see how it can possibly advance knowledge. What is to be learned from hearing the same orthodoxies sworn to again and again? As an educational process, debate between sects or parties will tend only to *polarize* ideas, pitting them against one another rather than clarifying what is at issue. At such a pass, knowledge is more likely to be advanced by independence and heresy. Elsewhere, for example, I have argued that the canon is a bogey, that there is nothing in the world about which it is true (or false) to say *this* is the canon or *that* is not.[2] In recent discussions of the canon, for *and* against, all that may be going on is an effort to relate various works of literature to one another. This relationship is then hypostatized as "the canon," but it is a blunder to speak of a relationship as itself a cultural achievement. And from this it follows that the entire debate over the canon has been misconceived. In the din of charge and countercharge, any such argument stands little chance of being heard. But if my argument is correct, the current debate is largely beside the point. And it would seem that inquiring into the question would take precedence, then, over teaching the debate. For it is precisely a question *about* aims, methods, procedures, criteria; it is a question about the disciplinary conditions of theoretical debate.

Last, theoretical debate will probably not teach students how to see through a disciplinary inquiry for themselves. It may satisfy the craving of professors for a more advanced discussion of issues than is possible in most undergraduate classrooms, but the likelihood is that students will be left feeling (in Graff's own words) baffled or cynical. In making his proposals, Graff says he is "drawing on a familiar format, the academic conference." Jetting off to conferences is becoming an increasingly indispensable part of professors' lives, "substitut[ing] for the kind of general discussion that does not take place at home." Graff proposes to restart the discussion at home, by means of a grand conference across the curriculum. "The idea," he says, "is to *thematize the semester.*" And to insure that students are not bored and passive listeners, Graff insists that they must actively participate, "from writing papers about the conference, to presenting some of the papers and responses in it, to planning and organizing the program itself."

It sounds wonderful, but it seems unlikely to come off as planned. What Graff overlooks is the fact that academic conferences are highly specialized forms of argumentative inquiry. It is one thing to settle on a theme for the semester, but quite another to know how to *thematize* anything at all. Again, this is a distinction to which Graff himself once appealed, and gives evidence now of having forgotten. In "Literature as Assertions" (1981), he wrote:

> Many students who have no difficulty comprehending literary works on the level of action and story are unable to perform the operations required to make conceptual sense of action and story. . . . All but the most receptive students of literature have difficulty performing the thematizing operations that come so easily to the practiced teacher and critic. (158)

The problem that Graff defines with such firmness here is unlikely to be solved by thematizing semesters and planning and organizing conferences. For it is *not* a question of how to get students to participate in scholarly debates, as if this were the ultimate experience of the life of the mind. And the answer is *not* for students to present papers and responses, making believe they are professors. The deeper problem is how to instill within students intellectual ambitions and rational habits; to school them in the use of selection procedures and criteria of adequacy.

Until they can think through an argument for themselves, it is unrealistic to expect them either to follow or participate in a debate.

And this is the tiresome little knot that, in my opinion, Graff fails to unmuddle. He asserts that "the best way to learn a foreign language is to live in the country in which it is spoken." And he treats the university as if it were such a country. But though this is enormously suggestive, in the end it is merely suggestive. Unless Graff is proposing a general course in conversational academese, his idea of a "language" is superficial. By conceiving it in terms of current debates over substantive claims to know real meanings and real truths, Graff simplifies language to its semantical component; and as the philosopher Nicholas Rescher points out, "a 'language' involves not merely rules of meaning and rules of truth (semantical rules) and rules of inferential transition (logical rules) but rules of assertion-entitlement (evidential rules) as well" (93). On this showing, the university is not a country with a single language, but a small continent, like Europe, which is crisscrossed by ancient linguistic enmities. For what counts as evidence in one discipline of university study is laughed off as superstition in another. An utterance from the past is treated as a historical fact in one department, a textual uncertainty or interpretive puzzle in another, a statement of truth or falsehood in a third. Not to attend to what entitles scholars to make different sorts of assertions is to acquire but a stuttering, fumbling use of the language (or languages) of intellectual life. Graff's model of education accounts for the semantics of rational controversy. On his model, students would profit from hearing the language of controversy spoken. But it is not clear whether or in what way his model contains any provision for enabling students to master logic and rules of evidence, especially in more than one area of controversy. It is not clear, on Graff's model, how students would ever learn to speak with any assurance for themselves.

I conclude with a few observations about what might be salvaged from Graff's proposals: (1) Graff's theory of education is a reminder that rational argument stands at the center of the academic enterprise, although Graff's own ideas suggest that what is immediately needed in theorizing about education is a more adequate conception of argument. If nothing else, it would seem better to conceive of arguments as occurring not *between* rival factions, but *into* shared questions. (2) Graff's earlier thinking pointed in this direction, toward a probative and dialectical conception of argument. More recently he appears to have abandoned theorizing about argument to concentrate upon institutional arrangements for a public debate. His earlier writing remains fundamentally sound, providing a basis for future work. But what will be required is more reflection than Graff has yet given to the aims, methods, procedures, and criteria of the various *disciplines* of argument. (3) In the meantime, Graff is probably right to emphasize the semantics of current scholarly disputes. Perhaps there is a better way, however. Instead of attending thematized conferences, it might be more productive to turn attention to the *themes* currently under dispute. Although questions may be formulated misleadingly, and although answers may be offered that do more to conceal than to illuminate, scholarly debates are an important clue to where the current problems in a discipline lie. (4) And on the evidence of Graff's proposals, the biggest problem facing education today is how to teach students to hold their own in intelligent argument.

A provisional solution might be to conduct classes upon the model of argument. Although Graff insists that "educational problems are systematic ones that involve not just individual teaching but the way that teaching is organized," until the system is reorganized individual teachers might begin to correct the problem by inviting students to contest the claims that they themselves make in class. As the British philosopher Martin Warner says in describing F.R. Leavis's pedagogical style, the teacher's "characteristic question 'This is so, isn't it?' is no mere rhetorical flourish, but an invitation to debate—where the response 'Yes, but . . .' must be accompanied by reasons, examples, new perceptions, and discriminations" (359). As a pupil of Graff—one of his last Ph.D. students at Northwestern—I can testify from sometimes bruising experience that this is precisely the manner in which he conceived his role as a teacher. I learned from Graff that to do him honor I must receive his teaching as an invitation to argue staunchly with him. At any rate, that is what I have tried to do in this essay.

NOTES

*Throughout this essay, the italics in any quotation are in the original. I am grateful to Craig Kallendorf, James Seaton, William E. Cain, and (as always) Jerry Graff for criticism and suggestions.

1. But see his response to Lorraine Clark's "Allan Bloom and Gerald Graff: On Mimesis as Freedom" (Buckley and Seaton 151–63). There Graff says that he has "changed [his] position" since writing *Literature Against Itself.*

2. See D.G. Myers, "The Bogey of the Canon," *Sewanee Review* 97 (1989): 611–21. In a letter of February 9, 1990, Graff told me that he was struck by the "curiously contradictory mix of conservative and nonconservative 'discourses'" in my essay. Since I did not conceive the essay in these terms (and cannot understand what it would mean to do so), I remain puzzled by his response.

WORKS CITED

Buckley, William K., and James Seaton, eds. *Beyond Cheering and Bashing: New Perspectives on "The Closing of the American Mind."* Bowling Green, KY: Bowling Green State University Popular Press, 1992.

Forster, E.M. *A Passage to India.* Harvest Book 35. New York: Harcourt Brace & World, 1924.

Graff, Gerald. "Interpretation on Tlön: A Response to Stanley Fish." *New Literary History* 17 (1985–86): 109–17.

————. *Literature Against Itself: Literary Ideas in Modern Society.* Chicago: University of Chicago Press, 1979.

————. "Literature as Assertions." In *American Criticism in the Poststructuralist Age.* Ed. Ira Konigsberg. Ann Arbor: Michigan Studies in the Humanities, 1981, 135–61.

————. "The Politics of Composition: A Reply to John Rouse." *College English* 42 (1980): 851–56.

Mill, John Stuart. *On Liberty.* Ed. Gertrude Himmelfarb. Harmondsworth, UK: Penguin, 1974.

Rescher, Nicholas. *Dialectics: A Controversy-Oriented Approach to the Theory of Knowledge.* Albany: State University of New York Press, 1977.

Toulmin, Stephen. *Human Understanding: The Collective Use and Evolution of Concepts.* Princeton: Princeton University Press, 1972.

Warner, Martin. *Philosophical Finesse: Studies in the Art of Rational Persuasion.* Oxford: Clarendon, 1989.

Professing Literature in 2001

James J. Sosnoski

> ... there is a discernible longing for intellectual community. ("Teach the Conflicts" 66)

> One of the oddest things about the university is that it calls itself a "community of scholars," yet organizes itself in a way that conceals the intellectual links of that community from those who don't already see them. I trace this oddity to what I call the course fetish, the assumption that the natural unit of instruction is the autonomous course, one not in direct dialogue with other courses. ("How Curricular Disconnection" [in this volume])

> Yet it is the individual classroom we have tended to focus on in educational reform discussions, a fact that our very use of the expression "the classroom" betrays. ("Teach the Conflicts" 57)

> That the teaching of literature is a collective enterprise may seem too obvious a point to need stating, but it is easily overlooked. ("The Future of Theory" 255)

In the April 18, 1992, issue of *Entertainment Weekly*, George Mannes describes "the fine art of transforming your house into a movie house." His essay recounts the fastest growing consumer technology—the home theater. This phenomenon, he notes, is not the result of a "hot tech fad" but rather of "a concept bringing together a variety of entertainment devices"—large-screen TVs, VCRs, CD drives, and surround-sound audio-sources. Integrated technology allows you, if you can afford the equipment, "to bring the thrills of the movie house into your home with big, sharp video screens and full, all-enveloping sound systems" (26). The rewards are captivating—"the fourth, or 'surround' channel, is what really captivates home-theater fans. Typically coming from a pair of speakers at the rear of a viewing room, the 'surround' channel contains mood-setting background sound, such as *Apocalypse Now*'s jungle noises and throbbing helicopters" (28).

Home theaters are merely one facet of the revolution that is making homes into electronic environments (EEs). The idea is a simple one—integrate all electronic devices into a system that produces an environment. Before long, home EEs will incorporate "virtual reality" technology to produce an experience so enveloping that it rivals physical experiences. But even persons without the new technology already enjoy many more virtual experiences than they recognize as such. Such encounters have a surprisingly long history in our culture. Producers of rock music have used virtual reality techniques for decades. (I recently read a review of a live concert that addressed the disappointment of fans in the musical quality of a singer's voice by arguing that recorded video performances in which her voice was enhanced by electronic devices were superb. The reviewer ended his comments with the remark, "Who cares if she can't sing?")[1]

Soon, classrooms will follow theaters into the home. Philips, for example, has released a compact disc interactive (CDI) technology which features educational discs as well as films, recordings, and games that can be run on its CDI players. With CDI you can play "The Palm Springs Open" but also explore "The Treasures of the Smithsonian." In the academy, "Explorations of the Virtual Classroom" were invited for the Ninth Conference on Computers and Writing, convened in May of 1993. Virtual universities are already under construction. Alpha University, which goes beyond the Bulletin Board Services of MegaByte U or the Electronic College of Theory, has been in development since November of 1991. David Downing and I have been coordinating its activities from its inception. We believe that proposals for future universities must be undertaken with virtual classrooms in mind. We live and work in a period of transition from print environments to electronic ones. As text-based learning, cultural study will be deeply affected by this transformation. So, it seems appropriate to consider Gerald Graff's curricular reforms in the context of electronic textbases.

Graff's proposals were influential in the building of Alpha University. As the headnotes indicate, Graff looks beyond the traditional classroom. "As long as it continues to be taught in a privatized space," Graff writes, "even the best-taught course is limited in its power to help students" ("Other Voices" 828). He advocates interrelated (networked) classrooms wherein teachers swap roles or organize the classes as symposia or conferences in ways that parallel work in LAN (local area) or WAN (wide area) electronic networks. However, bringing classrooms into homes reconfigures them as "private spaces." Moreover, when not monitored by surveillance devices, interactions in cyberspace ("a parallel universe created and sustained by the world's computers and communication lines" [Benedikt 1]) are impenetrably "private." There, persons often do not know and cannot identify each other. (The virus problem is one unhappy instance of such "networking" privacy.) Indeed, since future classrooms will be in cyberspace/time, those who wish to pursue Graff's proposals find themselves in a dilemma—will cyberspace/time make "classrooms" of the future even more privatized despite networking facilities? Will they, for instance, countermand academic ivory-towerism?

Graff's proposals for curriculum change, specifically for "foregrounding conflict," suit the virtual universities of the future. In Graff's argument, if we can break out of our self-imposed isolationism and "connect" with students, we can "restore" our "transformative" cultural role ("Other Voices" 831). At the outset of his project, Graff wrote:

> Embracing . . . new methods is no answer in itself, for they too have been unable to create a usable cultural context for literary study. The close, concrete reading of literary works, which remains one of the primary tasks of criticism, is not likely to recover the sense of mission that once informed it as long as it takes place in a vacuum—separated from historical, philosophical and social contexts. Thus a fusing of cultural inquiry and the most

> scrupulous textual attention would begin to restore to
> criticism a constructive role in the literary culture.
> (*Professing Literature* 10–11)

Graff has set out to construct a university that is not an "ivory
tower." Since he tells us in detail what professing literature *could*
be like in a reconstructed university, it seems appropriate to
inquire what it *can* be like in a virtual university. So, first I
describe those features of Graff's proposals most likely to be
affected in virtual classrooms. His new university features

1. a *learning community* in which
2. students *collaborate* with their teachers
3. on *cultural texts*
4. to resolve *"real-time" problems.*

Then, I offer some recommendations as "friendly amendments"
to Graff's recommendations.

Graff's University

Graff is the architect of a postmodern university. Whereas
the modern university was organized on the basis of a consensus
or conformity model, his is based on a conflict or difference
model. He hopes

> to reconceive educational coherence as a coherence of
> conflict rather than of consensus. . . . Such a rethinking
> would mean moving from the consensus model which has
> governed educational philosophy in the past to a conflict
> model, in which we would start from the assumption that
> we do not need agreement on first principles in order to
> make humanities education more accessible. ("What
> Should We Be Teaching" 199)

Such a fundamental change in the organizing principle of an
institution radically alters it.

Graff's proposal reverses the bonds that usually hold the
social relations in universities together. As he compellingly
argues, consensus could be the principle underlying the "Old
College" because it was predetermined by religious affiliation.

Although historians often describe the modern university as a democratic institution governed by consensus, Graff notes that consensus was never the norm ("The Future of Theory" 260). After a century of illusory discourse about common principles and shared aims, we should not delude ourselves further by basing our curricular proposals upon a consensus model. Instead, we should restructure the university (or, at least, the humanities) on the basis of our differences. Graff focuses almost entirely upon the pedagogical implications of this new order.

From a pedagogical perspective, a university is constituted by relations among teachers and students. The transmission of information (often called the "banking" theory of education) is an issue that has engaged educators since Paulo Freire published his influential *Pedagogy of the Oppressed* (1970) and has been vigorously renewed in our "information era." Graff rivets his attention on the "connectivity" issue in this debate. In "Colleges Are Depriving Students of a Connected View of Scholarship" (in this volume as "How Curricular Disconnection Disempowers Students"), Graff remarks that when students are not "connected" to the issues underlying faculty research, courses are less "intellectually stimulating" (A48). Without "connectivity," students soon forget and forgo their learning. For Graff, connectivity is more likely when students take part in the conversations going on in the intellectual communities to which their teachers belong.

Learning Communities

In the same essay, Graff envisions the curriculum as a forum for discussion, a "learning community" (A48).

> A learning community is any one of a variety of curricular structures that link together several existing courses—or actually restructure the curricular material entirely—so that students have opportunities for deeper understanding and integration of the material they are learning, and more interaction with one another and their teachers as fellow participants in the learning enterprise . . . all these efforts represent attempts to reorganize and redirect students' academic experience for greater intellectual and social

coherence and involvement. . . . In learning communities, students and faculty members experience courses and disciplines not as arbitrary or isolated offerings but rather as a complementary and connected whole. These interwoven, reinforcing curricular arrangements make it possible, then, for faculty and students to work with each other in less distant, routinized ways and to discover a new kind of enriched intellectual and social ground. (Gabelnick et al. 19)

Gabelnick, MacGregor, Matthews, and Smith, the authors of *Learning Communities: Creating Connections Among Students, Faculty, and Discipliness*, see Graff's proposal as one of many variants. ("One solution, offered by Gerald Graff, suggests that we 'teach the debate' over the canon instead of trying to resolve it through narrow definitions" [8].) To perceive Graff's proposals as "one of many variants" fits their taxonomy of learning communities. But this is misleading. Their five basic models of learning communities dovetail more easily with the modern university than with a "postmodern" one. From a "postdisciplinary" perspective (Harkin 124–138), their view of learning communities wherein methods are consensual matters is at its core "modern." Both Graff's view of learning and his view of community are more distinctively postmodern in their tolerance of difference and dissent. Graff writes:

As the disciplines have moved away from the positivism of the nineteenth century, knowledge has come increasingly to be visualized not as a unified structure, a pyramid of building blocks, but as a set of social practices, a conversation. Whether this spells the death of the concept of the disciplines as a "body of knowledge" is still very much open to debate—the kind of debate that I have been recommending we put in the forefront of education. ("Teach the Conflicts" 66)

Gabelnick et al. have a less supple sense of a "discourse community" than Graff (see Swales below).

In Graff's postmodern university, teachers and students discuss texts that have cultural significance. Neither the persons nor the texts are construed in "patterned isolation" from each other. However, this discussion community does not take a "united" front on the rationales of its own existence. Nor is it a "discourse community" in the sense which John M. Swales developed in *Genre Analysis,* which takes as its defining characteristic that the members have "a broadly agreed set of common public goals" (24–25). It comes closer to Swales's 1992 redefinition, in which he proposes that discourse communities have only "a discoverable set of goals":

1. A discourse community (d.c.) has a discoverable set of goals. These may be publicly and explicitly formulated and either generally or partially assented to by the members; they may be consensual; or they may be separate but contiguous (Old Guard and Young Turks; researchers and practitioners, as in the just-holding-together American Psychological Association).
2. A d.c. has mechanisms of intercommunication among members. There is no change here. Without mechanisms there is no community.
3. A d.c. uses its participatory mechanisms for a range of purposes: to provide performance-enhancing information and feedback; to channel innovation; to maintain the value and belief systems of the community; and to enhance its professional space.
4. A d.c. utilizes an evolving selection of genres in the furtherance of its set of goals and as instantiation of its participatory mechanisms.
5. A d.c. has acquired and continues to search for discourse-community-specific terminology.
6. A d.c. has an explicit or implicit hierarchical structure which manages the processes of entry into and advancement within the discourse community. ("The Concept of Discourse Community" 1)

Item 5 in Swales's definition of a discourse community matches an important point in Graff's view of the role of theory in the conflict model.

Collaborative Arguments

Graff recommends that students learn theorizing by "living the language" in a way that parallels the learning process of normal language acquisition—by living in the country in which the language is spoken. The living conversation of theory is, for Graff, debate. This is the work upon which teachers and students of cultural studies collaborate. Writings and readings in cultural studies are structured by debate. In its most rudimentary form, cultural study is constituted by cycles of arguments.

To collaborate is "to work together." Thus, teachers and students work on cultural issues together by writing out their readings of them. Agreeing or disagreeing about the social and cultural effects of "readings" is the work of collaboration. Hence, in Graff's proposals the crucial issue is how to disagree constructively. As he often points out, critics do not know how to disagree. For him, *debate is a constructive form of disagreement.*

To many this seems counterintuitive. Debates are often rationalized quarrels. In a postmodern critical climate wherein there are no grounds for refutation, debating would seem little more than a competition for truth (see Harkin). It's not competition for Graff; it's "dialogical." "To me," he writes,

> the bottom line in analyzing the institutional processes I discuss in *Professing Literature* is the results these processes produce at the student's end, not whether a culture of "argument" is or isn't maintained. More specifically, what matters to me is the extent to which educational institutions help students to see what is at issue in the political and cultural conflicts that they have a stake in. ("Gerald Graff's Response to His Critics" 91)

Cultural Texts

In Graff's recent essays, he construes "conflict" as "dialogical." Graff writes that

> in a dialogical curriculum, questions that challenge or redefine the premises of the discussion would not arise in

one class only to be abruptly dropped in the next, as tends to be the case now. Since such questions would have a chance to become part of other conversations besides the one taking place in the privacy of a single course, the more pertinent ones would figure to be sustained and reinforced. This is the case if only because the inevitable inequalities of authority in the pedagogical situation mean that questions like "So what?" "Who cares?" "Could you clarify that?" "How is that point relevant?" and "Why are we going on about this issue to the exclusion of that one?" are more likely to come from other faculty than from students, at least for the moment. ("Other Voices" 831–832)

In "Teach the Conflicts," Graff concludes that there is no alternative to consensus but to "agree to disagree." However, he is well aware that any group working together on a problem will sometimes agree and sometimes disagree. Agreement and disagreement are dialogical relations. Disciplinary discourse communities can be distinguished from other kinds of discourse communities, for instance concurrences (see below). A disciplinary community wherein consensus is achieved by argumentation (akin to Swales's original definition of a d.c.) is organized on an agreement-to-disagree priority to which agreements-to-agree are secondary. By contrast, a concurrence (akin to Swales's redefinition) is based on agreement-to-agree protocols which take priority over agreements-to-disagree. Protocols shape the various relations of agreement and disagreement in dialogical situations.

Yet how can a policy of "conflict" be a productive form of work?[2] Debate in a postmodern climate is far more likely to encourage an ever-widening range of diversity. As Graff notes, we have rarely if ever depended upon consensus in the humanities. For him, cultural studies provides ways of embracing diversity ("What Should We Be Teaching" 192; "The Future of Theory" 266). The recommendations of Terry Eagleton (*Literary Theory*) and William E. Cain (*The Crisis in Criticism*) for changes in the conduct of literary criticism combined with Raymond Williams's exemplary practice delineate for Graff a viable "cultural studies." How is it, then, that "cultural studies" can offer us a productive way of handling increasing diversity where other attempts have failed?

Reading Graff's work, one is tempted to think that the answer is that cultural studies can admit a diversity of conflicting methods. But Graff's analysis does not easily allow that inference. Theory has come under the sway of the field coverage principle. The "schools and movements" curricular scheme, which presupposes a pluralism of unified method- ologies or approaches, is thereby governed by both a consensus principle and a field coverage principle. A school is an "interpretive community" that appears to achieve "consensus" about its methods of reading. In his remarks about Fish's conception of interpretive communities, Graff doubts that consensus exists even at this level of our curricular system ("Co-optation" 179). His analysis invites distrust of the "schools and methods" view of literary study as a microscopic version of "field coverage." Is applying a method the "work" Graff would have students do? Is this what they are trained for? In such a view, students are destined to be future disciples (or should we say "clones"). Though it has seemed so to some of his critics, this is not the outcome Graff anticipates. What's the alternative?

Throughout his writings Graff insists that students should be active participants in academic disputes rather than passive spectators. In "Cultural Studies, Postmodernism, and Composition," John Schilb views students as potential collabo- rators which he deems consonant with Graff's proposals.

> *A composition program would therefore be a research program* examining various theories of "cultural studies" and "postmodernism," as well as how they diverge or mesh.
>
> This agenda might appear to threaten the field's current pluralism, the range of scholarly concerns and method- ological approaches it now exhibits. But they could be productively juxtaposed even as faculty undertake the collective study I have in mind. It could actually help writing teachers avoid the fragmentation that Gerald Graff has found plaguing literary scholars because they fail to admit and work through their conflicts. And just as Graff has proposed that literary studies foreground conflict in a way productive and involving for students, so *they should be enlisted in the project I am suggesting for composition,* not

conceived as mere recipients of its fruits. (174–175, emphasis mine)

Following Schilb's version of Graff's "conflict model," let me stipulate that the activity in which students engage is, in principle, collaborative; they are potential co-researchers. Understanding students as potential co-workers in research fits future classrooms. A different structure of authority governs educational electronic environments. In computer labs students handle virtual "learning community" situations more adeptly than their teachers. Even so, assuming that collaboration is the wave of the future, why *debate* together?

Problems That Derive from "Real-Time" Experiences

Where does debate lead us? The conflicts that Graff offers as instances of his model are not only derived from texts but also from extratextual concerns. As I have already noted, he writes that "the close, concrete reading of literary works, which remains one of the primary tasks of criticism, is not likely to recover the sense of mission that once informed it *as long as it takes place in a vacuum*—separated from historical, philosophical and social contexts" (*Professing Literature* 10–11, emphasis mine). The problems that texts presuppose "live" *outside* the discussion; namely, in our social or cultural experiences (*Literature Against Itself*). Texts are, in Kenneth Burke's famous phrase, "equipment for living."

Graff's university is a *learning community* in which students *collaborate* with their teachers on *cultural* problems that derive from "*real-time*" (extratextual) *experiences*. With these parameters in mind, let us consider what happens when Graff's university becomes a virtual university.

Graff's University and Alpha University

Alpha University (AU) is a virtual university. It exists in a virtual space/time continuum, not in real space or time. In his *Computer Glossary*, Alan Freedman defines virtual reality (VR) as "a simulated or conceptual environment." Through the aid of computers, for instance, scientists simulate weather patterns in order to understand real weather patterns in what has become known as "chaos theory." Architects test the design of buildings by simulating stress factors on computers. In addition, they can show prospective clients exactly what their new environments will look like. "Virtuality" has become a standard aspect of marketing even in hairdressing. There is, however, a dark side to the virtual reality phenomenon—for instance, virtual "news" wherein images and voices in databases are restructured to serve as VR scenarios for events that have transpired but for which there was no immediate coverage. Nonetheless, we can expect the rapid development of virtual classrooms. Will Graff's recommendations (e.g., to develop learning communities as the sites of cultural debates) work in virtual classrooms?

The problem Graff hopes to solve (classrooms as "privatized spaces") is exaggerated in virtual environments. Cyberspace is a highly "privatized space." As any subscriber to a computer list-service knows, writing and reading expand at a rapid pace in the differing tempo of cybertime. Placing your name on a list-service commits you to a deluge of mail because messages arriving at its site are sent to everyone on its list. Each morning your e-mail box is crammed with messages that arrive at an unaccustomed rate. The difficulties of reading available materials are amplified tenfold in cyberspace. Thus, an emphasis on disagreement would be likely to produce not only diversity but also endless controversy.

That productive work is accomplished by list-services is questionable—persons are so swamped with scattered "talk" that they cancel their subscriptions. Downloading material sent by a list-service parallels tape-recording telephone conversations on party lines. This form of networking is not collaborative. It is not an instance of an exemplary learning community. The level at which assumptions and conceptions are shared is indeed minimal. Moreover, as Graff notes, the assumption that humanists share assumptions does not hold up even in real time.

Debates on "computer party lines" tend toward a chaotic state. Everyone is talking at the same time to no one in particular but to everyone in general. This propagates pandemonium. In such an environment, the tendency for critics to behave as "schools unto themselves" is magnified. In virtual classrooms "conversations" tend toward solipsistic cybercism or critical self-envelopment because they lack the constraints of real-time dialogue (e.g., a listener's bored countenance). If Graff's aim is not "to bring conflicts to a consensual resolution, but to exploit the conflicts themselves as an organizing principle" ("The Future of Theory" 261), we have to ask: is such an aim feasible in cyberspace/time?

To avoid the list-service problem, we developed *Cycles*, a set of research protocols that form "a cooperative document editing tool," for Alpha University. The model was inspired by a 1988 review of Lotus Corporation's Notes, a major business networking software.

> Lotus Corp's new program Notes is a "group productivity tool" that lets co-workers share documents and graphics across local area and wide area networks. Notes is intended as a vehicle to enable a wide range of knowledge workers to share their ideas and comments on projects. The package acts as a cooperative document editing tool that records all input. Several large companies and about 200 Lotus employees have put Notes to a variety of uses, including tracking the product's own development. The software gathers and archives input from multiple departments, pulling together material for large-scale brainstorming. Action items are suggested and then tested against the reactions of corporate reviewers. Project members don't have to meet as often when they can interact this way. (Hogan 14)

Cycles merges the protocols of classrooms, research projects, and journals into "cycles" of dialogues linked by cross-references and indexes so that they can be searched and reassembled productively. Taking Graff's view of the classroom as a dialogical site of debate, we record the ongoing dialogue among the researchers in a journal-like circular comprised of "letters to the editor" through which projects are negotiated at every stage (see below). Like Lotus Corporation's Notes, *Cycles* functions as a cooperative group project that records its communications in a collaborative document which is continuously edited with the aim of publication. It takes the complex process individuals undertake in their research and makes every step collaborative. All the researchers enter their "notes" into the same database. Through a series of editing protocols these notes are revised toward making recommendations for specific actions. *Cycles* participants communicate with each other while tracking the communication as an electronic exchange interfaced with editing programs that record it in journal-like formats. Many of the traditional protocols and techniques of scholarly communication merge with each other. *Cycles* has some of the characteristics of a journal, an edition, a conference, a phone call, a videotape, a computer instruction program, and a classroom.

We construe classes in AU as research projects in which students are co-researchers with their teachers, lending their skills to the projects. Each class project starts with the shared perception of a problem and discussion of various ways of handling it. Since these discussions are recorded and edited, the "conversations" and "debates" teachers and students enjoy become a "journal" of their research activity. Let me offer three examples of the *Cycles* model.

David Downing, who has been collaborating with me on AU, gave graduate students registered for his "Theory and Pedagogy" course in the fall of 1992 the option of writing letters to me, the editor of *Cycles*, describing problems they had as teachers who were at the same time students. Ann Ott wrote a letter about "the awful graduate course" she had taken at another university in which she was asked to accomplish more than was physically possible in a semester. Shortly afterward, Bill Thelin wrote me about student apathy. His letter was followed by one from Karrie Szatek about student resistance. I wrote back, pointing out the connections among their observations. They decided to form a cycle to discuss the problem of student apathy and resistance. Bennis Lathan, Cathy Haskell, Laura French, and Celene Seymour (all of whom had written to me about other problems) found themselves more interested in the issues Ann, Bill, and Karrie had articulated and so joined their cycle. As a part of an ongoing class, this cycle constituted a research group focused on the problem of student apathy and resistance. David Downing and I are co-researchers in the project. Moreover, in response to students' e-mail letters, I referred them to Graff's "Other Voices, Other Rooms," which argues that student apathy is related to the lack of connectivity in our curricula. The project is still in process.

One of the precursors to *Cycles* was a collaboration between four graduate students (Kathy Burkland, Terry Cooper, Kim Gannon, and Les Epstein) and myself on the dilemma of being "taught teachers." As students, an expressive pedagogy was *prescribed* to them in a graduate seminar. They experienced this prescriptive pedagogy as a contradictory restraint. They had no voice in the classroom of their professor who insisted that they give voice to freshmen in their own classrooms. When they approached me, I suggested that we take their dilemma as a research project and organize a symposium, inviting well-known scholars and our own graduate faculty to join us in a discussion of the problem. At the time, I did not understand my pedagogy to be in line with Graff's proposals. In retrospect, I do.

Two years later, Marian Sciachitano and Rory Ong approached me to teach a seminar on "theory." I agreed on the premise that the seminar be organized not on the principle that we cover theory as a "field" (again, this is a retrospective realization) but along the lines of the "taught teachers" research group. They agreed, and we formed the Miami University Theory and Pedagogy Research Group. The course began with the seminar participants (now including Bob Broad, Holly Roberts, Dan Dawson, Cher Uhl, and Don Armstrong) articulating their problems in dealing with theory. On the one hand, theory had important consequences in their graduate training, and, on the other, in their teaching. These situations did not always match up well. This research group has its counterpart in AU where Steven Horvath, Jennifer Gehrman, Margery Vagt, and Peter Naruscewicz have discussed the same problem. (I might add that Craig Frey and Don Paul Palutis formed another cycle concerned with graduate students who were not teaching assistants.) Once problems are "on the table," we work with their "connections." Sometimes these function extramurally. For instance, David Downing invited the Miami University theory and pedagogy group to visit with his "Theory and Pedagogy" seminar at Indiana University of Pennsylvania

(IUP). We presented our seminar papers to David's class and interested faculty. Eventually, four papers from this research group were published in an issue of *Works and Days* edited by Mark Hurlbert.

These research groups are instances of the "learning community" for which Graff calls. Moreover, because it is an electronic medium, *Cycles* is also an instance of "multicourse conferencing" in Graff's sense, as the Lotus Notes analogy makes clear. It is also an electronic form of "teacher swapping." In addition, it enjoys some of the features of teleconferencing. Though I have visited the IUP campus, which is the current site of the "Student Apathy and Resistance" project, most of our dialogue has taken place in cyberspace. And, as the project continues, we expect other teachers and students at different universities to join in.

Cycles is not a "privatized classroom" even though we work in an electronic environment. Without going into the complex details of the database and how the materials are collected, stored, retrieved, indexed and edited (which are not germane to the purposes of this essay), I will simply mention that we have made "adjustments" to Graff's delineation of intellectual communities in order to circumvent the problems cyberspace/time introduces, in particular the problem of the privatization of learning. There are two interrelated cyberspace problems that are connected to privatization—solipsism and discursive violence. Let me take up the problem of violence first.

Anyone who has taught in a computer classroom is likely to be familiar with the discursive violence known as "flaming." Since cyberspace is opaque, speakers can remain anonymous. Anonymity lends itself to discursive violence. Insults, crude jokes, mean-spirited criticisms, anger, resentment, and other negative interpersonal emotions are often vented in cyberspace. The problem is an exaggeration of the more familiar one in which the anonymous reviewers of essays, books, and tenure and promotion documents use their anonymity to level hurtful critiques at colleagues. Such practices, known euphemistically as "refutation," destroy open dialogue. This issue is intensified in cyberspace and raises this question: how can we create "productive disagreement" in electronic environments?

If the disagreeing parties in a controversy take as their starting point the mutual recognition of a problem, they can be productive. However, unless all the parties involved care about the resolution of the problem *more than* about their own stake in how the problem is conceived or approached, then the conflicts lapse into quarrels about terms and methods. There has to be a willingness to let one's own conceptual frameworks be changed by negotiation. This is impossible unless the parties care more about the resolution of the problem than about their own egos.

In AU, care rather than rejection is the key to overcoming the "resistance to conflict" syndrome to which Graff often alludes. AU offers its registrants a "safe space," inspired by the phenomenology of caring Milton Mayeroff presents in *On Caring*. At its core is the premise that "in caring as helping the other grow, I experience what I care for (a person, an ideal, an idea) as an extension of myself and at the same time as something separate from me that I respect in its own right" (5). He goes on to contrast caring to "dogmatically clinging to a belief" (5), a state wherein we are unable to experience others as having worth in their own right. He writes that in caring, "I experience the other as having potentialities and the need to grow; I experience an idea, for instance, as seminal, vital, or promising" (6), and he contrasts this experience of "trust" to one that gives a feeling of power and provides "something to dominate"(7). Conflicts of interest that occur in AU are negotiated through protocols of care.

By introducing an ethos of caring we emend Graff's proposals by shifting from a text-centered view of literary study to a person-oriented view.

> Alpha University has as its aim the creation of an environment conducive to the understanding of other human beings. It is governed by a protocol of caring. As a consequence, all of its projects, including *Cycles*, are organized on the principle of care for others. AU is dedicated to building a more caring environment in which to live. The strategy involved in its design is simple. Once the building of such an environment is deemed feasible, the hope is that it will spread by imitation. If persons involved in AU find this environment fulfilling, hopefully they will not only maintain it but help it grow and

> encourage others to be involved. AU is a self-selecting institution. Unlike a corporate institution, it is founded not for profit but for the benefit of its builders. Every person who works in this environment works to make it a more caring one. Thus all the members of AU are its builders because the single task of AU is to build a just and caring environment. Like persons who enjoy living in their homes and work hard to maintain, repair, and remodel them, so too, the inhabitants of AU work to maintain, redesign and renegotiate the interpersonal relations that constitute AU because they enjoy being in its environs. (Sosnoski, "Starting a Cycle")

But this shift from text-centricity to persons does not by itself make conflicts productive (socially transformative).[3] As I mentioned earlier, there is a tendency toward intellectual solipsism in EEs familiarly described as a tendency to "get lost in cyberspace." Once inside the privatized world of on-line databases in which the only interaction necessary involves concepts and keystrokes or clicks, persons can dwell within this simulated world as a private *weltanschauung*. In the study of texts located in cyberspace, reading can be highly solipsistic. To use Gregory Ulmer's term somewhat ironically, all stories become "mystories" (82–112).

What is outside cyberspace? We could say real experiences. This answer would perturb many postmodern thinkers. They would persuasively argue that there is no metadiscursive grounding to thought. The realism invoked here, however, is not a logical or metadiscursive conception. It is simply a reference to persons in a physical world contrasted to their personae (roles) in virtual classrooms. The realism involved is not epistemological but practical. Yet, since virtuality is a conceptual environment in cyberspace/time, which is a simulacrum of the physical world, we need to maintain the distinction between physical and virtual.

AU anchors itself in physical pain and joy. In EEs, we have to anchor problems outside cyberspace in persons. We cannot allow cybernetics to take over intellection. However difficult it may become to tell the difference between virtual reality and physical events, pain (if not joy) will demarcate that difference.

Since these events occur in real time, they anchor our work and provide what Graff calls "coherence of conflict." Let me explain.

The three interrelated seminar/research groups I mentioned at the beginning of this section were grounded in concrete problems—the painful experiences of students were the starting points. Rather than begin with a pedagogical discourse (for instance, "expressive" pedagogy), we made actual teaching experiences our point of departure. This move provoked further research. Moreover, our seminars were not organized according to the "field coverage principle" wherein a professor presents various schools and methods to graduate students as a transmission of the current state of theoretical knowledge. Rather, students started with concrete pedagogical problems and then used available theoretical formulations to help understand them.

The problem orientation of these research groups, which is maintained in AU's cycles, grounds research in mutually recognized pains and joys which counters the tendency of EEs to privatize intellectual projects. From this perspective, pain and joy are the real problems underlying the debates in AU's cycles. We name this way of organizing collaborative research "concurrence." We emend Graff's conflict model by introducing "concurrence protocols."

A concurrence is an event in which several persons, because they mutually recognize a problem (or a joy), get together to change (or maintain) that situation. Concurrence is not based on consensus. It is not required that all those concurring agree on fundamental principles. On the contrary, the differences among those concurring *are* the values they bring to the collaboration. The paradox in this situation is that the more diverse the disagreement, the more perspicuous the problem becomes because there are more perspectives involved. Rather than strive for conceptual agreement, persons are encouraged to look for coincidences in understanding amid their differences. Whereas in the procedures of disciplines anomalies are heuristic, in the protocols of concurrence coincidences are. When concurring, persons do not apply preconceived methods. Instead, they allow events to break down the conceptual frameworks they bring to them. These articulations of the problem are negotiated. Agreement and disagreement are in continuous dialogical relation. Whereas at one moment several articulations exhibit striking coincidences and govern the group's plans for action, at another stage, different views of the problem pertain, especially when the pressures of experience break down the *always temporary* frameworks in use. Even continuing disagreements help sharpen the perspectives of the persons to whom they are addressed if they are "careful" disagreements. Concurrence depends upon *care* for the other members in the group who work to come to terms with mutually recognized pains and joys. Without such care, disagreements cripple research groups.

Controversies or conflicts that inspire debate in literary studies are rooted in experiences of pain and joy. In negotiating them, researchers build cultures. Concurrences, as intertextual relations, are nothing less than building blocks of cultures. We need to incorporate interactions that are not divorced from imagination and emotion into the design of future universities. Our link to the public is through their cultural pains and joys. Imagination and emotion are "fields" we all too often neglect in cultural studies. They are indispensable in EEs. The over-intellectualized analyses that disciplinary mechanisms have occasioned in our work will only be exaggerated in EEs.

At this historical juncture, as Graff's work makes us aware, we are faced with a crucial alternative—consensus or conflict. There is another interrelated dilemma: Program or be reprogrammed!

NOTES

1. Unfortunately, I did not save the newspaper in which the concert was reviewed.

2. I am indebted to Don Bialostosky for this formulation of the question.

3. See David Downing's "The Cultural Politics of Graff's History of Literary Studies" (*Critical Exchange* 23, Summer 1987, 45–63) for an excellent account of the potential for social transformation in Graff's work. Written in 1987, it anticipates many of the emendations Graff has made to his initial articulation of the conflict model.

WORKS CITED

Benedikt, Michael, ed. *Cyberspace: First Steps*. Cambridge, MA: MIT Press, 1991.

Cain, William E. *The Crisis in Criticism: Theory, Literature, and Reform in English Studies*. Baltimore: Johns Hopkins University Press, 1984.

———. *"Literature Against Itself* Briefly Revisited." *Critical Exchange* 23 (Summer 1987): 31–36.

Downing, David. "The Cultural Politics of Graff's History of Literary Studies." *Critical Exchange* 23 (Summer 1987): 31–36.

Eagleton, Terry. *Literary Theory: An Introduction*. Minneapolis: University of Minnesota Press, 1983.

Freedman, Alan. *The Computer Glossary*. New York: AMACOM, 1981.

Freire, Paulo. *Pedagogy of the Oppressed*. Trans. Myra Bergman Ramos. New York: Continuum, 1970.

Gabelnick, Faith, Jean MacGregor, Roberta S. Matthews, and Barbara Leigh Smith. *Learning Communities: Creating Connections Among Students, Faculty, and Disciplines. New Directions for Teaching and Learning, Number 41*. San Francisco: Jossey-Bass, 1990.

Graff, Gerald. "Colleges Are Depriving Students of a Connected View of Scholarship." *The Chronicle of Higher Education* (February 13, 1991): A48.

———. "Co-optation." *The New Historicism*. Ed. H. Aram Veeser. New York: Routledge, 1989. 168–181.

———. "The Future of Theory in the Teaching of Literature." *The Future of Literary Theory*. Ed. Ralph Cohen. New York: Routledge, 1989. 250–67.

————. "Gerald Graff's Response to the Critics." Special Issue on the Work of Gerald Graff. Patricia Harkin, ed. *Critical Exchange* 23 (Summer 1987): 91–93.

————. *Literature Against Itself: Literary Ideas in Modern Society*. Chicago: University of Chicago Press, 1979.

————. "Other Voices, Other Rooms: Organizing and Teaching the Humanities Conflict." *New Literary History* 21 (1990): 817–839.

————. *Poetic Statement and Critical Dogma*. Chicago: University of Chicago Press, 1980.

————. *Professing Literature: An Institutional History*. Chicago: University of Chicago Press, 1987.

————. "Taking Cover in Coverage." *Profession 86* (1986): 41–45.

————. "Teach the Conflicts." *South Atlantic Quarterly* 89.1 (Winter 1990): 51–67.

————. "The University and the Prevention of Culture." *Criticism in the University*. Eds. Gerald Graff and Reginald Gibbons. Chicago: Northwestern University Press, 1985.

————. "What Has Literary Theory Wrought?" *The Chronicle of Higher Education* (February 12, 1992): A48.

————. "What Should We Be Teaching—When There's No 'We'?" *The Yale Journal of Criticism: Interpretation in the Humanities* 1 (1988): 189–211.

Graff, Gerald, and Reginald Gibbons, eds. *Criticism in the University*. Chicago: Northwestern University Press, 1985.

Harkin, Patricia. "Arguing a History: Gerald Graff's *Professing Literature*." *Critical Exchange* 23 (Summer 1987): 77–90.

————. "The Post-disciplinary Politics of Lore." *Contending with Words*. Eds. Patricia Harkin and John Schilb. New York: MLA, 1990.

Hogan, Mike. "Top of the News." *PC World* 6 (May 1988): 14.

Hurlbert, Mark, ed. *Works and Days* 8, 2 (Fall 1990).

Mannes, George. "How Theatrical." *Entertainment Weekly* (April 18, 1992).

Mayeroff, Milton. *On Caring*. New York: Harper & Row, 1971. 5–7.

Schilb, John. "Cultural Studies, Postmodernism, and Composition." *Contending with Words: Composition and Rhetoric in a Postmodern Age*. Eds. Patricia Harkin and John Schilb. New York: MLA, 1991. 173–189.

Sosnoski, James. "Starting a Cycle" (brochure). 1992. N.P.

Swales, John M. "The Concept of Discourse Community: Dog, Cash Cow, Problem Child or Star?" Lecture handout. University of Toledo Rhetoric Symposium, 1992.

———. *Genre Analysis: English in Academic and Research Settings.* Cambridge: Cambridge University Press, 1991.

Ulmer, Gregory. *Teletheory: Grammatology in the Age of Video.* New York: Routledge, 1989. 82–112.

III. Afterword

In Defense of Teaching the Conflicts

Gerald Graff

Having amply had my say at the front of this volume, I will try to confine myself here to some brief responses to several of the most persistent criticisms that have been directed at the idea of "teaching the conflicts," including those presented by contributors to this volume. I want at the outset, however, to express my deep gratitude and appreciation to the contributors, and above all to Bill Cain, for honoring me with a volume on my educational work.

I have noticed that my arguments tend to get a cool reception from several kinds of people: (1) those who see so little fundamentally wrong with the established educational system that changes of the kind I propose seem unwarranted, if not inexplicable; (2) those who see so much fundamentally wrong with the established educational system that my proposals seem superficial; (3) those who see no likelihood of significant improvement in the extent to which students may be socialized into the discourses of the academy; (4) those who believe that socializing students into the discourses of the academy is a bad thing.

By contrast, my analyses and proposals tend to receive the most understanding reception from those who share my root intuition that both today's academic culture and today's student body possess an immense potential that has yet to be realized, largely because of an atomized curriculum that belies the social and dialogical nature of intellectual work. I also like to think that my proposals appeal most to those who are able to think about the culture wars and the current problems of education from the point of view of students rather than that of professors, legislators, and public moralists.

I would like to address one common misunderstanding at the outset, however, by pointing out that in an important sense educational institutions are *already* "teaching the conflicts" right now, insofar as they are exposing students every day to an increasingly diverse and conflicted range of views. The choice, in other words, is not between teaching the conflicts and not doing so, but between teaching the conflicts well, or teaching them badly, representing what in fact are conversations in so disjunctive and disconnected a fashion that students have trouble recognizing them as dialogues, much less actively entering into them.

So the point of teaching the conflicts is not to get teachers to do something totally different from what they have been doing, but rather to enable them to do it better, in a way that would give students a greater chance to enter the academic intellectual conversation. As I argue, students cannot very well be expected to join an intellectual community that they rarely see, or see only in disconnected glimpses. This is why, though my emphasis ostensibly is on *conflict*, it is ultimately on *community* and the need for a more integrated curriculum.

Another frequent criticism directed at my work is that teaching the conflicts would divert students' attention from truly important texts and ideas to the presumably narrow and petty controversies of professional academics. In conservative versions of this criticism (i.e., David Bromwich, Harold Fromm), academic conflicts are said to come between students and the great texts and ideas with which education should directly acquaint them. In "oppositional" versions of this criticism, academic conflicts are said to be too genteel and apolitical to have much bearing on the deep social divisions of American culture.

Of course such characterizations of academic conflicts as narrow, pedantic, or genteel would have often been justified a generation or two ago. But they seem to me to have become increasingly obsolete as the academy has been opened to a far wider diversity of concerns and viewpoints than formerly, and as narrowly positivistic specialization has lost caste in many fields. Teaching the conflicts in the university of the 1990s, where feminists and multiculturalists are a significant presence, is a different proposition from what it would have been in 1950, when the prevailing conflicts would have operated within assumptions determined by a more culturally homogeneous elite.

The conflicts of the present culture war seem to me very far from being petty, superficial, or merely "academic" in the bad sense, and certainly far from being apolitical. I agree with Paul Berman's remark in the introduction to his anthology, *Debating PC*, that the culture war "has managed to raise nearly every important question connected with culture and education—the proper relation of culture to a democratic society, the relation of literature to life, the purpose of higher education." I would add that any questions the culture war has *not* raised can be quickly arrived at by taking it as a starting point—including the question of whether the concerns of present academic culture are narrow, petty, and merely intraprofessional.

What the critics fail to consider is that just because one *starts* with a relatively local or restricted (or overly binary and polarized) set of conflicts does not mean that one has to end there. Indeed, part of the point of teaching the conflicts is to enable narrow and rigid conceptions of what the conflicts *are* to be challenged and displaced. The challenge of teaching the conflicts is to see if we can elevate our current debates, moving them beyond the admittedly unedifying level at which they have often become stalled.

In the aloof distaste they express for the conflicts of the present academic scene, critics like Bromwich and Fromm simply refuse to take any responsibility for improving the current state of discussion. These critics speak as if they somehow stood outside the contentions of their pitiful contemporaries, as if they looked down on the scene from a superior height. In fact, these critics are as much inside the conflict as anyone, and whatever pettiness it may contain is their responsibility as much as anyone's. Though the culture war has indeed become squalid enough, I become tired of critics who condescend to today's debates and thereby do nothing to help us elevate them.

These critics are also mistaken in thinking that critical analysis, theory, and debate about a text in some way *compete* with that text. It is this disastrous assumption that has induced literature teachers to withhold the discourses of criticism and theory from their students, thereby leaving them with no models of the kind of critical discourse they are expected to produce in literature classes.

Fromm imagines that students will be better off if we "simply" get them "to read a massive number of books, not only for 'their own sake' but to provide foundations of knowledge on which to base future opinions." But after all, we ask our students not just to read books but to find something to *say* about them, and when what they say is too close to their own idiom and not close enough to those of the intellectual culture, they are punished. Screening students from the critical debates that are swirling around them (and that their instructors are enmeshed in, whether they know it or not) only leaves them without the critical languages that students are punished for not being able to speak.

As long as many students possess neither the critical vocabularies nor the contexts to read and talk about those books in the analytical ways the academy requires, this "just read the books" prescription has traditionally resulted in failure. Ironically, the attempt to rescue the great books by isolating them from the critical discourses that surround them helps drive students to *Cliffs Notes*, the only place they can get the Critspeak that has been withheld from them. It is true that the effect of teaching the conflicts *can* be to divert attention in a disabling way from the texts about which the conflicts rage. But if thoughtfully managed, the effect should be to arouse interest in books by students who now lack an incentive for reading them, as well as to supply those students with contexts for discussing books that they now lack.

The fear that teaching the conflicts about books will cause the books themselves to lose out rests on a false polarity between books and discussions about books. You would think that those who complain that books are being beaten out by other media in the competition for students' attention would be able to imagine how an interesting climate of debate around a book could give students a reason for reading and talking about it.

Whereas Bromwich and Fromm find current academic conflicts too sordidly embedded in interest-group politics to be of any legitimate interest to students, critics further to the left imply that those conflicts operate at too lofty a height, too remote from what Carl Freedman calls "the gritty unpleasantries" of real social struggles. While I much appreciate Freedman's generous treatment of my work, this criticism seems to me an odd one coming from those who, in other contexts, would maintain that no discourse is innocent, that all discourses "inscribe" power relations. If this is the case (as I think it is), and if people like Freedman who believe it is the case are well represented on university faculties (as they often are), then there is little danger that foregrounding today's conflicts in the curriculum would be the arid intellectual exercise that Freedman anticipates. Even if it did become an arid exercise on occasion, the presence of such critics as Freedman would ensure that this very objection would become part of the dialogue.

Of course, if "dialogue" seems to you a poor substitute for the kind of "transformative" education some today insist on—I am thinking of Paulo Freire, Henry Giroux, and many proponents of "cultural studies"—then teaching the conflicts may indeed sound like tame stuff. My view, however, is that the transformative model advanced by Freire, Giroux, and others cannot be institutionalized without resorting to the sort of authoritarian, undemocratic methods that have in some cases at least given legitimacy to charges of "political correctness" and "thought police."

Freire's "pedagogy of the oppressed," though it pretends to be based on teacher-student "dialogue," in fact promotes a pseudo-dialogue in which only a single political outcome counts as authentic teaching and learning. Freirean pedagogy presupposes students who are already willing to define themselves as "oppressed" (as seems to have been the case with the Latin American peasants Freire has worked with) and instructors who already aspire to become "transformative intellectuals." In other words, it is a pedagogy that preaches to the already converted, positioning everyone else as complicitous with the status quo and therefore not worth addressing.

Teaching the conflicts, by contrast, assumes that, as Gregory Jay has argued, the definition of categories such as the disenfranchised and the dominant, oppressed and oppressor, should be a *product* of the pedagogical process, not its unquestioned *premise*. It therefore assumes that the success of any academic "oppositional" project in the United States must depend heavily on *persuasion*, and that effective persuasion demands entering into respectful dialogues with the unconverted—even taking the risk that *they* may end up converting *us*. It also assumes that in a society and an academic scene in which a continuing dialogue about the politics of culture has been largely nonexistent, merely raising political *issues* would be a significantly "radical" step, and a more democratic one, than a transformative pedagogy that simply reproduces authoritarianism from the left side of the spectrum.

But then, precisely because teaching the conflicts would submit the issues in the culture war to democratic discussion, its political outcome is not predictable. This fact, I would like to think, explains the hostility toward the idea that has come from journals like *Heterodoxy* and *The New Criterion* as well as from the ultraleft. Neither of these groups can be expected to favor an arrangement that asks them to grant any legitimacy to opposing factions, much less to risk entering an argument they would not be guaranteed to win.

I should add, however, that, given the great diversity in kinds of educational institutions across the country, teaching the conflicts would necessarily be implemented in many different ways, with varying political and philosophical colorations, and varying degrees of centrality in the overall curriculum. It is not a question of all institutions or instructors doing the same thing, but of adapting a certain body of principles to the exigencies of very different local situations.

In closing, a few further comments on criticisms made by various contributors.

Harold Fromm accuses me of having "portrayed the average undergraduate as a somewhat dazed, simpleminded innocent, staggering aimlessly from class to class while his various instructors spout incompatible dogma which the student is afraid, or too naive, to question."

I think I do at times veer toward such a caricature. My excuse is that many students are indeed confused by the enormous shifts in assumption and method as they move from one class to the next. If they do not always "stagger aimlessly" it is because they acquire the technique of giving each teacher what he or she "wants," even when it conflicts with what the last teacher wanted. In any case, the reason for my admittedly one-sided emphasis on the struggling or confused student is that this is the type of student who particularly interests me.

I am grateful to John Schilb for pointing out that one of the central conflicts we need to teach is the one that has always existed between the culture of students and that of the academy. He is right in suggesting that students in this way "may even desirably transform the rhetorics of the academy."

In other words, teaching the conflicts should not be an entirely one-way or top-down socialization of students into the superior discourses of the academy (as I sometimes seem to suggest—a criticism also made here by Patrick J. Hill and Andrea A. Lunsford and Suellynn Duffey). It should involve a critique of those academic discourses from the perspectives of students.

I very much like Schilb's practical suggestions for courses that would engage the tensions between student cultures and academic cultures. David Shumway of Carnegie Melon University has been teaching a course in "Student Cultures" that is similar to what Schilb outlines.

Andrea A. Lunsford and Suellynn Duffey have not got me quite right when they say I "reject" dialogism, though I do say that "'the classroom' [cannot] become effectively dialogic as long as it is not itself in dialogue with other classrooms." And I do have to concede their essential point, which is that I give short shrift (or no shrift at all) to the so-called "collaborative learning" format (as usefully developed by writers like Ken Bruffee, John Trimbur, and Lunsford herself with Lisa Ede [*Singular Texts/Plural Authors: Perspectives on Collaborative Writing* (Carbondale: Southern Illinois University Press, 1990)]). I agree with Lunsford and Duffey that there are numerous ways to imagine dialogical pedagogy, including at the level of the single classroom. Particularly promising is the strategy of "peer tutoring," in which the quicker students become intermediaries between the instructor and the other students.

I find something potentially ominous in Patrick J. Hill's proposal that we "re-train the faculty" to be responsive to cultural diversity and differing learning styles, a proposal that seems to me ironic given Hill's otherwise critical view of top-down modes of instruction.

Of course a lot depends here on how the "re-training" is conceived. But in a highly conflicted academic environment, the question inevitably arises of who will get to retrain whom. Maybe I am unfair, but the tone of Hill's comments suggests to me the assumption that now that we know where the forces of light and justice reside, it is up to us on the virtuous side to retrain the not yet enlightened.

I think of those compulsory reeducation workshops at some campuses that have lately aroused tremendous resentment against the cause of cultural diversity, and sometimes with good reason. I for one would be insulted by attempts to "reeducate" me in this fashion, even if I believed in the content of the reeducation (as in this case I do). The problem, it seems to me, is that you don't effectively change minds, especially resistant ones, by "retraining"; you are more likely to change minds and overcome resistance by holding an open discussion in which people feel free, if they want to, to say they think "empowerment" is a crock.

Faculty discussion sessions, then, in which currently disputed issues can be debated frankly and openly, seem to me infinitely preferable to any program of "retraining," and I think the difference is very important.

D.G. Myers complains that "debate between sects or parties will tend only to *polarize* ideas, pitting them against one another rather than clarifying what is at issue." Yes, this *can* be the result, all right, but must it be? Surely we have all experienced debates in which polarization gave way to some degree of understanding and clarification. Here I think *third* and *fourth* parties are often necessary for displacing the entrenched binaryism of us vs. them oppositions. Good moderators are useful too.

Why should we always assume that our academic debates are doomed to be sterile and paralyzed (a prediction that will certainly fulfill itself)? Again, instead of adopting an aloof fatalism which disclaims any responsibility, why not begin seriously reflecting on how we might improve the quality of our debates?

Myers also raises the question of "how to instill within students intellectual ambitions and rational habits . . . ," and he wonders how on my model "students would ever learn to speak with any assurance for themselves." This of course remains the key question at the center of all learning theory—how can students be helped to make the qualitative leap from their paradigm to another (a move that does not exclude reciprocal critique of the academy).

Myers seems to think that this leap can only be made if we teach students formal "logic and rules of evidence." But I don't believe anybody has ever learned "rational habits" by studying formal logic. It seems to me that we best learn these habits in the same way that we best learn foreign languages, by associating with speakers of those languages in circumstances that allow for a good deal of practical give and take.

My own interest in the conference or symposium as an untapped pedagogical resource comes from my having been a person who started really to learn the discourses of the academy when I started to attend academic conferences. The maturation that can be observed in the increasing number of graduate students who now attend academic conferences suggests that this is an idea worth pursuing further.

James Sosnoski's account of how he and his colleagues have been using computer and video technology to overcome the isolation of the traditional autonomous classroom seems to me extremely important, since it is obvious that these new technologies will play a major role in the classrooms of the future. Given the capacity that we will soon possess to develop a single "course" that can be accessed by virtually every student in the country, it will soon be possible to increase enormously and significantly the amount of common experience students will be able to share. Such a development in my view could be of immense aid to teachers, who now must construct the contexts of their courses entirely by themselves and without help, and it could make possible the saving of billions of dollars in the costs of education. It would also pose serious questions about who will control the content of this common experience—another reason, I believe, for rethinking educational structures in terms of difference and debate rather than consensus.

Contributors

Gerald Graff is George M. Pullman Professor of English and Education at the University of Chicago, where he moved in 1991 after teaching for twenty-five years at Northwestern University. He is the author of *Professing Literature: An Institutional History* (1987) and *Beyond the Culture Wars: How Teaching the Conflicts Can Revitalize American Education* (1992).

William E. Cain, professor of English at Wellesley College, is the author of *The Crisis in Criticism* (1984) and *F. O. Matthiessen and the Politics of Criticism* (1988). He has recently edited a selection of abolitionist writings by William Lloyd Garrison (forthcoming from Bedford Books).

Suellynn Duffey directs the First-Year Writing Programs at Ohio State University and has focused her scholarship on literacy, basic writing, and revision.

Lynette Felber is an assistant professor of English at New Mexico State University. She has published essays on Elizabeth Gaskell, Anthony Trollope, Anthony Powell, critical theory, and the profession of literary studies. She is the author of *Novels Without End: Genre, Gender, and Narrative in the British Roman-Fleuve* (forthcoming).

Carl Freedman teaches in the English department at Louisiana State University. He is the author of a book on George Orwell, a forthcoming book on critical theory and science fiction, and many articles on aspects of modern culture and theory.

Harold Fromm, whose essays and reviews appear regularly in the *Hudson Review* and from time to time in many other journals, is the author of *Academic Capitalism and Literary Value* (1991). He also writes frequently on ecological subjects. In 1994 he will be a visiting professor at the University of Illinois, Chicago.

Patrick J. Hill, while at Stony Brook in the State University of New York system, founded the Federated Learning Communities, a problem-focused, interdisciplinary alternative to curricular organization, since replicated at a dozen or so colleges and universities. From 1983 to 1990 he served as provost at the Evergreen State College, the institution which inspired the experiment at Stony Brook. He is now teaching at Evergreen and completing a book on democracy and higher education.

Deborah H. Holdstein, professor of English and rhetoric at Governors State University, coordinates the English program and directs the writing program. She is the author of numerous essays and books, including *On Composition and Computers* (1987) and a coedited collection, *Computers and Writing: Theory, Research, Practice* (1990). With David Bleich, she is also editing a collection of essays on composition, teaching, and academic institutions.

Timothy D. Johnston is professor of psychology, associate dean of the College of Arts and Sciences, and director of the Center for Critical Inquiry in the Liberal Arts at the University of North Carolina at Greensboro. He is coeditor (with Alexandra P. Pietrewicz) of *Issues in the Ecological Study of Learning* (Erlbaum, 1985) and has published empirical and theoretical studies on the development and evolution of animal behavior.

Andrea A. Lunsford is Distinguished Professor of English and vice chairperson for rhetoric and composition at Ohio State University. She is currently editing a collection on women and rhetoric, titled *Reclaiming Rhetorica*, and coediting an innovative reader with John Ruszkiewicz, *The Presence of Others*. Her previous books include *Singular Texts/Plural Authors* (with Lisa Ede), and, with Robert Connors, *The St. Martin's Handbook*.

Steven Mailloux, professor of English and comparative literature at the University of California, Irvine, is the author of *Interpretive Conventions: The Reader in the Study of American Fiction* (1982) and *Rhetorical Power* (1989), and the coeditor of *Interpreting Law and Literature: A Hermeneutic Reader* (1988). He has recently edited a collection titled *Rhetoric, Sophistry, Neopragmatism* (forthcoming from Cambridge University Press).

D.G. Myers, assistant professor of English at Texas A & M University, earned his Ph.D. at Northwestern University under Gerald Graff. He has published essays in the *Journal of the History of Ideas, Commentary, New Criterion, Sewanee Review,* and elsewhere. He is completing a history of creative writing and creative writers in the American university.

John Schilb teaches in the English department at the University of Maryland, College Park. He has coedited *Constellations: A Contextual Reader for Writers* (HarperCollins, 1992) and two collections published by the Modern Language Association, *Contending with Words: Composition and Rhetoric in a Postmodern Age* (1991) and *Writing Theory and Critical Theory* (forthcoming). Currently he is writing a book entitled *Reading and Writing Between the Lines: Literary Theory and Composition Theory.*

James J. Sosnoski is a professor of English at Miami University and the executive director of Alternative Educational Environments. He has written extensively on literary criticism and theory and on the institutions of literary studies.

Index

academic
  conferences, 39, 133
  departments, 6–7, 13–14,
    95–99
  disciplines, 100, 159–60
African-American literature,
  xi, xxix–xxx
American literature, xi–xiv,
  xxix

budget crisis, in higher
  education, 124–25

canon, xi–xvi, xxi, 20–24, 36,
  47, 54–56, 131–32, 171–
  72, 185–86
classroom, 25, 30, 59, 164–
  65, 175
close reading, xxvii, 5
collaboration, xxiv–xxv
collaborative learning, 225–
  26
composition programs,
  xxxv–xxxvi, 60, 63–64,
  87, 95–99, 109–20, 123–
  25
conflict,
  in higher education, x, 10,
  28–29, 49

in society, 136–42
conflict model, ix, xxxii,
  xxxiii, 17–41, 80, 85, 95–
  99, 105, 179–90, 202,
  219–28
core courses, xxxvii, 163–76
critical approaches to
  literature, 17–19
cultural history, 14
cultural studies, 14, 82–84
culture wars, x, xxi–xxii
curriculum, x, xxxii, 3–5, 7,
  10, 25, 37, 40–41, 45–50,
  56, 70, 72, 97, 117–20,
  124–25, 185

debate, as principle for
  reform, xix, xxiv, xxx–
  xxxi, 56–57
deconstruction, 75
dialogics, 34–35, 56–59, 109,
  116, 166–67

electronic environment for
  learning, xxxviii, 193–
  213
empiricism, 61–62